Optimizing Strength Training

Designing Nonlinear Periodization Workouts

William J. Kraemer, PhD

Professor of Kinesiology
Professor of Physiology and Neurobiology
Human Performance Laboratory
Department of Kinesiology
University of Connecticut
Storrs, CT

Steven J. Fleck, PhD

Chair, Sport Science Department
Colorado College
Colorado Springs, CO

Human Kinetics

Library of Congress Cataloging-in-Publication Data

Kraemer, William J., 1953-
  Optimizing strength training : designing nonlinear periodization workouts / William J.
Kraemer, Steven J. Fleck.
    p. cm.
  Includes bibliographical references and index.
  ISBN-13: 978-0-7360-6068-4 (soft cover)
  ISBN-10: 0-7360-6068-5 (soft cover)
  1. Weight training. 2. Exercise. 3. Periodization training. I. Fleck, Steven J., 1951- II. Title.
  GV546.K73 2007
  613.7'13--dc22

                                        2007011833

ISBN-10: 0-7360-6068-5
ISBN-13: 978-0-7360-6068-4

Acquisitions Editor: Mike Bahrke; **Developmental Editor:** Judy Park; **Assistant Editor:** Heather M. Tanner; **Copyeditor:** Jan Feeney; **Proofreader:** Darlene Rake; **Indexer:** Bobbi Swanson; **Permission Manager:** Carly Breeding; **Graphic Designer:** Fred Starbird; **Graphic Artist:** Denise Lowry; **Cover Designer:** Keith Blomberg; **Photographer (cover):** AJ Macht, courtesy of the Indianapolis Colts; **Photographer (back cover):** Monte Isom/SportsChrome; **Photographer (interior):** © Human Kinetics unless otherwise noted. Photos on pages 2, 35, 62, 95, 108, 126, 127, 128, 129, 130, 132, 133, 134, 135, 136, 142, 153, 169, 190, 192, and 206 courtesy of Dr. William J. Kraemer and his colleagues: Disa L. Hatfield, Jakob L. Vingren, Maren Fragala, Jen-Yu Ho, Brittny Boyd, Cassandra E. Forsythe, Linda M. Yamamoto, and Dr. Barry A. Spiering. **Photo Asset Manager:** Laura Fitch; **Photo Office Assistant:** Jason Allen; **Art Manager:** Kelly Hendren; **Illustrator:** Tammy Page; **Printer:** Total Printing Systems

Printed in the United States of America   10 9 8 7 6

The paper in this book is certified under a sustainable forestry program.

Human Kinetics
Website: www.HumanKinetics.com

United States: Human Kinetics
P.O. Box 5076
Champaign, IL 61825-5076
800-747-4457
e-mail: info@hkusa.com

Canada: Human Kinetics
475 Devonshire Road, Unit 100
Windsor, ON N8Y 2L5
800-465-7301 (in Canada only)
e-mail: info@hkcanada.com

Europe: Human Kinetics
107 Bradford Road
Stanningley
Leeds LS28 6AT, United Kingdom
+44 (0)113 255 5665
e-mail: hk@hkeurope.com

For information about Human Kinetics' coverage in other areas of the world,
please visit our website: www.HumanKinetics.com

To my wife Joan and to our children Daniel, Anna, and Maria
for their love and support.

-WJK

I would like to thank my parents Marv and Elda Fleck for their love and
support, but also for instilling in me that with training, the ability to perform
physical tasks does improve. I would also like to thank my wife Maelu
for allowing me the freedom and time to complete this book.

-SJF

Contents

Preface

We are very excited about *Optimizing Strength Training: Designing Nonlinear Periodization Workouts,* a revolutionary approach to periodization of resistance training. This book is the product of both scientific research and practical experiences with athletes and subjects in studies over the past several years.

The nonlinear concept of periodization came together in 2001 when Dr. Kraemer moved to the University of Connecticut at Storrs. Studies done at Ball State University and Pennsylvania State University over the previous 12 years were put into practice in nonlinear periodization by Coach Gerard Martin and Andrea Hudy in UConn's strength and conditioning program.

Studies had shown that long seasons and long-term training might best be served by a flexible approach using a variety of workouts within a short period of time. This is emphasized in sport in the academic situation with student-athletes, as many factors affect the quality of training on a given day (e.g., schoolwork, classes, practices, competition schedules, and illness). Individualization is also a vital part of nonlinear periodization because not everyone progresses at the same rate, nor is each person ready to perform the same type of workout on a given day. This underscores the importance of quality of training, efficient use of time, and use of the most effective workout for the day. Furthermore, for optimal physical development of each trainee, training goals must be identified and many aspects must be trained.

As discussed in chapter 1, with classic strength and power periodization, intensity and volume have minimal variation over a 1- to 4-week microcycle. In contrast, in one 7- to 10-day nonlinear cycle a trainee might do several types of workouts.

Chapter 2 covers the training principles you need to understand before designing and implementing a program (i.e., specificity of training, progressive overload, and frequency). Chapter 3 covers the classic variables that quantify a workout: choice of exercise, order of exercise, intensity (resistance used), number of sets, and rest between sets and exercises. These variables are the periodized factors and are involved in the concept of variation in resistance training.

Chapter 4 covers practical aspects of using the nonlinear approach to periodization. Most important is the overall plan, even for flexible nonlinear periodization, in which you do an assessment on the day of the workout to see if the trainee is capable of the workout. Merely going through the motions is not conducive to effective training; the advantage of nonlinear periodization is the flexibility involved in choosing the workout for a particular day. In the overall plan and goals of the mesocycle, which typically is about 12 weeks, you must make sure that the workout is optimal for that day, whether it is a power workout, a heavy-day workout, or an active rest day.

Chapter 5 explores workout design for the various types of workouts used (e.g., power days, heavy days, light days) in the nonlinear periodization approach. Included is a base program, which prepares the body for the stress of resistance training.

Chapter 6 presents information on fitness assessments. If you do not evaluate a trainee's progress, you will not know when or even whether a program has met its goals. Chapter 7 discusses various tools, such as workout logs and equipment commonly used in a program and necessary for optimal implementation. Ultimately this book will allow you to understand the concepts and then the implementation of the concepts, which will lead you to success in resistance training.

The most important chapter in *Optimizing Strength Training: Designing Nonlinear Periodization Workouts* is chapter 8. Using the case studies presented, you can apply your knowledge in using the nonlinear approach to periodization. You will learn how to respond to various situations and see if you can use some creativity in your approach. Coaches, fitness instructors, and personal trainers can use the case studies to make this a revolutionary approach to resistance training.

We hope you find the nonlinear approach to periodization as exciting and revolutionary as we and others have. Personal trainers, high school coaches, college coaches, and NBA and NFL strength coaches and trainers have used these tools to meet the demands of their individual situations. This is the future of strength training, and we wish you the best as you take charge and implement a program using the concepts we discuss in this book. You can customize the information for your own situation and needs. We wish you good luck and good training.

Acknowledgments

We would like to thank all the people who have contributed to the evolution of this book. Many athletes and coaches have worked with us; we thank them for their valuable interactions on this new concept of nonlinear periodization. We also are indebted to our colleagues and friends who have allowed us to hone this concept into a solid paradigm for use. As with any system of training, implementation of the nonlinear program has a tremendous amount of flexibility, depending on a client's goals and abilities. We thank the strength and conditioning staff at the University of Connecticut, most notably head strength and conditioning coach Gerard Martin and coach Chris West for using the system of training in its early stages and contributing their insights on its varied use and evolution in the hands of practitioners. We thank Andrea Hudy, now a coach at the University of Kansas, for training her basketball teams at UConn with this approach. Coach Sue Whiteside at Penn State participated in our research on this program with her tennis team many years ago; she showed that nonlinear programming was the only way to go with such a long season and demanding schedules. Coach Jon Torine of the Indianapolis Colts had the courage to use this new approach to training on a professional team and demonstrated its success; we are indebted to him and all of our coaching colleagues. Our fellow investigators have shown that periodization, no matter what the format, is superior to constant-set training. Our thanks also go to Dr. Howard G. Knuttgen for his input on the conceptual design of figure 4.2. Finally, we are grateful to our friends at Human Kinetics: Dr. Mike Bahrke believed in our new concept of training, and Ms. Judy Park worked tirelessly in pulling it all together. We hope that the book puts knowledge in your hands and allows you to reach your strength and conditioning goals.

CHAPTER 1

Periodization of Resistance Training

Many people performing resistance training, whether they are fitness enthusiasts or professional athletes, have reached points in their training at which little or no increase in muscle size, power, or strength occurs. Such a training plateau occurs even though they train intensely. Training plateaus have most likely occurred since athletes started serious training. Likewise, probably since athletes started serious training, they and their coaches have made changes in their training programs in an attempt to bring about continued fitness gains and avoid training plateaus. With experience, coaches and athletes have learned what changes to make in training programs and when to implement those changes. The changes made resulted in the development of planned long-term training programs and planned changes in training programs. Terms to describe planned long-term training variation are *cycling, chronic program manipulation,* and *periodization. Periodization* is the most popular term for planned training variation.

Changes in resistance training in virtually any acute program variable can be used as part of a periodized training plan. Thus choice of exercise, order of exercise, number of repetitions per set, number of sets, lengths of rest periods between sets and exercises, and intensity of exercises can all vary in a program. In addition, the number of training sessions per day, the velocity of training, the number of training sessions per week, and planned short-term (e.g., 1-2 weeks) rest breaks or low-intensity or low-volume training periods can all be incorporated into a periodized training program. Although all of these types of changes can be made, changes in training volume (i.e., number of sets, number of repetitions per set, training sessions per week, training sessions per day) and training intensity (i.e., percent of the maximal resistance that can be used for 1 repetition) have

From the perspectives of health, fitness, and performance, there are many reasons to use a periodized resistance training program.

The 2005 International Powerlifting Federation World Championships. Photo courtesy of Disa L. Hatfield.

received the most study by sport scientists and are typically used as the basis of any periodized training program.

Besides continued long-term gains in muscle size, strength, and power, there are other reasons to use a periodized resistance training program. Planned variation in training for many individuals will also help keep the training program psychologically interesting. If a trainee simply goes through training sessions and does not attempt to perform the session at the needed intensity and volume because of boredom, fitness gains will stagnate. Another reason to use a periodized training program is the prevention of overuse injuries. Performing the same exercises at the same training intensity and volume for long periods can eventually result in an overuse injury.

EASTERN EUROPEAN INFLUENCE ON PERIODIZATION TRAINING

Anecdotal evidence indicates that some American weightlifters were using periodized training as early as the 1960s. However, coaches, athletes, and sport scientists from the former Eastern Bloc countries are normally credited with developing and researching the concepts of periodized training. The goal of elite athletes is to peak, or have the best possible performance, at major competitions, such as national championships, world championships, or the Olympic Games. So one original major goal of periodized training, including periodized resistance training, was to ensure peaking for major competitions. For resistance-trained athletes, such as Olympic weightlifters and shot putters, that meant that maximal strength and power must peak for major competitions. For the goal of peaking to occur, the training program had to ensure that strength and power were optimally developed, muscular hypertrophy occurred, and there was adequate recovery between training sessions so that successive training sessions could be performed at high intensity.

It may be that part of the success and domination of athletes in former Eastern Bloc countries in some sports indicates that periodized training does result in strength and power gains over a year of training and even over the careers of athletes. One of the concepts of periodized training was training variation. Thus the training program had to provide variation in the psychological and physiological stress of physical conditioning and competition. This was necessary in order to bring about the adaptations needed for long-term increases in the physical condition of an athlete that were critical for success in his or her particular sport. Training variation, such as progressing toward greater training intensities, was also essential for peaking the athlete for major competitions.

Sport scientists and coaches from the former Eastern Bloc carefully monitored their athletes' training volume and intensity and came to the conclusion that training volume and intensity of successful athletes followed a particular pattern over the course of a training year (see figure 1.1). At the start of the competitive year when preparation for competition was just beginning, training volume was high and training intensity low. As the competitive year progressed, training volume decreased and training intensity increased. Before major competitions, training intensity was at its highest and training volume was at its lowest. Additionally, training intensity also showed a decrease immediately before major competitions. This decrease in training volume and intensity was thought to be necessary for psychological as well as physical recovery immediately before a major competition so that the best possible performance would occur at the major competition. Skill training for the particular sport also showed a pattern similar to that of training intensity. However, skill training peaked slightly closer to the major competition than training

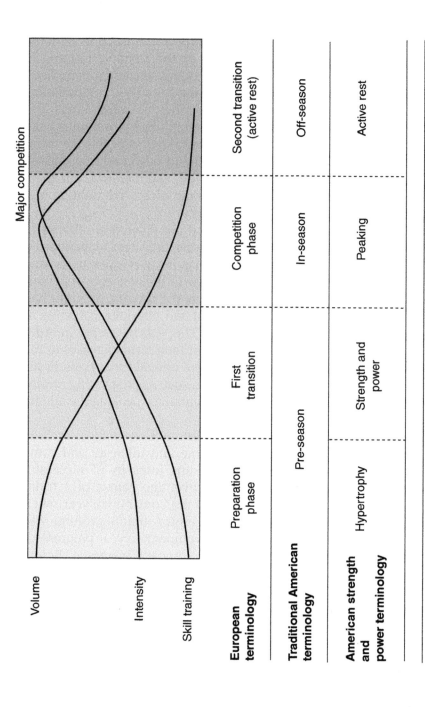

Figure 1.1 Training intensity and volume pattern with strength and power periodization.

Reprinted, by permission, from S.J. Fleck and W.J. Kraemer, 2004, *Designing resistance training programs*, 3rd ed. (Champaign, IL: Human Kinetics), 213.

intensity did. But similar to training intensity, skill training decreased immediately before major competitions. This general pattern of skill training, intensity, and volume was used in developing training programs for particular sports and individualized training programs for each athlete.

Originally, because there were relatively few major competitions in a competitive year, the pattern of increasing training intensity and decreasing training volume of one training cycle took place over an entire year. Then, as more competitions were added to the competitive year, the time frame for completing an entire training cycle was gradually shortened. Today, the entire pattern of decreasing training volume and increasing intensity takes place in 3 to 4 months. Thus the entire pattern is repeated three or four times per year. As the year progresses, training intensity and volume ideally are progressively higher at the start of successive training patterns than they were at the start of previous patterns because the athlete is now in better physical condition. Likewise, as the pattern is repeated over an athlete's career, training intensity and volume at the start of each year are also higher because physical condition during the athlete's career also increases.

The complexity of periodized strength training has evolved to meet the needs of particular sports and guarantee the success of individual athletes. However, periodization is still based in the concepts of training variation, sport specificity, and individualization of the training program.

CLASSIC STRENGTH AND POWER PERIODIZATION

Intensity and volume of weight training for classic strength and power periodization follow the pattern developed by the sport scientists and coaches from the former Eastern Bloc (figure 1.1). If this pattern of training intensity and volume is outlined in terms of sets of an exercise and repetitions per set, many variations are possible. One popular variation is presented in table 1.1. The changes in the repetitions per set account for the greatest change in training intensity and volume. The recommended repetitions per set are supposed to be performed with the use of repetition-maximum weights (RM) or very close to RM weights. Typically after an athlete completes the entire training cycle, a short period (1-2 weeks) of active recovery consisting of low-intensity and low-volume weight training, no weight training, or

Table 1.1 Classic Strength and Power Periodization Model

Training phase		Hypertrophy	Strength	Power	Peaking	Active recovery
Workout variables	Sets	3-5	3-5	3-5	1-3	Light physical activity
	Repetitions/ set	8-12	2-6	2-3	1-3	
	Intensity	Low	Moderate	High	Very high	
	Volume	Very high	High	Moderate	Low	

light physical activity takes place. This allows both psychological and physiological recovery in preparation for the next training cycle.

The active recovery phase does not necessarily mean complete cessation of all training; this phase is typically relatively short in length. If all training ceased for a long period, detraining, or loss of training adaptations, would occur. If the active recovery phase is too long, the trainee would enter the next training cycle in a physical condition at or significantly below where he or she started the cycle just completed. This potentially means that the trainee will be in no better physical condition as the years of training progress. The length of the active recovery phase also depends in part on the individual needs of the trainee. For example, an active recovery phase several weeks in length for a veteran international-class athlete who has just won a world championship medal may not be detrimental to the upcoming competitive year. However, an active recovery phase of similar length for a less experienced athlete who is trying to become competitive at the international level and is just starting to prepare for a world championship may not be beneficial.

As the concepts of classic strength and power periodization developed and research in sport science was performed concerning the efficacy of this training pattern, specific terminology was developed to describe various time periods or training phases within a periodized training program. Macrocycle typically refers to 1 year of training. Mesocycle refers to 3 to 4 months of a macrocycle. Using the European terminology, the preparation phase, first transition phase, competition phase, and second transition phase would all be mesocycles. A microcycle refers to 1 to 4 weeks of training within a mesocycle, although today many people use *microcycle* to refer specifically to 1 week of training.

Traditional American terminology also can be applied to the strength and power periodization model. The preseason corresponds to the preparation and first transition phase of the European terminology. In-season corresponds to the competition phase, and the off-season corresponds to the second transition and active recovery phases. When describing the classic strength and power periodization model, Olympic weightlifters and similar athletes, such as shot putters, use a slightly different terminology than the traditional American terminology, called the American strength and power terminology. The American strength and power terminology is used in table 1.1 to describe various training phases of the strength and power periodization model. Each training phase, no matter what terminology is used, has specific training goals. For example, the preparation phase is used for developing muscle hypertrophy and strength in preparation for the transition (first transition phase) to power and maximal strength development necessary for success during the competition phase. These same goals are applied to the traditional American term *preseason*. The American strength and power terminology perhaps is the most descriptive of the training goals of each training phase. The goals during the strength and hypertrophy phases are to develop strength and muscle size, respectively, while goals of the strength and power phases are to develop maximal strength and power, respectively. Although maximal strength, power, and hypertrophy are related within the context of the American strength and power terminology as the number of repetitions per set decrease, there is a gradual switch toward development of maximal, or one-repetition maximum (1RM), strength and power. Thus the major goal of the peaking phase is to develop maximal, or one-repetition maximum, strength and power. The goal of the classic strength and power model is to develop maximal (1RM) strength and power, which are necessary for success in sports such as Olympic weightlifting and discus throwing. This goal is in part accomplished by a gradual change to lifting heavier and heavier weights for fewer repetitions. The goal of emphasizing power as the training cycle progresses is also typically accomplished by changes in the exercises performed. Thus as the training cycle progresses, fewer sets of the back squat and more sets of the power clean or power snatch might be performed.

The training phases presented for the American strength and power terminology do allow variation within each phase and a gradual switch in training emphasis or goals as the training phase progresses. For example, during the strength phase, repetitions per set at the beginning of the phase would be 5 or 6, whereas at the end of the phase

Snatches and snatch variations like the power snatch pull require the development of power in order to be successfully completed.

© Mike Powell/Allsport Concepts/Getty Images

repetitions per set might be in the range of 2 to 4. This means that training intensity has increased while training volume has decreased. The number of sets within each training phase also allows for changes in training volume. For example, on one day in the strength phase, the back squat might be performed for 5 sets while on another day only 3 sets might be performed. These types of training emphases change by performing different exercises, and variation in training intensity and volume can be applied to all training phases.

EFFICACY OF CLASSIC STRENGTH AND POWER PERIODIZATION

When examining any training program, including resistance training programs, the first question that should be asked is whether the resistance exercise program causes the desired physiological adaptations. For resistance training programs, that includes increases in strength, local muscular endurance, muscle hypertrophy, and power. The next question is whether the program results in greater increases in those variables compared to the increases with other training programs. The answer to these questions concerning the classic strength and power periodization model is yes. Qualitative reviews (Fleck, 1999; Fleck, 2002) conclude that the majority of research projects demonstrate that the classic strength and power model brings about greater increases in maximal strength and power than low-volume (single-set) and higher-volume (3-6 sets), nonvaried (same number of sets and repetitions per set for the entire training period) training programs. Meta-analyses also conclude that periodized resistance training brings about greater increases in strength than nonvaried training programs (Rhea & Alderman, 2004). The majority of studies on periodization in this meta-analysis are variations of the strength and power periodization model, although a few of the studies use other periodization models (i.e., nonlinear models). A meta-analysis is a statistical procedure by which the results of all studies examining a particular topic, such as periodized weight training compared to nonvaried training models, can be statistically analyzed and a quantitative conclusion reached.

Not only does strength and power periodization result in greater strength and power increases than nonvaried models, but the majority of studies also indicate that this type of training brings about greater increases in fat-free mass, indicating greater muscle hypertrophy and greater decreases in percentage of body fat than nonvaried training models (Fleck, 1999; Fleck, 2002). Fewer studies have examined body composition changes due to strength and power periodization than studies examining strength and power changes, so conclusions concerning body composition changes must be viewed with some caution. It is important, however, to note that whenever a significant difference between strength and power periodization and nonvaried models occurs, it is always in favor of the periodized training program.

Figures 1.2 and 1.3 present the maximal strength results of one study comparing the strength and power periodization model to two nonvaried training models. Training was performed 3 days per week for 16 weeks. The two nonvaried models were 5 sets of 10 repetitions at approximately 79% of 1RM and 6 sets of 8 repetitions at approximately 83% of 1RM. The periodized program consisted of four 4-week training phases. The training phases were 5 sets of 10 repetitions at approximately 79% of 1RM, 6 sets of 8 repetitions at approximately

83% of 1RM, 3 sets of 6 repetitions at approximately 88% of 1RM, and 3 sets of 4 repetitions at approximately 92% of 1RM. Bench press and squat 1RM were determined every 4 weeks. In the bench press (figure 1.2), the periodized program demonstrated superiority at 8, 12, and 16 weeks of training compared to the two nonvaried programs. Both nonvaried programs appear to be in a training plateau from week 4 to week 12. Both nonvaried programs also demonstrated relatively small percentages of increase in bench press 1RM compared to the strength and power periodization training.

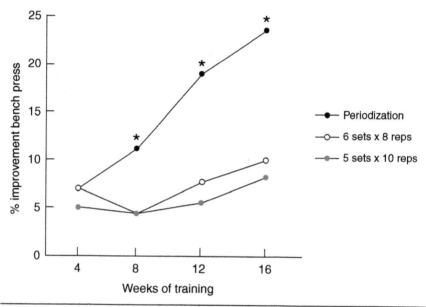

Figure 1.2   Results of a study comparing the strength and power periodization model to two nonvaried training programs for gains in the bench press in American football players. * = Significant difference from nonperiodized programs.

Data from D.S. Willoughby, 1993, "The effects of meso-cycle-length weight training programs involving periodization and partially equated volumes on upper and lower body strength," *Journal of Strength and Conditioning Research* 7:2-8.

In the squat (see figure 1.3), the periodized model and the 6 sets of 8 repetitions training model both showed significantly greater gains than the 5 sets of 10 repetitions after 4, 8, and 12 weeks of training. However, it was not until after 16 weeks of training that the periodized model showed a significantly greater gain in squat 1RM than both of the nonvaried training programs. The results demonstrate several important aspects of strength increases due to weight training. Not all muscle groups or exercises will respond to the same extent (i.e., period-

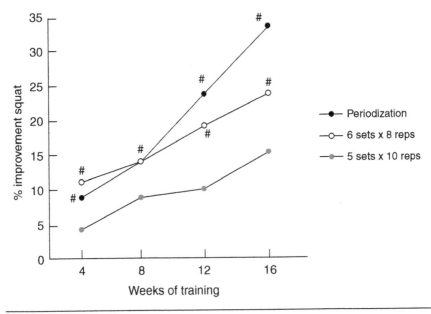

Figure 1.3   Results of a study comparing the strength and power periodization model to two nonvaried training programs for gains in the squat exercise in American football players. * = Significant difference from nonperiodized programs. # = Significant difference from 5 sets of 10 repetitions program.

Data from D.S. Willoughby, 1993, "The effects of meso-cycle-length weight training programs involving periodization and partially equated volumes on upper and lower body strength," Journal of Strength and Conditioning Research 7:2-8.

ized bench press increased approximately 24% while squat increased approximately 34%) or in the same time frame to a training program. Over short training periods (4 weeks in bench press and 12 weeks in squat), periodized training may not show superiority over nonvaried programs. Additionally, in order for physiological adaptations to occur, such as muscle hypertrophy and optimal neural recruitment resulting in strength gains, sufficient training time must be allowed, and the time necessary for training models to show different results (if they exist) may not be the same for different muscle groups.

The mechanisms resulting in greater strength gains caused by periodized training are not completely elucidated. However, a meta-analysis concludes that the effectiveness of periodized training is independent of the performance of greater volume or intensity with periodized training compared to nonvaried programs (Rhea & Alderman, 2004). Additionally, variations in training, independent of increases in training volume and intensity, may increase the overload experienced by the neuromuscular system by continually applying an unaccustomed training stress, which may result in greater fitness gains. With periodized training, the unaccustomed training stress occurs when the number of repetitions per set or number of sets of an exercise changes from one training phase to the next and within each training phase. Although the mechanisms by which strength and power periodized training brings about greater increases in strength, power, and changes in body composition than nonvaried training models are not completely clear, it is clear this type of training is more effective than nonvaried training models.

NONLINEAR PERIODIZATION

The exact origin of nonlinear periodization, also termed *undulating periodization,* is unclear, but it is a more recent development than the classic strength and power periodization model. Nonlinear programs may have originated in the late 1980s with 2-week training periods using various training zones to meet the needs of athletes (Poliquin, 1988). Likewise, nonlinear programs may have originated in the late 1970s and early 1980s with strength coaches designing programs to meet the needs of American football players. In these training plans, two very different types of training days were developed. The different training days were termed hypertrophy and functional strength days. On the functional strength days, multijoint exercises (power clean, squat) were performed using lower numbers of repetitions (4-6 repetitions per set), while on the hypertrophy days more single-joint exercises (arm curls, knee curls) were performed using higher numbers of repetitions (8-12 repetitions per set). Additionally, it was noted that when more mesocycles were used in a macrocycle, better results were achieved. Essentially that meant that the different patterns of loading had a greater frequency of exposure as microcycles shifted from 4 weeks to 2 weeks; some now use 1-week microcycle changes.

Although many variations of the nonlinear training model can be developed to meet the needs and goals of a trainee, the following is a representative model. If weight training is performed 3 days per week, three different RM training intensities, or repetition maximum (RM) zones, will be used on each of the 3 training days. On the first, second, and third training day of the week, training zones of 4 to 6, 12 to 15, and 8 to 10 repetitions per set using RM resistances will be performed, respectively. Other training zones, such as a very heavy (1- to 3RM) zone, can be included in the training program's design

On a hypertrophy workout day, predominantly single-joint exercises, such as arm curls, are performed using higher numbers of repetitions (8-12) per set.
© University of Connecticut Office of Athletic Communications.

if they meet the needs and goals of the trainee. In addition, percentages of the 1RM can be used for certain lifts addressing the same types of loading ranges. Care must be taken because the percentage of 1RM and the RM vary depending on the muscle mass involved in an exercise and for machines versus free weights (e.g., 80% of 1RM in a squat may result in only 8 to 10 repetitions, whereas in the leg press 15 to 20 repetitions may be possible at the same percentage of 1RM) (Hoeger et al., 1987; 1990; Shimano et al., 2006).

Note that training zones are *not* necessarily performed sequentially such that training volume and intensity follow a consistent pattern of increasing or decreasing over time. For example, during 1 week of training, the zones might be performed in the sequence of 4 to 6, 12 to 15, and 8 to 10 repetitions per set. During the next week of training, the sequence of zones might be 8 to 10, 4 to 6, and 12 to 15 repetitions per set. With nonlinear training, long periods (weeks) using the same training intensity and volume are not performed. Thus the need for a high training volume phase (hypertrophy phase), as used in the classic strength and power model, is avoided. Another advantage of the nonlinear model is ease of administration. Once training zones have been chosen that meet the goals of the training program, they are simply alternated on a session-by-session basis. So continuing with the current example, if, during the course of a season during one week only two weight training sessions can be performed because of a competition, the first training session of the next week might use the training zone that was not used during the previous week and the sequence of training zones begins with that training zone. There are other possible ways to make the decision concerning which training zone to use, such as if there is lingering fatigue resulting from the weekend competition, which minimizes the ability to develop maximal power. In that case if a power training zone is part of the training program, it might be advisable to use a different training zone for the first training session of the week after the competition.

However, once training zones have been decided, it does not mean that over time different training zones cannot be incorporated into the training program. For example, during the early preseason, a very heavy or a power training zone might not be used. But, during the late preseason, a very heavy or power training zone might be used. Thus the choice of training zones to use at a particular point in the training program can be changed to meet the goals and needs of the trainee as training progresses. Similar to the classic strength and power training model, planned light training periods or rest periods can also be incorporated into nonlinear training programs. Typically these recovery periods are scheduled approximately every 12 weeks of training.

Nonlinear periodization offers advantages over classic strength and power periodization in some training situations. A major goal of the strength and power periodization model is to reach a peak in strength and power at a particular time. For many sports with long seasons, such as basketball, volleyball, tennis, ice hockey, and baseball, success is dependent on physical fitness and performance throughout the season. When resistance training for general fitness, peaking maximal strength and power at a certain point may not be important, but continued gains in strength and power are important training outcomes. Training goals for many sports and for general fitness need in part to focus on development and maintenance of physical fitness throughout the season or throughout the year. For sports with long seasons, peaking maximal strength and power at the end of the season in preparation for major competitions, such as conference tournaments or other major tournaments, is important. However, using the classic strength and power periodization model for those sports presents some difficulties. If a classic strength and power model is used as a program approach in the off-season and preseason, the peaking phase will occur at the start of the competitive season. This may ensure the best possible performance at the start of the competitive season; however, strength and fitness must be maintained throughout the season. If the peaking phase occurs at the end of the competitive season in preparation for major competitions or tournaments, then high-volume resistance training must be performed during the beginning of the competitive season. That may result in less-than-optimal performance at the beginning of the season because of fatigue and could result in losses in early competitions. If those early games are lost, qualification for tournaments at the end of the season may be jeopardized. Thus the application of the classic strength and power periodization training model for many sports and activities presents some difficulties in the training program's design.

Nonlinear periodization is more flexible in how and when a peak in performance is created, depending on the goals of a particular mesocycle. It also allows for more frequent exposure to different loading stimuli (e.g., moderate, power) within a particular weekly workout profile. It does not progress in a planned linear increase in intensity with a reduction in volume as seen in the linear model, but it varies training volume and intensity in such a way that consistent fitness gains occur over long training periods.

EFFICACY OF NONLINEAR PERIODIZATION

Studies have examined the efficacy of nonlinear periodization. To date, all studies indicate that it does result in significant fitness gains and results in greater gains than other training models provide. The earliest of the studies was 24 weeks in length. It involved training Division III collegiate football players and compared a session-to-session nonlinear pattern to a low training volume one-set training model (Kraemer, 1997). The one-set program consisted of training 3 days per week using two different groups of exercises on alternating training days and forced repetitions. The nonlinear training model consisted of training 4 days per week using two different training sessions alternated on a training-session basis. One training session was a strength and power session and consisted of primarily multijoint exercises using a 3- to 5-, an 8- to 10-, or a 12- to 15RM training zone. The other session was a hypertrophy session and consisted of both single-joint and multijoint exercises always using an 8- to 10RM training zone. The nonlinear model resulted in significantly greater gains in tests of strength, local muscular endurance, and power (table 1.2). Although both training programs resulted in a significant decrease in percentage of body fat, the nonlinear model resulted in a significantly greater decrease (nonlinear 17.9% to 12.0%; single-set model 17.1% to 15.9%). Both training models also resulted in a significant increase in total body mass. However, again the nonlinear model resulted in a significantly greater gain in body mass (nonlinear model 104 kg to 111 kg; single-set model 103 kg to 104 kg) than the single-set model.

Women's Division I tennis players have been trained using the nonlinear model, and the results were compared to a nonvaried, low-volume one-set model and a higher-volume three-set model. In the first of these studies a one-set circuit program of 8 to 10 repetitions at an 8- to 10RM resistance performed 3 days per week was compared to a nonlinear model performed 4 days per week over 9 months of training (Kraemer et al., 2000). Both groups of tennis players trained 2 or 3 days per week depending on their competitive schedules. The nonlinear model consisted of performing 2 to 4 sets using training zones of 4 to 6, 8 to 10, and 12 to 15 repetitions per set alternated on a session-by-session basis. Both groups performed the same series of single-joint and multijoint exercises. The nonlinear model generally used all three training zones only for the multijoint exercises, while the single-joint exercises were always performed using 8 to 10 repetitions per set. The resistance used in the nonlinear model was adjusted to allow only the desired number of repetitions per set (RM training zone). The nonlinear model demonstrated a greater percentage of gains in measures of strength and power than the single-set model (table 1.2). A significant decrease in percentage of body fat (nonlinear 22 to 18%; single set 22 to 21%) and an increase in fat-free mass were shown by the nonlinear model, while the single-set model showed no significant changes in these measures. Perhaps most important, the nonlinear model demonstrated a significant increase of 30% in serve velocity while the single-set model demonstrated a nonsignificant change of 4% in serve velocity. It is also important to note that in the majority of test variables, the nonlinear model demonstrated significant increases from pretraining to 4 months of training, from 4 months to 6 months of training, and from 6 months to 9 months

Table 1.2 Nonlinear Training Studies

Reference	Mean age (yrs) and sex	Training length	Frequency per week	Sessions	Intensity	Exercises trained	Tests	Percentage of increase
Kraemer, 1997		24	3	Sets: 1 Repetitions: 8 to 10 with forced reps	8- to 10RM	20	Bench press Leg press Bench press reps at 80% 1RM Leg press reps at 80% 1RM Vertical jump Wingate power	13* 6* 37* 22* 7* 5*
			4	Undulating periodization strength session Sets: 2 to 4 Repetitions: 12 to 15, 8 to 10, 3 to 5 Hypertrophy session Sets: 2 to 4 Repetitions: 8 to 10	12- to 15-, 8- to 10-, 3- to 5RM 8- to 10RM	21	Bench press Leg press Bench press reps at 80% 1RM Leg press reps at 80% 1RM Vertical jump Wingate power	29*[a] 20*[a] 56*[a] 41*[a] 23*[a] 55*[a]
Kraemer et al., 2000	19 F	36	2 or 3	Sets: 1 Repetitions: 8 to10	Close to 8- to 10RM	14	Bench press Shoulder press Leg press Wingate power Vertical jump	10* 14* 7* 1 5

(continued)

Table 1.2 *(continued)*

Reference	Mean age (yrs) and sex	Training length	Frequency per week	Sessions	Intensity	Exercises trained	Tests	Percentage of increase
			2 or 3	Undulating periodization Sets: 3, 2, or 4 Repetitions: 4 to 6, 8 to 10, or 12 to 15	Close to RMs	14	Bench press Shoulder press Leg press Wingate power Vertical jump	25* 28* 18* 14* 48*
Marx et al., 2001	22-23 F	24	3	Sets: 1 Repetitions: 8 to 12	8- to 12RM	2 alternating groups of 10 exercises	Bench press Leg press Bench press reps at 80% 1RM Leg press reps at 80% 1RM Wingate power Sit-ups in 1 min Vertical jump 40 yd sprint	12* 11* 10* 19* 4 13* 10* +1

	4	Undulating periodization strength sessions/wk Sets: 2 or 3 Repetitions: 3 to 5, 8 to 10, or 12 to 15 Hypertrophy sessions Sets: 2 or 3 Repetitions: 8 to 10	3- to 5-, 8- to 10-, or 12- to 15RM 8- to 10RM	Undulating sessions 7 Constant 8 to 10 reps Session 12	Bench press Leg press Bench press at 80% 1RM Leg press reps at 80% 1RM Wingate power Sit-ups in 1 min Vertical jump 40 yd sprint	47[*a] 32[*a] 24[*a] 64[*a] 27[*a] 42[*a] 40[*a] −6[*a]
Kraemer et al., 2003	36	Nonvaried Sets: 2 or 3 Repetitions: 8 to 10	8- to 10RM	3 alternating groups of 11 or 12 exercises	Bench press Leg press Wingate power Vertical jump	17[*] 17[*] 18[*] 37[*]
		Undulating periodization alternating sessions Sets: 2 or 3 Repetitions: 4 to 6, 8 to 10, or 12 to 15	4- to 6, 8- to 10-, or 12- to 15RM	3 alternating groups of 11 or 12 exercises	Bench press Leg press Wingate power Vertical jump	23[*] 19[*] 12[*] 50[*b]

[*] = Significant change pre- to posttraining.

[a] = Significant difference from 1-set group.

[b] = Significant difference from nonvaried group.

of training. The single-set model demonstrated a significant increase from pretraining to 4 months of training and then showed no further significant change or was in a training plateau.

The second study training female Division I tennis players compared the nonlinear model to a nonvaried three-set model over 9 months of training (Kraemer et al., 2003). The three-set model always trained using 8 to 10 repetitions per set at RM resistances. The nonlinear model trained with three sets using three alternating training zones on a session-by-session basis of 4 to 6, 8 to 10, and 12 to 15 repetitions per set at RM resistances. Both groups trained 2 or 3 days per week, depending on their competitive schedules. Few significant differences in strength and power were noted between groups after the 9 months of training (table 1.2). However, whenever a significant difference between groups was noted, it was in favor of the nonlinear training model. Additionally, testing was performed after 4, 6, and 9 months of training; whenever a significant difference was noted between groups at those time points it was in favor of the nonlinear model. It is also important to note that the nonlinear model showed a greater number of significant gains between pretraining and 4 months training, 4 to 6 months of training, and 6 to 9 months of training, indicating more consistent fitness gains as the training progressed. Both groups also demonstrated significant increases in fat-free mass and decreases in percentage of body fat; no significant differences were noted between groups. Perhaps most important to this group of athletes, the nonlinear program resulted in significantly greater increases (22 to 36%) in serve, backhand, and forehand velocities compared to the nonvaried training increases of 14 to 17% in the same sport-specific measures.

The nonlinear model has also been compared to a low-volume single-set model in the training of typical college-aged females over 6 months (Marx et al., 2001). The single-set group trained 3 days per week using 8 to 10 repetitions per set at RM resistances. Two different circuits were performed by the single-set model on an alternating session-by-session basis. The nonlinear group trained 4 days per week with 2 to 4 sets. Two days per week a strength session composed of primarily multijoint exercises was performed with the use of alternating training zones of 3 to 5, 8 to 10, and 12 to 15 repetitions per set at RM resistances. The other two training sessions per week were hypertrophy training sessions performed always for 8 to 10 repetitions per set at RM resistances. At the end of the 6 months of training, the nonlinear group demonstrated significantly greater increases in measures of strength, power, and motor performance than the nonvaried group (table 1.2). The nonlinear group also demonstrated significantly greater increases in fat-free mass (8 vs. 2%) and percentage of body fat (-7 vs. -2.5%) than the single-set group. Additionally, in the majority of variables, the nonlinear training group demonstrated significant changes from pretraining to 4 months of training and from 4 months of training to 6 months of training while in all variables the single-set group demonstrated significant gains from pretraining to 4 months of training with no significant increase from 4 to 6 months of training. This shows that the nonvaried training resulted in a training plateau after 4 months of training while the nonlinear training showed continued fitness gains over the 6 months of training, which underscores the efficacy of nonlinear training.

Nonlinear periodization has even been shown to be effective during a competitive season. Silvestre and colleagues (2006) demonstrated that strength and power can be maintained or even increased with a nonlinear resistance training protocol over a competitive soccer season. Such uses of the nonlinear method enhance the ability of athletes to physically develop their bodies—even during a competitive season, when detraining can occur.

Collectively these studies demonstrate that the nonlinear training model results in significantly greater changes in body composition, strength, and power than nonvaried training models. These changes with the nonlinear training model are consistent and progressive even after months of training. Additionally, changes in fitness parameters are apparent in untrained individuals as well as in trained athletes.

EFFICACY OF SESSION-BY-SESSION VARIATION

One aspect of any periodized training program that needs to be considered is how often training intensity and volume should be changed. With nonlinear resistance training, volume and intensity are changed dramatically from one training session to the next. Some insight concerning the efficacy of using session-to-session changes in training volume and intensity, such as used in nonlinear periodization, can be gained by examining the results of several studies. The first of these studies compared strength gains during training with the use of a classic strength and power model, a nonvaried multiset model, and a biweekly nonlinear model over 12 weeks (Baker et al., 1994). With a biweekly nonlinear model, three training zones are used, but rather than alternately use training zones on a session-by-session basis, training zones are alternated every 2 weeks. Although all groups significantly improved in bench press 1RM (12-16%) and squat 1 RM (26-28%), no significant differences were observed between the groups. Results indicate that a biweekly nonlinear periodization model and a classic strength and power model result in similar changes in strength.

The second study compared a session-by-session nonlinear program with a classic strength and power periodization program over 12 weeks of training (Rhea et al., 2002). Both groups trained 3 days per week and performed three sets of each exercise per training session. The nonlinear program performed one session per week at 8, 6, and 4RM resistances. After the 12 weeks of training, the session-by-session nonlinear program resulted in significantly greater increases in bench press 1RM (29 vs. 14%) and leg press 1RM (56 vs. 26%) than the strength and power periodized model, indicating session-by-session nonlinear programs result in greater strength increases than a variation of the classic strength and power training model.

Collectively these two studies indicate that a session-by-session nonlinear program results in greater strength gains than a classic strength and power model, while a biweekly nonlinear program results in significant but equivalent strength gains compared to a variation of the classic strength and power model. Although comparison of results from two separate studies is tenuous, results of these two studies suggest session-by-session nonlinear programs cause greater strength gains than biweekly nonlinear programs.

IMPETUS FOR THE FLEXIBLE NONLINEAR APPROACH TO PERIODIZATION

As discussed previously, research supports the use of a classic strength and power training model. Anecdotal evidence also supports the classic strength and power periodization model and a reduction in the number of mesocycles in the macrocycle indicating that a greater variation in volume and intensity appears to be beneficial to the training adaptations. Several other factors also spurred the growth of nonlinear periodization methods at the grassroots level. Personal trainers always try to keep workouts exciting to their clients and have discovered that their clients need more variation in training routines to keep boredom at a minimum. Finally, the physical and mental challenges that athletes face outside of the weight room also demand a training system that responds to athletes' immediate needs for training on a given day.

Consequently, the practicality and increasing popularity of the nonlinear approach to periodized resistance training have been due to several factors:

1. It allows more variety in a workout sequence.
2. It allows athletes to more quickly pick up a workout sequence after illness or injury.
3. It causes less boredom in the day-to-day workout routines.
4. It is adaptable to the diverse situations of a given training day and gives trainees the most effective type of workout.
5. It allows more frequent rest of some muscle tissue due to the use of various resistance loadings.

One possible problem associated with any training program is determining whether a trainee can perform the scheduled session with the desired training volume and intensity. To help address this question, researchers working with the University of Connecticut men's and women's basketball players in 2001 to 2004 showed that new variations in the nonlinear approach to periodization of resistance training were successful and that even newer variations of nonlinear periodization were still possible. This work resulted in what has been termed *flexible nonlinear periodization*. The flexible nonlinear approach allows for the trainer and athlete to choose the workout when the athlete reports to the weight room. While still in an experimental stage of development, the practical concept consists of several steps:

1. Conducting a coaching analysis of the athlete's fatigue status at the time of the workout
2. Testing for physical performance status on the day of the workout
3. Monitoring of the initial resistance and set performances in the workout compared to prior efforts
4. Choosing, modifying, or switching the workout based on the results of steps 1 to 3
5. Having an overall plan for the mesocycle so that workouts in a 7- to 10-day cycle can be checked off or accomplished

In sports, more frequent variation was needed for the longer-season sports, such as basketball, tennis, hockey, and wrestling, in which athletes could not peak for just a single competition.

Both nonlinear periodization and flexible nonlinear periodization have advantages over other weight training programs that make them applicable to a variety of training situations and populations. These populations include both fitness enthusiasts as well as various groups of athletes.

SUMMARY

Eastern European coaches and sport scientists are normally credited with developing the concepts of periodization of training, including the classic strength and power periodization of resistance training model. Classic strength and power periodization of resistance training follows a general pattern of decreasing training volume and increasing training intensity as a training cycle progresses. Sport science research demonstrates the classic strength and power periodization training model does result in greater fitness gains than nonvaried resistance training can provide. Although nonlinear periodization is a relatively new strength training model, it does result in significant gains in strength, power, body composition, and motor performance. Data also indicate that nonlinear periodization results in significantly greater changes in fitness variables compared to nonvaried and even strength and power training models. Current research indicates that when a nonlinear program is used, the training zones should be alternated on a session-by-session basis. Building on the concepts of training variation used with classic strength and power periodization of resistance training, both the nonlinear periodization training and the flexible nonlinear periodization programs have emerged as very effective training models.

CHAPTER 2

Training Principles

Principles of weight training apply to all resistance training programs, including nonlinear periodization training programs. To completely understand nonlinear program design, you need to understand all of the principles of resistance training. This is true for experienced practitioners as well as beginning students of resistance training program design. All principles presented are discussed from the perspective of their application to resistance training program design, including the nonlinear program design. The nonlinear periodization method involves the creation of unique and specific workouts that address the goals of a training program as well as the goals of a resistance training cycle.

SPECIFICITY

As with all types of physical training, there is a high degree of task specificity with resistance training (American College of Sports Medicine, 2002; Kraemer & Ratamess, 2004). Task specificity refers to the movement pattern and strength or power output necessary for successful completion of a specific physical task. Physiological adaptations brought about by a particular resistance training program are specific to the training program performed. Therefore, the best training program to use to become better at a specific task, such as a certain sport or physical activity, mimics the characteristics of the task (e.g., velocity of movement, angles used, type of muscle actions) and brings about physiological adaptations necessary for higher proficiency in the specific task.

Physiological adaptations brought about by performance of resistance training are specific to the muscles trained, types of muscle action (eccentric, concentric, isometric), speed of movement, range of motion, and energy source (aerobic, anaerobic) (American College of Sports Medicine, 2002; Kraemer & Ratamess, 2004). Because of the specificity of training, each resistance training program emphasizes unique physiological adaptations. Perhaps the simplest explanation of specificity is the adaptations are brought about predominantly in the muscle groups trained. Training of the lower body (i.e., legs) does not necessarily bring about increased strength or power of the upper body (i.e., arms). The performance of a squat, sometimes thought of as a lower-body exercise, does bring about some increased strength in the muscles of the upper and lower back because of the support of the load. However, most lower-body exercises, such as the leg press and knee extension, cause minuscule or even nonexistent physiological adaptations in the upper body. Training adaptations are all specifically related to the demands for recruitment of muscle tissue caused by the performance of the exercise movement with a specific resistance.

There are many types of training specificity. A well-designed resistance training program for any sport or activity takes into account training specificities. Taking advantage of training specificities can result in a better-designed resistance training program for a particular sport and can result in greater performance increases in the sport for which the training program is intended. Ultimately, the amount of transfer from the resistance training program to the functional activity, everyday task, or athletic skill is an important part of the benefits of a resistance training program.

Muscle Action

Specificity in muscle action is important in planning resistance training programs for particular sports. For example, eccentric strength (muscle lengthening under tension) may be just as important as concentric strength (muscle shortening under tension) for the performance of some tasks. Good powerlifters not only lift heavier resistances but also lower the resistance, or perform the eccentric portion of repetitions, in the bench press and squat at a slower velocity than less successful lifters (Madsen & McLaughlin, 1984; McLaughlin, Dillman, & Lardner, 1977). Figure skaters not only need to jump high to perform jumps, but they also must land those jumps in a graceful and controlled manner, which requires eccentric strength. Therefore, these athletes need to include some specific eccentric training in their resistance training programs. Speed of movement with a certain resistance is dependent on power output. If one major goal of a resistance training program is to increase maximal vertical jump ability, then the training program would include exercises specific to the lower body with an emphasis on velocity of movement and power output, such as the jump squat, power clean, and plyometric exercises.

Range of Motion

Normally most resistance training exercises are performed through the greatest range of motion allowed by the body positions and joint angles of a particular exercise. This results in strength and power gains throughout the range of motion. Generally the goal of a resistance training program is to increase strength and power throughout the range of motion in a joint. This allows increased strength and power to be applied throughout the range of motion of other tasks, such as the vertical jump or throwing a ball. Joint angle–specific strength gains

For volleyball training, some squat sets using heavier resistances and squat jump–type exercises may be performed only through the range of motion used when performing a vertical jump.

are perhaps most apparent with isometric training where strength gains obtained at a certain joint angle may only result in significant increases in strength 5 to 20° on either side of the joint angle at which training was performed (Fleck & Kraemer, 2004). Although most resistance training exercises are performed throughout the greatest possible range of motion, it is possible to use range-of-motion specificity in some situations by performing exercises through a limited range of motion (Fleck & Kraemer, 2004).

Energy Source

Resistance training is normally thought of as an anaerobic activity. However, there are two anaerobic sources of energy. Intramuscular stores of high-energy phosphates (adenosine triphosphate—ATP—and phosphocreatine) are the most powerful of the energy sources; they supply the greatest amount of energy per second, but there are very limited amounts of these substances stored intramuscularly. Therefore some muscle fibers are depleted or at least partially depleted of high-energy phosphates in a matter of seconds. Depletion of high-energy phosphates in some muscle fibers is a major reason it is impossible to perform two repetitions with the one-repetition maximum (1RM) of an exercise. When some muscle fibers cannot generate their maximal force or power because of high-energy phosphate depletion, it is impossible to generate sufficient force or power to complete two repetitions with a 1RM resistance.

High-energy phosphates are the energy source of maximal strength and power expression. Typically during training for maximal strength or power expression, relatively few repetitions are performed (1-5) per set of an exercise and long rest periods are used between sets to allow recovery of the intramuscular high-energy phosphates so that they can once again be used for energy in successive sets. Thus when performing a heavy resistance training session (4- to 6RM) in a non-linear program, relatively long rest periods between sets and exercises are used. When performing a session using lighter resistances (12- to 15RM), shorter rest periods (2 minutes or shorter) can be used.

The second anaerobic energy source is anaerobic metabolism of carbohydrate (i.e., breakdown of glucose or glycogen), resulting in the production of lactic acid. Lactic acid is a substance that is a by-product of the chemical reactions of anaerobic glycolysis and is associated in part with the burning feeling when sprinting as fast as possible for 400 meters or on completion of several sets using a 10RM resistance and short rest periods (1 minute) between sets. The lactic acid energy source is less powerful (supplies less energy per second) than high-energy phosphates, but it can supply energy for a longer period of time in an all-out sprint or near-maximal power activity. This energy source can supply energy for up to 2 minutes (Wilmore & Costill, 2004) in a near-maximal power output activity. The high rate and use of ATP result in proton production, which causes an increase in acidosis and brings about fatigue (Robergs, Ghlasvamd, & Parker, 2004). Lactic acid is a good marker of this process but may not be directly responsible for fatigue. Also, it is does not produce muscle soreness, as many athletes and coaches often believe (Robergs, Ghlasvamd & Parker, 2004). Some activities, such as sprinting 400 meters or performing repeat sprints during a relatively high-intensity game such as basketball, require the ability to generate energy by anaerobic metabolism, resulting in high use of ATP and therefore fatigue.

Sprinting requires a high use of ATP and results in release of lactic acid.

Performing sets of an exercise with short rest periods (1 minute) between sets and successive exercises in a training session using moderate resistances (approximately 10RM) results in higher concentrations of blood lactic acid representative of the high level of use of ATP and increasing acidosis; this concentration is higher than it would be during sets with heavier resistances (5RM) or with longer rest periods (3 minutes) between sets and exercises (Kraemer et al., 1990; 1991; 1993). Thus, when emphasizing the ability to generate high levels of acidosis indicated by lactic acid, generally moderate resistances (i.e., 8- to 10RM or 75-85% of 1RM) and short rest periods (i.e., 1-2 minutes) between sets and exercises are used. Careful progression is needed when reducing the amount of rest between sets and exercises in order to eliminate unwanted symptoms such as dizziness, nausea, and fainting during a resistance training session. Short rest periods range from 1 to 2 minutes; and when relatively moderate loads are used (8- to 10RM or 70-85% of 1RM), dramatic elevations in muscle and blood lactate along with symptoms frequently occur. Extremely short rest periods (less than 1 minute) using similar resistance loads result in even more dramatic symptoms that need to be carefully monitored (Kraemer et al., 1987).

Cardiorespiratory Endurance

Typical heavy resistance training has a minimal impact on cardiorespiratory endurance or markers of cardiorespiratory endurance, such as peak oxygen consumption (Kraemer et al., 1995). Therefore resistance training is typically not used as a means of increasing cardiorespiratory endurance. Perhaps the type of resistance training that brings about the greatest increase in peak oxygen consumption is circuit training using moderate resistances and short rest periods between successive exercises. Circuit training causes increases in peak oxygen consumption of approximately 4 and 8% in males and females, respectively, over short training periods (8 to 20 weeks) (Gettman & Pollock, 1981). This, however, is substantially lower than the 15 to 20% increase in peak oxygen consumption caused by traditional aerobic training over the same period. The lack of an increase in peak oxygen consumption does not, however, mean that resistance training does not increase endurance activity performance. Increases in endurance activity performance, such as 5- to 10-kilometer run times, have been caused by the addition of resistance training to a conditioning program in untrained individuals, moderately trained individuals, and highly trained endurance athletes (Hickson, 1980; Hickson et al., 1988; Marcinik et al., 1991; Bastiaans et al., 2001; Paavolainen et al., 1999). Interestingly, these increases in performance occur despite no increase in peak oxygen consumption. The increases in performance have been attributed to an increase in the lactic acid threshold. Lactic acid threshold is the pace that can be maintained with minimal increase in tissue lactic acid or increasing acidity. This information indicates that resistance training may bring about increased performance in endurance sports and activities requiring a substantial cardiorespiratory endurance component for success, such as basketball and soccer, even if peak oxygen consumption is not significantly increased. This does not imply that athletes requiring cardiorespiratory endurance should not perform cardiorespiratory endurance training, but that resistance training should be a part of their total training program to bring about improved running economy and metabolic efficiency. The previous information indicates that resistance training programs, including nonlinear periodization programs, are of value not only to athletes who need strength and power for success but also to athletes dependent on cardiorespiratory endurance for success. In fact, one might hypothesize that nonlinear models using not just heavy resistance sessions but also lighter resistance sessions could optimize performance in events typically thought of as heavily dependent on cardiorespiratory endurance for success.

PROGRESSIVE OVERLOAD

Progressive overload is a concept developed by U.S. Army physician Thomas Delorme in the 1940s as he worked in hospitals to physically rehabilitate soldiers from their injuries incurred during World War II. This concept has been a principle in resistance training. The term *progressive resistance training* was suggested by his wife during a dinner conversation (personal communication with Dr. Terry Todd, University of Texas). The principle underscores the need for greater demands to be placed on the body during successive workouts over time if improvement is to be achieved (DeLorme & Watkins, 1948).

An important corollary to the principle of progressive overload is the need for variation in training, which provides periods of planned rest and variation in the exercise stress. Thus, progressive overload refers to the gradual increase of training stress placed on the body during any physical training program, including resistance training. Once an athlete adapts to the demands of a specific training program, if the athlete does not adjust some element of the program to make the training more difficult to perform, then continued adaptations, such as continued increases in strength, will not occur. The most common way to apply progressive overload in a resistance training program is to increase the resistance used in performing a specific number of repetitions per set of an exercise. Once muscle hypertrophy has occurred, less muscle mass is recruited for an exercise using the same absolute weight compared to before hypertrophy had taken place (Ploutz et al., 1994). This indicates that in order to recruit the same percentage of the muscle's mass, the resistance used must be increased when performing a specified number of repetitions. Thus progressive overload must be applied for maximal muscle fiber recruitment if the maximal amount of muscle mass is to be used when performing an exercise. If progressive overload is not applied, not all muscle fibers will be recruited, resulting in minimal physiological adaptations in those fibers. If physiological adaptations are minimal, strength gains and muscle hypertrophy will also be minimal.

Although the most common way to apply progressive overload is to increase the resistance used in performing a specific number of repetitions, there are other ways in which progressive overload can be applied, such as the following:

- Increase the number of repetitions performed using a specific resistance.
- Increase the speed with which the concentric portion of a repetition is performed if a training goal is to increase maximal power and increased velocity can be accomplished in a safe manner.
- Shorten rest periods between sets and exercises so that more total work is performed in the same total training time; this may be especially important if a training goal is to increase local muscular endurance.
- Lengthen rest periods between sets and exercises and increase the resistance used. Because of the longer rest periods, more recovery occurs, thus allowing the use of a heavier resistance. This may be important if a training goal is to increase maximal strength and power against heavy resistances.
- Increase training volume by increasing the number of sets or number of repetitions per set, within reasonable limits.
- Use any combination of the previously mentioned methods to apply progressive overload.

Progressive overload appears to be a necessary component of a resistance training program if continued gains in strength and power, local muscular endurance, and other physiological adaptations are desired. It has been recommended that small changes in training volume and intensity (up to 5%) be used when applying progressive overload (American College of Sports Medicine, 2002). However, larger changes in training volume and intensity have been used successfully in programs designed for advanced athletes. Therefore the maximum amount of change in training volume and intensity when applying progressive overload needs further study. No matter how progressive overload is applied, careful monitoring of the trainees' tolerance to the increased training stress needs to occur to ensure that the increased training stress results in continued fitness gains without harm.

A key point in the use of nonlinear periodization is that the changes in training volume and intensity between workouts can be quite large.

While the changes between a light 12- to 14RM training day and a heavy 3- to 5RM training day might be quite large in both intensity and volume, it is the progression for each of these specific workouts over time that needs to be carefully changed and gradually progressed.

However, the context of the increase in volume and intensity is relative to the specific workouts. This concept applies to any progressive overload concept described previously.

More dramatic changes in volume and intensity can occur in beginners over time as they rapidly improve in many training features because of their untrained status and great potential for gain. Conversely, advanced athletes (those with many years of resistance training experience) have already used a high percentage of their adaptational potential. In highly resistance-trained athletes, the challenges in exercise prescription to improve the trainable variables require even more knowledge and attention to detail. The quality of the workout, then, has the greatest importance. Thus the flexible nonlinear training model, where testing before a session in part determines the decision about what type of session to perform on a given day, becomes paramount for optimizing training adaptations.

TRAINING FREQUENCY

Training frequency is the number of training sessions per week in which a particular muscle group is trained or emphasized in a session. The need for this definition is made apparent by body-part training routines. A body-part routine is a program structure in which individual body parts or muscle groups are emphasized in individual training sessions, such as training the arms, legs, shoulders, chest, and back on Monday, Tuesday, Wednesday, Thursday, and Friday, respectively. In this type of training program, a particular body part is trained only 1 or 2 days per week, but training sessions actually occur 5 or 6 days per week because all muscle groups are trained 1 or 2 days per week.

Optimal Training Frequencies

Optimal training frequency is dependent on factors such as training volume, intensity, exercise selection, level of conditioning, and ability of a muscle group to recover. For example, many national- and international-class Olympic weightlifters train two times per day 5 or 6 days per week. In fact, frequencies as high as 18 sessions per week have been reported in Olympic weightlifters (Zatsiorsky, 1995). The rationale for use of such high-frequency training is that shorter, more frequent training sessions allow recovery and nutrient intake between sessions, which allow for reduced fatigue levels at the end of training sessions and therefore higher-intensity training overall. Thus frequent, short-duration sessions consider the quality of the workout as vital for improvement. However, Olympic weightlifters use resistance training to physically prepare for competitions; and because competition involves lifting weights in certain types of lifts (snatch and clean and jerk), they also practice sport-specific techniques when they perform these exercises in training. Many elite powerlifters also typically train 4 to 6 days per week. Again, similar to Olympic weightlifting, some lifts (bench press, back squat, and deadlift) for these athletes also constitute sport-specific technique training. Thus they have the luxury of training the specific exercise movements to be used in their competitions.

Other athletes (e.g., basketball players, tennis players, soccer players) perform resistance training to physically prepare their bodies for their specific competitions. In addition, they must also perform other types of sport-specific conditioning and skill practice to thoroughly prepare for competition. Some bodybuilders and elite weightlifters also use double-split training routines (2 training sessions per day with emphasis on different muscle groups), which may result in 8 to 12 training sessions per week. However, rest and recovery of individual muscle groups are allowed, even though total training frequency is quite high. Even though some elite weightlifting athletes use very high total-training frequency, training frequency of individual muscle groups is substantially lower than the total-training frequency. When examining training frequency of elite Olympic weightlifters, powerlifters, and bodybuilders, also consider that these athletes' genetic makeups might allow such frequent training sessions and that it may have taken years of training to prepare them to tolerate the training frequencies they use. Thus, careful progression to higher frequencies should be based on toleration, need, and progression in training background.

Training frequency of an individual muscle group is the major determinant of how much rest and recovery for a muscle group are allowed between resistance training sessions. However, muscle recovery between resistance training sessions for most athletes is also dependent on the other types of physical training being performed, such as aerobic training, interval sprint training, sport practice, and sport-specific conditioning. Ultimately recovery between any training session, including resistance training sessions, will be in large part dependent on physical recovery between all types of sessions. Thus for most athletes, frequency of other types of training sessions determines frequency of resistance training sessions. Too much total training within a weekly training cycle can create reductions in performance or acute overtraining. The flexible nonlinear method can rapidly adjust to such complex demands on a daily basis, adding further efficacy to this training approach.

Recommendations for Frequency

Whether the emphasis is on muscular strength and power, hypertrophy, or local muscular endurance, the following are the recommended training frequencies (American College of Sports Medicine, 2002). Novice weight trainers should train using a total-body routine 2 or 3 days per week. Intermediate weight trainers, if using a total-body training session, should also train 2 or 3 days per week. If intermediate weight trainers use upper- and lower-body split programs or other types of split or body-part programs, training frequency for individual muscle groups should be 1 or 2 days per week, but this will result in a total-training frequency of 3 or 4 days per week. Advanced weightlifters can train 4 to 6 days per week in part because of the use of upper- and lower-body split programs or other types of body-part programs and may benefit from using more frequent training, such as two training sessions per day, so long as adequate recovery occurs between sessions and appropriate recovery steps are taken to minimize the risk of overtraining. A frequency of 1 or 2 days per week is effective as a maintenance frequency for trainees already engaged in a resistance training program.

An extensive meta-analysis supports the previously recommended frequencies for untrained and trained lifters. The meta-analysis concludes that for untrained individuals and trained individuals a frequency of 3 and 2 days, respectively, per week per muscle group is optimal (Rhea et al., 2003). In the meta-analysis, Rhea and colleagues hypothesize that the optimal training frequency may be lower in trained individuals than in untrained individuals because the studies of trained individuals used higher training volumes. Results of the meta-analysis also indicate that optimal training frequency may vary with training status and training volume.

Frequency must always be considered as the frequency of working a particular muscle group. Training frequency may change throughout the course of a season for an athlete. Whatever the frequency used in weight training, the total program, including all other types of training sessions, must be considered because training forms that do not involve weights will affect recovery between weight training sessions.

In the off-season, frequency of weight training may be 3 or 4 days per week. However, when sport-specific training volume increases during the in-season, frequency of weight training may be only 2 or 3 days per week.

© University of Connecticut Office of Athletic Communications.

To date, research concerning the nonlinear periodization model has used training frequencies ranging from two to four sessions per week, and these frequencies have resulted in significant fitness gains (see chapter 1). Note that these frequencies fall within the ranges of training frequency discussed and recommended previously.

SUMMARY

When implementing a nonlinear periodization training program, consider all the information concerning the training principles of specificity, progressive overload, and training frequency. Use of this information helps in designing a program that meets the specific goals and training needs for a sport or activity. All nonlinear programs, especially those for athletes, need to take into account the various types of specificity. Thus you must consider muscle action, range of motion, and energy source when designing a nonlinear program for a specific group of athletes or for improving performance in a task. You will need to apply the principle of progressive overload in some way as fitness gains occur in the performance of a nonlinear periodization program. Depending on the point in a training cycle, training frequency with nonlinear programs is typically two to four sessions per week. Applying information about these training principles will allow the implementation of a nonlinear program that meets the needs and goals of athletes or fitness enthusiasts.

CHAPTER 3

Acute Program Variables

A cute program variables are factors that can be changed during any resistance training session or varied over time in a periodized program. The acute physiological responses and chronic adaptations to a resistance training program over time depend on the five acute program variables (Kraemer, 1983):

1. Exercise choice
2. Exercise order
3. Number of sets of an exercise
4. Training intensity
5. Length of rest periods between sets and exercises

As with all resistance training programs, choices concerning workout variables, such as what exercises to perform, should be made based on the training goals for the nonlinear program. Applying information concerning workout variables in the design of a nonlinear training program is necessary if the program is to achieve and meet training goals with the least amount of effort and training time.

EXERCISE CHOICE

The choice of exercises to perform during a training session and as training progresses is an important consideration because the selection of muscle groups to train is in large part determined by the exercises performed. Therefore you would need to include exercises that train the muscle groups in which any physiological adaptations (e.g., increases in strength, power, or size) are desired. If you want to increase strength in the hamstring and quadriceps muscle groups, you need to include exercises for both muscle groups in the training program. If adaptations are desired in all major muscle groups of the body, then at least one exercise for each major muscle group must be included in the training session.

There are, however, some other considerations when choosing what exercises to perform. One of the choices is whether to use a machine exercise or a free-weight exercise for a particular muscle group. Free-weight exercises typically involve the use of a barbell or a dumbbell. Many strength training professionals prefer free-weight exercises. Free-weight exercises require that the resistance be balanced in all three planes of movement (sagittal, transverse, and coronal) and require the use of additional muscles to balance the resistance, as is required of movement during everyday tasks. So free-weight exercises resemble movement and muscle recruitment in the real world to a greater extent than machine exercises do. If you are training to improve athletic performance, which takes place in a three-dimensional world, advocates of free weights believe that training in a manner resembling movement in the real world will result in greater carryover to performance in the real world.

Generally, resistance training machines restrict movement to only one plane. For example, the typical overhead press machine allows only up-and-down movement. Movements to the left and right and forward and back are restricted. But now there are machines that allow some movement in two planes. Some advocates of the use of resistance training machines believe that by restricting movement to only one plane, greater recruitment of the muscles involved in that movement will take place and so the greatest possible adaptations in those muscle fibers will occur. In reality, both advocates of free-weight and exercise machines are correct, depending on the desired training outcome. Both free-weight and machine exercises have a place in most resistance training programs. For example, many training programs include the free-weight squat, machine knee extension, and machine knee curl exercises. Some exercises, such as the knee extension, cannot be performed safely with free weights. Thus, some machine exercises may be included in a training program because it is impossible to perform a similar exercise in a safe manner with free weights. Correct exercise technique with machine exercises has been generally regarded as easier to learn because of the restriction of movement to only one plane. And machines in general are considered safer than free-weight exercises (American College of Sports Medicine, 2002). These last two considerations are important for individuals just beginning a weight training program because machines allow trainees to use the resistances necessary to bring about adaptations in a shorter time. After trainees have learned the basic exercise technique, they can make the transition to more free-weight exercises if desired.

Another choice is whether to perform single-joint or multijoint exercises. Single-joint or single-muscle-group exercises, such as the triceps extension and calf raise, require movement of one joint and train only one major muscle group. Multijoint or multimuscle-group exercises, such as the leg press and bench press, require movement at more than one joint and train several muscle groups with the same movement. Both types of exercises have been shown to be effective for increasing muscular strength and hypertrophy in the muscle group or muscle groups trained. Generally, single-joint exercises target adaptations in specific muscle groups and are thought to pose less of a risk of injury because of the reduced level of skill and exercise technique required for correct performance compared to multijoint exercises. The maximum weight possible for a certain number of repetitions of

Performance of a back extension exercise for the low back musculature will increase the maximal weight possible in squatting exercises for many individuals.

a multijoint exercise is limited by the weakest muscle or the muscle group that fatigues most quickly in the multijoint exercise. For example, squat exercises are typically limited by the musculature of the low back. This is apparent in the forward lean of the trunk when a set is carried to failure and when attempting to lift the maximal weight for one repetition (1RM). The limiting effect of the weakest muscle group in a multijoint exercise means that generally the weakest muscle group receives the greatest training stimulus. In many situations it is possible to use a combination of single-joint and multijoint exercises if the goal is to increase the maximum weight in a multijoint exercise.

Multijoint exercises, such as the squat, power snatch, and clean pull, involve a large muscle mass and complex neural activation and coordination of the involved muscle mass. Because a large muscle mass is involved, it is possible to use heavier resistances than with single-joint exercises, where a smaller muscle mass is involved. Because of these factors, multijoint exercises have been thought of as the most effective exercises for increasing total-body strength and power (Fleck & Kraemer, 2004). Additionally, power-oriented total-body exercises, such as the power clean and power snatch, have been regarded as the most effective exercises for increasing total-body power because of the fast velocity at which these exercises are performed and the necessity of developing force quickly to successfully complete a repetition (Garhammer, 1991). So if the goal of training is to increase total-body strength or power, multijoint exercises should be included in the training program. Multijoint exercises, because of the large muscle mass involved, have also shown the greatest metabolic responses (Ballor et al., 1987) and the greatest acute response of some hormones, such as increased growth hormone (Kraemer & Ratamess, 2003). The acute metabolic and hormonal responses of multijoint exercises have direct implications for their use when the goals of a program target increased local muscular endurance, fat-free body mass, and reductions in body fat (Kraemer & Ratamess, 2004).

Another consideration involved in exercise choice is whether or not to perform different exercises for the same muscle group. Different exercises for the same muscle group, such as types of abdominal exercises or quadriceps exercises, result in different recruitment patterns of the muscles involved in the exercise (Maffiuletti & Lepers, 2003; Willett et al., 2001). Varying the foot or hand position in an exercise will also change the recruitment pattern in an exercise. For example, using a wide or narrow grip in the bench press, various hand positions in the lat pull-down, or different widths in stance when performing a squat all vary recruitment patterns during the exercise (Barnett et al., 1995; Escamilla et al., 2001; Signorile et al., 2002). Varied recruitment patterns means that different portions of the muscle (i.e., different muscle fibers) are emphasized during the exercise. To develop all portions of the muscle or muscle group, it may be necessary to perform more than one exercise for the same muscle group in the training program. The exercises performed for a particular muscle group can be changed every 4 to 6 weeks, or different exercises for the same muscle group can be performed during alternating training sessions.

A general rule to remember is that every time you change the angle, you change the exercise. Bodybuilders know that targeting a muscle from various angles will dimensionalize the development of the muscle (i.e., it will recruit and therefore build up muscle fibers in more than one portion of a single muscle). Most exercise programs use what can be called *normative movements,* which stimulate the primary angle of an exercise (e.g., most people perform the flat bench press, but the decline bench press trains the same muscles with a different recruitment pattern). So muscle recruitment changes when slightly different exercises are used to train the same muscle groups. However, muscle recruitment will also change with varied hand and foot positions while performing a particular exercise (e.g., toes pointing in or out while performing a knee extension). The choice of exercise angles should reflect the angles that are typical for movement at a particular joint, but you should also keep in mind the movement angles used in a sport or task. The angle of the exercise will affect the muscle tissue that is stimulated in that exercise. In addition, this is why proper exercise technique and positioning are so important in a resistance training program. Grip width (e.g., close-grip bench press) and width of foot placement (e.g., sumo stance in deadlift) all affect how that muscle will be stimulated because of the body's mechanical structure. Thus, the choice of exercise dictates what motor units (i.e., motor neuron and associated muscle fibers) are stimulated in a resistance exercise program. If a motor unit is not stimulated, it will not adapt. The adaptations from the repeated stimulation of the muscles' motor units improve muscular fitness.

It is important to consider the inclusion of both bilateral (both limbs) and unilateral (single limb) exercises in a program to make sure proper balance occurs in the development of the body. Unilateral exercises play an important role in maintaining equal strength in both limbs. Disparity in muscle force production can develop when one limb works harder on every repetition than the other limb, which can lead to an obvious deficit in force production and muscle imbalances between limbs.

Each type of exercise (machine, free weight, single joint, and multijoint) has unique beneficial characteristics; therefore many programs consist of a combination of all of these types of exercises. However, the needs of a trainee and goals of a training program might dictate the use of one exercise type in a particular training program. Exercise choice may also change over time in a training program because of a characteristic of a particular exercise type. For example, power-oriented exercises may be favored over strength-oriented exercises in a particular cycle of periodized resistance training, or power-oriented exercises may be used more in the late preseason than in the off-season of a program. In nonlinear periodization it is important to create mesocycles with specific types of training priorities for the 12-week cycle, and exercise choices can help to mediate this aspect of a nonlinear program.

EXERCISE ORDER

Traditional exercise order dictates performing large-muscle-group or multijoint exercises before performing small-muscle-group or single-joint exercises. The rationale for this order of exercises is that by performing the multijoint exercises first or early in a training session, a superior training stimulus is presented to the muscles involved in the multijoint exercises. This is thought to be mediated by a greater neural, metabolic, hormonal, and circulatory response, which may augment training of muscles or exercises later in the training session. Exercises performed later in the training session are affected by fatigue resulting from performance of the exercises early in the training session (Sforzo & Touey, 1996; Simao et al., 2005). This results in the performance of fewer repetitions at any particular weight or use of a lighter weight to perform the same number of repetitions when an exercise is performed late in a training session. This appears to be true for both multijoint and single-joint exercises whenever they are preceded by exercises involving the same muscle group or even exercises for different muscle groups. When single-joint exercises for the same muscle groups involved in the bench press and squat are performed before the bench press and squat, there is a 75% and 22% decline in performance, respectively (Sforzo & Touey, 1996). This indicates that the lower-body musculature may be more affected by preceding exercises than the upper-body musculature. Thus sequencing of exercises may be of particular importance when considering the lower-body musculature. The traditional exercise order—performing multijoint exercises early in a training session or before single-joint exercises involving the same muscle groups—does result in the ability to use a heavier resistance for the desired number of repetitions or performance of more repetitions at the training resistance when performing the multijoint exercises. So over time it may result in greater total-body physiological adaptations. Generally in a nonlinear program, multijoint exercises are performed early in a training session.

Minimizing fatigue when performing multijoint exercises (such as the squat and deadlift, which emphasize total-body strength) and power-oriented exercises is an important consideration. Performing these exercises early in the training session allows the use of the heaviest resistance for the desired number of repetitions, which may be necessary for maximizing total-body strength, power, and even hypertrophy (Kraemer & Ratamess, 2004). Multijoint exercises also require greater neural coordination than single-joint exercises. Therefore, when training for strength and power, performing these exercises early in a training session, before fatigue sets in, may enhance

When prescribing power-oriented exercises such as the power snatch and clean pull, which emphasize total-body power, minimizing fatigue is an important factor.

© Mike Powell/Allsport Concepts/Getty Images

exercise performance by optimizing neural recruitment. When the major training goal is local muscular endurance, the sequencing of multijoint exercises before single-joint exercises may not be as important. The accumulation of metabolic by-products (such as lactic acid) results in fatigue, which is a stimulus for the development of local muscular endurance.

Fatigue is also a consideration when performing exercises in an alternating sequence or a stacked sequence. An alternating sequence refers to performing exercises for alternating muscle groups in succession, such as the typical arm-to-leg exercise order. A stacked sequence refers to performing exercises for the same muscle group in succession, such as the typical arm-to-arm or leg-to-leg order. Stacked exercise orders have generally been used when the training goal is muscular hypertrophy. An order of alternating muscle groups allows for some recovery of one muscle group while another is performing the subsequent exercise. This is true when exercises are performed in a set-repetition manner (performing all sets of one exercise before performing the next exercise) or when exercises are performed in a circuit manner (performing one set of an exercise and then one set of the next exercise in the circuit). This is especially true when short rest periods are used between sets or exercises (60 seconds or shorter) because high concentrations of blood lactic acid will occur with short rest periods (Kraemer et al., 1990; 1991). The accumulation of blood lactic acid and fatigue is an important consideration when a trainee is just beginning weight training, starting to use short rest periods between sets and exercises, or starting to use a stacked exercise order. In all of these situations the trainee must allow sufficient time for physiological adaptations to occur, which allow toleration of the high blood lactic acid concentrations. This can be accomplished in several ways, including gradually shortening the rest periods between sets and exercises and gradually altering the exercise order to a stacked exercise order, such as performing several exercises in a session in a stacked order and other exercises in an alternating exercise order. So when making changes in length of rest periods in a nonlinear program, athletes and trainers need to monitor fatigue and exercise performance carefully.

Whenever a new exercise (particularly one that a trainee has never performed) is added to a training program, it should occur first or very early in the training session. This allows the learning of proper exercise technique before fatigue affects the trainee's ability to concentrate. Therefore, the trainee is able to learn correct technique as quickly as possible. Multijoint exercises are generally thought of as being more neurally complex (Chilibeck et al., 1998) and therefore learning correct exercise technique for these types of exercises may take longer than learning correct technique of single-joint exercises. The fast velocity of movement involved in power-oriented exercises, such as the power clean, may also result in the need for more time to learn correct exercise technique. So whenever an exercise is added to a training program, the trainer and trainee must allow sufficient time to learn correct exercise technique so that injury does not occur. If correct exercise technique is not initially mastered, it will compromise the resistance that can be used safely and effectively in that exercise.

Exercises can also be arranged with the use of a priority system. In a priority system the exercises performed first or early in the training session focus on the major goals for the training sessions. If upper-body strength is the major goal of a training session, then the upper-body exercises would be performed early in the training session before the onset of fatigue caused by performance of other exercises. This allows the trainee to concentrate on correct exercise technique and use the heaviest possible resistances when performing the priority exercises. A corollary to the priority system is the performance of power-oriented exercises early in the training session. This allows the trainee to develop and train maximal power before fatigue hinders the development of maximal power. However, for some sports, power-oriented exercises may be performed later in the session to improve the ability to develop power in a slightly fatigued state. For example, volleyball and basketball players not only should have a high maximal vertical jump, but they also must be able to jump late in a game when they are fatigued. Because of this, performance of some power-oriented exercises later in the training session will enhance the ability to develop near-maximal power in a slightly fatigued state.

A recent study has shown that the exercise order can also facilitate the power of an exercise despite the reductions in total work and number of repetitions performed in a set (Spreuwenberg et al., 2006). When the squat exercise was placed first in a workout, a higher number of repetitions could be performed with 85% of 1RM. Conversely, when the squat was performed at the end of the workout, fewer repetitions could be performed. But since it was placed after the hang clean exercise, a higher power output was observed during the repetitions that were completed. This indicates that fatigue produces one type of effect on an exercise at the end of the workout, but the

Performance of power training late in a training session may be important for athletes who have to generate power under conditions of partial fatigue.

choice of the exercises may interact with the order of the exercises to produce other acute effects on the characteristics of the workout (e.g., change power output and velocity of the exercise via facilitation of the movement).

Since the order of exercises affects the outcome of a training program, the exercise order needs to correspond with the specific training goals. In general, the sequence of exercises for both multiple- and single-muscle-group exercise sessions should be as follows:

1. Large-muscle-group exercises before small-muscle-group exercises
2. Multijoint before single-joint exercises
3. Alternating of push and pull exercises for total-body sessions
4. Alternating of upper-body and lower-body exercises for total-body sessions
5. Explosive (power) lifts (e.g., Olympic lifts) before basic strength and single-joint exercises
6. Exercises for weak areas of the body (priority) before exercises for strong areas of the body

7. Most intense to least intense (particularly when performing several exercises consecutively for the same muscle group)

The order of exercises in a nonlinear periodization program is used in conjunction with the other acute program variables to create the various styles of workouts necessary for bringing about the desired variation in the program. Exercise order can be used to emphasize certain muscle activation patterns and to rest other muscle fibers used at exercise angles needing more recovery.

NUMBER OF SETS

The number of sets does not have to be the same for all exercises in a workout program. In reality, the number of sets performed for each exercise is one variable in what is referred to as the calculation of volume of exercise (i.e., sets × reps × resistance). As such, one of the major roles of the number of sets performed is to regulate the volume performed during a particular exercise protocol or training program. In studies examining resistance-trained individuals, multiple-set programs have been found to be superior for improvements in strength, power, hypertrophy, and high-intensity endurance. The number of sets necessary for gains in maximal strength has received considerable study. Several factors need to be considered concerning the number of sets necessary for bringing about optimal physiological adaptations. Not all exercises in a training session need to be performed for the same number of sets. Additionally, the number of sets performed can be varied to address a trainee's specific goals. For example, if a specific muscle group is being emphasized in the training session, more sets of exercises in which that muscle group is recruited can be performed. Training status may also affect how many sets are necessary for optimal adaptations. For example, the number of sets necessary for maximal strength gains may be different between untrained and highly trained individuals.

The number of sets performed is one of the factors affecting training volume (i.e., sets × repetitions × resistance). The number of sets does affect the nervous, metabolic, and muscular acute response to resistance training (Kraemer & Ratamess, 2004). For example, the acute growth hormone response is greater with multiple-set than with single-set training sessions. Gains in strength and muscle hypertrophy have been shown with single-set and multiple-set training programs. However, the majority of studies demonstrate greater strength gains with multiple-set programs, and no study comparing single sets to multiple sets has shown single sets to result in greater maximal strength gains (Fleck & Kraemer, 2004). Several meta-analyses clearly demonstrate that multiple-set programs result in greater strength gains than single-set programs (Peterson, Rhea, & Alvar, 2004; Rhea, Alvar, & Burkett, 2002; Rhea et al., 2003; Wolfe, LeMura, & Cole, 2004). A meta-analysis is a statistical procedure in which the results of all studies examining a particular topic, such as number of sets needed to cause maximal strength gains, are compared in order to reach a quantitative conclusion. This allows a quantitative conclusion to be reached concerning the question being asked, in this case the relationship between strength gains and the number of sets performed. Several of the meta-analyses also indicate more specific recommendations concerning the optimal number of sets. For untrained and trained individuals, 4 sets appear to be optimal for increasing strength (Rhea et al., 2003). Another meta-analysis indicates that for highly trained individuals, 8 sets per muscle group are optimal for bringing about maximal strength gains (Peterson, Rhea, & Alvar, 2004). Additionally, the number of sets necessary for optimal strength gains does not appear to be different between males and females (Wolfe, LeMura, & Cole, 2004).

During the initial weeks of training (6-15 weeks), untrained individuals show the same increases in strength, regardless of whether single- or multiple-set programs are performed (Wolfe, LeMura, & Cole, 2004). This indicates that initially untrained individuals can perform single-set programs and show the same strength gains as those achievable with multiple-set programs. However, after a short initial training period, if maximal strength gains are to be achieved, multiple-set programs must be employed. The probable reason for no initial difference in strength gains in untrained individuals with multiple- or single-set programs is that both types of programs initially bring about relatively equivalent neural adaptations, and initially neural adaptations cause the majority of strength gains in untrained individuals. After this initial training period, multiple sets are necessary for bringing about further physiological adaptations resulting in maximal strength gains (American College of Sports Medicine, 2002). It is also possible with a single-set or low-volume program to use changes in exercise choice, exercise order, and number of repetitions per set to bring about training variation so that during short training periods near-optimal physiological adaptations can occur. However, eventually higher-volume programs must be used in order to bring about optimal adaptations.

Multiple sets have also been recommended for bringing about optimal increases in local muscular endurance and hypertrophy (American College of Sports Medicine, 2002; Fleck & Kraemer, 2004). Collectively qualitative as well as quantitative analyses of information concerning the optimal number of sets demonstrate that multiple sets for both trained and untrained individuals are necessary for bringing about maximal training adaptations over long training periods. During the initial training period of untrained individuals, single-set programs can be used. Eventually, however, after an initial short training period, multiple-set programs need to be incorporated to bring about maximal adaptations. It is also possible to emphasize specific muscle groups or exercises by performing more sets (e.g., up to 8 per muscle group in highly trained individuals). Training adaptations in specific muscle groups can also be deemphasized or capped (maintained) by performing fewer sets per exercise or muscle group over short training periods, such as during an in-season maintenance resistance training program.

Generally nonlinear programs involve the performance of multiple sets of an exercise. However, in a nonlinear periodization program, a trainee can use a low-volume-program day involving performance of fewer sets to allow for recovery. Varying the number of sets of an exercise functions as a volume modulator of the exercise stress in a nonlinear periodization resistance training program.

TRAINING INTENSITY

Intensity of resistance training, or the amount of resistance used when performing resistance training, may be the major stimulus related to training adaptations, such as increased strength and local muscular endurance. Typically repetition maximums (RMs), or the resistance that allows the performance of only a specific number of repetitions per set with correct exercise technique, are used in determining the resistance. Generally an RM target, such as 10RM, or an RM target zone, such as 6- to 8RM, is used. The resistance used is then increased as the lifter's strength increases so that the lifter continues to train at the chosen RM target or RM target zone.

Research (Fleck & Kraemer, 2004) supports the concept of an RM continuum (figure 3.1). The continuum relates RM resistances to broad training effects, such as increased strength and power and low-intensity endurance. An inverse relationship exists between the resistance used and the number of repetitions performed to failure. Thus when a heavy resistance is used, it is possible to perform only a few repetitions, whereas when a lighter resistance is used, it is possible to perform more repetitions to failure. Training studies indicate that resistances corresponding to 1- to 6RM are the most conducive to increasing maximal dynamic strength (Fleck & Kraemer, 2004). Significant strength increases have been reported with the use of resistances corresponding to 8- to 12RM; however, this resistance range appears to be most effective for increasing muscular hypertrophy. Even lighter resistances, such as 12- to 15RM, result in small significant increases in maximal strength; however, this RM range is most effective in increasing local muscular endurance. As trainees move away from the 1- to 6RM range, strength gains decrease until they are practically negligible when 25RM resistances or lighter are used. Because of the adaptations emphasized by the use of varying RM resistances, varying resistances within the training program, such as those used in periodized training, are most effective for bringing about continued strength and power gains (Fleck, 1999; Rhea & Alderman, 2004) and possibly other adaptations (American College of Sports Medicine, 2002). Note that the typical RM zones used in a nonlinear program encompass all the repetition ranges emphasizing major training outcomes, such as strength and power, hypertrophy, and local muscular endurance (4- to 6-, 8- to 10-, 12- to 15RM zones).

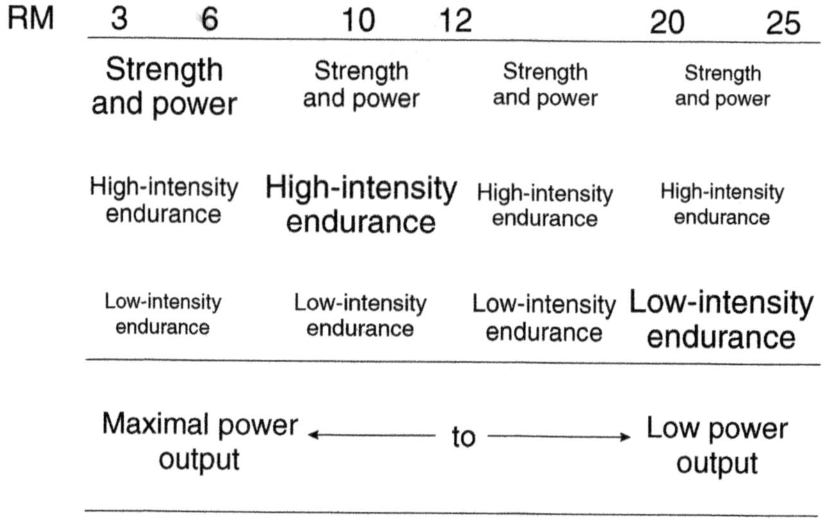
RM 3 6 10 12 20 25
Strength and power
Strength and power
Strength and power
Strength and power
High-intensity endurance
High-intensity endurance
High-intensity endurance
High-intensity endurance
Low-intensity endurance
Low-intensity endurance
Low-intensity endurance
Low-intensity endurance
Maximal power output
to
Low power output

Figure 3.1 Theoretical repetition maximum continuum.

Reprinted, by permission, from S.J. Fleck and W.J. Kraemer, 2004, *Designing resistance training programs,* 3rd ed. (Champaign, IL: Human Kinetics), 167.

Another method of determining the resistance to be used is to use a certain percentage of 1RM to perform a specific number of repetitions per set. This method requires the determination or estimation of 1RM at regular intervals. If 1RM is not determined on a regular basis, particularly when beginning a training program, the percentage of 1RM used decreases because the trainee is becoming stronger. This results in a lower percentage of 1RM used and therefore a lower training intensity. From a practical perspective, use of percentages of 1RM to determine the resistance used for many exercises is not administratively effective because of the amount of time that must be dedicated to determining or estimating the 1RMs of all the exercises performed. Therefore an RM target or RM target zone is used in nonlinear programs with increases in resistance to maintain training at the RM target or within the RM target zone, which is a more efficient way to determine the resistance to be used.

Charts or equations are often used in predicting the 1RM based on the number of repetitions performed to failure with a submaximal resistance. Unfortunately, most of the charts and equations assume a linear relationship between the number of repetitions performed and the resistance used. However, that is not the case. Such charts and equations should be used only as a rough estimate of the true 1RM for a particular exercise.

In examining machine exercises, the number of repetitions performed to failure using various percentages of 1RM varies drastically from one exercise to the next (table 3.1). In fact, in some exercises, even though a relatively high percentage of 1RM is used if a set is carried to failure, a great number of repetitions can be performed. For example, trained females, defined as people who weight-train all major muscle groups 3 times per week for a minimum of 2 months, can perform approximately 57 repetitions of the leg press using 60% of 1RM (table 3.1). This raises a question: Even though a relatively high percentage of 1RM is used, does this type of training result in optimal strength and power gains? Examination of the repetition maximum continuum indicates that strength and power are not emphasized when performing this number of repetitions per set, but low-intensity endurance is emphasized. Therefore use of true RMs or RM zones may be a better method of determining training resistances for most exercises.

Table 3.1 also indicates that training status may also affect the number of repetitions that can be performed at a certain percentage of 1RM. This idea is clearly demonstrated by a study showing that in the leg press, powerlifters could perform 22 repetitions (a 22RM) when

Table 3.1 Number of Repetitions That Can Be Performed With a Machine Using a Selected Percentage of 1RM

	40% $\bar{x} \pm SD$	60% $\bar{x} \pm SD$	80% $\bar{x} \pm SD$	1RM[b] $\bar{x} \pm SD$
Untrained males n = 38				
LP	80.1 ± 7.9A[a]	33.9 ± 14.2A	15.2 ± 6.5A	137.9 ± 27.2
LD	41.5 ± 16.1B	19.7 ± 6.1B	9.8 ± 3.9B	59.9 ± 11.6
BP	34.9 ± 8.8B	19.7 ± 4.9B	9.8 ± 3.6B	63.9 ± 15.4
KE	23.4 ± 5.1C	15.4 ± 4.4C	9.3 ± 3.4BC	54.9 ± 13.3
SU	21.1 ± 7.5C	15.0 ± 5.6C	8.3 ± 4.1BCD	40.9 ± 12.6
AC	24.3 ± 7.0C	15.3 ± 4.9C	7.6 ± 3.5CD	33.2 ± 5.9
LC	18.6 ± 5.7C	11.2 ± 2.9D	6.3 ± 2.7D	33.0 ± 8.5
Trained males n = 25				
LP	77.6 ± 34.2A	45.5 ± 23.5A	19.4 ± 9.0A	167.2 ± 43.2
LD	42.9 ± 16.0B	23.5 ± 5.5B	12.2 ± 3.72B	77.8 ± 15.7
BP	38.8 ± 8.2B	22.6 ± 4.4B	12.2 ± 2.87B	95.5 ± 24.8
KE	32.9 ± 8.8BCD	18.3 ± 5.6BC	11.6 ± 4.47B	72.5 ± 19.8
SU	27.1 ± 8.76CD	18.9 ± 6.8BC	12.2 ± 6.42B	59.9 ± 15.0
AC	35.3 ± 11.6BC	21.3 ± 6.2BC	11.4 ± 4.15B	41.2 ± 9.6
LC	24.3 ± 7.9D	15.4 ± 5.9C	7.2 ± 3.08C	38.8 ± 7.1
Untrained females n = 40				
LP	83.6 ± 38.6A	38.0 ± 19.2A	11.9 ± 7.0A	85.3 ± 16.6
LD	45.9 ± 19.9B	23.7 ± 10.0B	10.0 ± 5.6AB	29.2 ± 5.6
BP	–[c]	20.3 ± 8.2B	10.3 ± 4.2AB	27.7 ± 23.7
KE	19.2 ± 5.3C	13.4 ± 3.9C	7.9 ± 2.9BC	26.7 ± 7.8
SU	20.2 ± 11.6C	13.3 ± 8.2C	7.1 ± 5.2C	19.3 ± 8.3
AC	24.8 ± 11.0C	13.8 ± 5.3C	5.9 ± 3.6C	13.8 ± 2.7
LC	16.4 ± 4.4C	10.5 ± 3.4C	5.9 ± 2.6C	15.8 ± 3.7

	40% $\bar{x} \pm SD$	60% $\bar{x} \pm SD$	80% $\bar{x} \pm SD$	1RM[b] $\bar{x} \pm SD$
Trained females $n = 26$				
LP	146 ± 66.9A	57.3 ± 27.9A	22.4 ± 10.7A	107.5 ± 16.0
LD	81.3 ± 41.8B	25.2 ± 7.9CB	10.2 ± 3.9C	34.8 ± 6.0
BP	–[c]	27.9 ± 7.9B	14.3 ± 4.4B	35.6 ± 4.9
KE	28.5 ± 10.9C	16.5 ± 5.3ED	9.4 ± 4.3CD	40.3 ± 10.2
SU	34.5 ± 16.8C	20.3 ± 8.1CD	12.0 ± 6.5CB	23.8 ± 6.4
AC	33.4 ± 10.4C	16.3 ± 5.0ED	6.9 ± 3.1ED	17.3 ± 3.8
LC	23.2 ± 7.7C	12.4 ± 5.1E	5.3 ± 2.6E	21.7 ± 5.0

LP = leg press (knees apart at a 100° angle for the starting position); LD = lateral pull-down (resistance pulled behind the head to the base of the neck); BP = bench press; KE = knee extension; SU = sit-up (horizontal board, feet held in place, knees at a 100° angle, and resistance held on chest); AC = arm curl (low pulley); LC = leg curl (to 90° of flexion).

[a] Letters indicate significantly different groupings: alpha level = 0.05; same letter = no difference.

[b] 1RM expressed in kg.

[c] Data unobtainable due to resistance limitations on the Universal gym equipment.

Reprinted, by permission, from S.J. Fleck and W.J. Kraemer, 2004, *Designing resistance training programs*, 3rd ed. (Champaign, IL: Human Kinetics), 169; adapted, by permission, from W.W.K. Hoeger, et al., 1990, "Relationship between repetitions and selected percentages of one repetition maximum: A comparison between untrained and trained males and females," *Journal of Applied Sport Science Research* 4: 47-54.

using 80% of 1RM (Kraemer et al., 1999), whereas untrained individuals could perform only 12 repetitions (a 12RM) in a leg press using this same percentage of 1RM. It is also clear from table 3.1 that there is a great deal of individual variation (large standard deviation) in the number of repetitions that can be performed using a specific percentage of 1RM. For example, the average number of repetitions at 80% of 1RM for trained males was 19.4. However, the range of the number of repetitions was actually between approximately 11 and 28. Additionally, a certain percentage of 1RM with free-weight exercises will allow fewer repetitions than the same percentage of 1RM on a similar exercise performed on a machine (squat versus leg press). This is most likely due to the need for greater balance and control in three planes of movement during a free-weight exercise. But with resistance training machines, control of movement is generally needed in only one plane of movement. This difference may also be due to limiting the involvement of the weakest muscle group with the machine exercise compared to the free-weight exercise. For example, when performing a leg press, the involvement of the low back is minimized compared to when performing a squat. The number of repetitions to failure will also vary depending on other training variables, such as exercise order (Sforzo & Touey, 1996; Simao et al., 2005), training volume within a training session and over time, training frequency, muscle action type, repetition speed, and length of rest periods (Kraemer & Ratamess, 2004). Thus if a certain number of repetitions at a certain percentage of 1RM is used in prescribing training, the percentage or number of repetitions should be considered as a guideline and not as an absolute rule.

Throughout the training program, the absolute resistance is then adjusted to match the changes in strength so a true RM target or RM target range resistance continues to be used. Performing every set until failure occurs can be stressful on the joints, but it is important to ensure that the resistance used corresponds to the targeted number of repetitions. This is because performing 3 to 5 repetitions with a resistance that allows for only 3 to 5 repetitions compared to a resistance that would allow 13 or 15 repetitions produces quite different training results. Squeezing out the last repetition of the set may not be as important as making sure the loading is perceptually within a 3-repetition zone. With practice, most trainees can detect that they could do only one more repetition. This is important with aging because joint stress, recovery, and neural inhibition may be greater and toleration of such repeated practices might be detrimental to optimal progress.

In a study using free weights, Shimano and colleagues (2006) examined the number of repetitions that could be performed at 60%, 80%, and 90% of 1RM in the back squat, bench press, and arm curl in trained and untrained men (see table 3.2). The researchers found that more repetitions were performed during the back squat than the bench press or arm curl at 60% 1RM for trained and untrained men. At 80% and 90% 1RM, there were significant differences between the back squat and other exercises; however, differences were much less pronounced. No differences in number of repetitions performed at a given exercise intensity were noted between trained and untrained subjects (except during bench press at 90% 1RM). The number of repetitions performed at a percentage of the 1RM is much different than is observed when using a machine that has a fixed path of movement and less demand for balance and coordination. The numbers

Table 3.2   Number of Repetitions at 60%, 80%, and 90% of 1RM

	60%	80%	90%
	UNTRAINED		
Back squat	35.9 ± 13.4 #,+,‡,†	11.8 ± 1.8 +,‡	6.5 ± 1.8 †
Bench press	21.6 ± 4.2 #,+,†	9.1 ± 2.7 +	6.0 ± 1.5 *
Arm curl	17.2 ± 3.7 #,+	8.9 ± 3.9 +	3.9 ± 2.1
	60%	80%	90%
	TRAINED		
Back squat	29.9 ± 7.4 #,+,‡,†	12.3 ± 2.5 +,‡	5.8 ± 2.3‡
Bench press	21.7 ± 3.8 #,+	9.2 ± 1.6 +	4.0 ± 1.3
Arm curl	19.0 ± 2.9 #,+	9.1 ± 2.8 +	4.4 ± 1.9

Values are mean ± SD.

* = $p < 0.05$ vs. corresponding trained group.

‡ = $p < 0.05$ vs. corresponding bench press value.

† = $p < 0.05$ vs. corresponding arm curl value.

= $p < 0.05$ vs. corresponding 80%.

+ = $p < 0.05$ vs. corresponding 90% value.

Data from Shimamo et al., 2006, "Relationship between the number of repetitions and selected percentages of one repetition maximum in free weight exercises in trained and untrained men," *Journal of Strength and Conditioning Research* 20:819-823.

of repetitions then fall more in line with what has been theoretically used when percentages of the 1RM are talked about in lifting circles, as much of the anecdotal evidence comes from free-weight experience. Interestingly, though, there were minimal differences between trained and untrained subjects. Therefore, relative load has a fundamental effect on the number of repetitions allowed, since more repetitions can be performed at a lighter load, and this relationship is not appreciably affected by the training status of the subject.

From this study the following recommendations were put forth for using the percentage of 1RM method for determining the loading for an exercise. If exercise prescription is based on a percentage of 1RM, follow these guidelines:

1. Very high-intensity loads (> 90% 1RM) should be used for strength gains in free-weight exercises.

2. Athletes should be regularly tested for 1RM strength, because changes in 1RM will have an effect on the absolute load prescribed during training.

3. The number of repetitions performed at a given percentage of 1RM is dependent on the absolute muscle mass involved (more muscle mass equates to more repetitions to failure at a percentage of 1RM); therefore, when strength coaches prescribe loads based on percentage of 1RM, they should be aware of the amount of muscle tissue involved in each of the specific lifts.

Using RM-zone-based prescriptions is recommended with nonlinear programs to ensure that the appropriate load is being used for a desired result. However, percentage of 1RM can also be used for exercise prescription when free weights are employed to approximate an appropriate exercise intensity.

Finally, meta-analyses indicate that training status affects the percentage of 1RM necessary for bringing about optimal strength gains. Optimal strength gains are brought about in untrained individuals when approximately 60% of 1RM is used (Rhea et al., 2003), whereas trained individuals' use of 80 to 85% of 1RM results in optimal strength gains (Rhea et al., 2003; Peterson et al., 2004). All of these factors make it clear that the percentage of 1RM used in training should be only a guideline for the training intensity. Use of target RMs or target RM zones is easier and allows the emphasis of various training outcomes, such as maximal strength and power and low-intensity endurance. For all of these reasons, nonlinear periodization uses RM training zones for the description of the resistance used in training.

In a nonlinear periodization program the resistance used is the most important variable in program design because it dictates the amount of motor units that are activated and in turn the amount of muscle fibers that are stimulated in a workout. As discussed later in the text, this relates to the concept of size principle of motor unit recruitment, which is a basis of nonlinear periodization theory.

LENGTH OF REST PERIODS

The length of rest periods between sets and exercises influences the hormonal, metabolic, and cardiorespiratory responses to a resistance training session (American College of Sports Medicine, 2002; Kraemer & Ratamess, 2004). The duration of rest periods also affects the amount of recovery that occurs between sets and exercises, thereby affecting the amount of fatigue experienced as the training session progresses. For example, if 3-minute rest periods are allowed between sets of the leg press and bench press, 10 repetitions per set for 3 sets can be performed (Kraemer, 1997). However, if only 1-minute rest periods are allowed between sets, 10, 8, and 7 repetitions per set in consecutive sets are performed.

Increases in maximal strength have been shown to be greater when longer rather than shorter rest periods are used (Robinson et al., 1995; Pincivero et al., 1997). For example, when 3-minute rest periods rather than 30-second rest periods are used over 5 weeks of training squats, 1RM increased 7 and 2%, respectively (Robinson et al., 1995). Additionally, performance of successive sets is highly dependent on recovery of anaerobic (intramuscular adenosine triphosphate and phosphocreatine) energy sources, and it takes approximately 3 minutes for this anaerobic source of energy to be almost completely rebuilt or recovered. If sufficient time is not allowed for recovery of this anaerobic energy source, the number of repetitions performed in successive sets with heavy resistances will decrease.

Short rest periods (approximately 1 minute) result in several significant physiological changes. With 1-minute rest periods between sets and exercises (especially when using 10RM resistances and performing 10 repetitions per set), acute hormonal changes, such as increased growth hormone in the blood, are significantly greater than with 3-minute rest periods (Kraemer et al., 1990; Kraemer et al., 1993). Although acute hormonal changes are not a direct assessment of muscle hypertrophy, these acute hormonal changes have generally been regarded as significant for development of muscle hypertrophy and have shown significant correlations to the development of muscle hypertrophy in both fast-twitch and slow-twitch muscle fibers (McCall et al., 1996). When using 10RM resistances, 1-minute rest periods between sets and exercises result in a significantly greater blood lactate response than with 3-minute rest periods and when using 5RM and either 1-minute or 3-minute rest periods (Kraemer et al., 1990; Kraemer et al., 1993). The ability to buffer and tolerate decreases in pH and hydrogen ions from the high levels of ATP hydrolysis is indicated by high concentrations of blood lactate, which might be a contributor to the development of local muscular endurance due to resistance training. Local muscular endurance is typically defined as the maximal number of repetitions that can be performed using a specific resistance (absolute endurance), such as 100 pounds (45 kilograms) or relative resistance (relative endurance), such as number of repetitions at 75% of the 1RM. Nevertheless, use of shorter rest periods contributes to improved ability to tolerate the high acidic conditions of exercise that occur beyond a few repetitions.

Because of the previously mentioned factors, it has been recommended that, when training to emphasize increases in maximal strength and power, rest periods of 2 to 3 minutes between sets and exercises be used for multijoint exercises (American College of Sports Medicine, 2002). In some cases this may have to be extended to longer rest periods if very heavy resistances are used. When performing single-joint exercises and training to emphasize increases in maximal strength, rest periods of 1 to 2 minutes can be used. The recommended length of rest periods when emphasizing increases in maximal strength and power applies to beginning, intermediate, and advanced lifters. When training to emphasize local muscular endurance, 1- to 2-minute rest periods should be used when using resistances allowing performance of 15 to 20 repetitions per set, and

Length of rest periods between sets and exercises does affect the physiological responses to resistance training. Therefore, as with all training variables, length of rest periods should be controlled to emphasize specific training goals.

1-minute rest periods should be used when using resistances allowing 10 to 15 repetitions per set. The recommendations for emphasizing local muscular endurance also apply to beginning, intermediate, and advanced lifters. When beginning and intermediate lifters train to emphasize muscle hypertrophy, rest periods of 1 to 2 minutes are recommended. However, when advanced lifters train to emphasize hypertrophy, 2- to 3-minute rest periods may be used when multijoint exercises are performed, and 1- to 2-minute rest periods can be used when performing single-joint exercises.

However, keep in mind that short-rest resistance training programs can cause greater psychological anxiety and fatigue because of the greater discomfort, muscle fatigue, and high metabolic demands of the session (Tharion et al., 1991). Therefore, psychological ramifications of using short-rest workouts must be carefully considered and discussed with athletes or clients before the training program is designed. The increase in anxiety appears to be associated with the high metabolic demands found with short-rest exercise protocols (i.e., 1 minute or less). Despite the high psychological demands, the changes in mood states do not constitute abnormal psychological changes and may be a part of the normal arousal process before a demanding workout.

The key to length of rest periods is the observation of symptoms of loss of force production in the beginning of the workout and clinical symptoms of nausea, dizziness, and fainting, which are direct signs of the inability to tolerate the workout. When such symptoms occur, the workout should be stopped and longer rest periods used in subsequent workouts. With aging, a decreased ability to tolerate decreases in muscle and blood pH underscores the need for gradual progression when cutting lengths of rest periods between sets and exercises. Rest periods may be thought of in these ways:

- Very short rest periods: 1 minute or shorter
- Short rest periods: 1 to 2 minutes
- Moderate rest periods: 2 to 3 minutes
- Long rest periods: 3 to 4 minutes
- Very long rest periods: 5 minutes or longer

The more rest that is allowed between sets and exercises, the heavier the resistance and the greater the number of repetitions that can be performed at a specific RM load. Improvements take place for a given rest period when the body's bicarbonate and phosphate blood and muscle buffering systems are improved from the gradual incorporation into the program of shorter rest periods.

The variable of rest plays an important role in the creation of the various workouts in a nonlinear periodization resistance training program. It sets up the impact on force production based on metabolic demands and buffering systems that are necessary for high-intensity competitions. Shortening the rest periods in any workout will create a completely different "fingerprint" of exercise stimuli that affect adaptations. Careful progression when shortening rest periods in any training cycle is necessary. This precaution avoids overstressing the trainee or compromising the quality of the workout caused by a reduced toleration of metabolic demands, resulting in lower force and power production.

SUMMARY

All information concerning acute program variables should be applied when designing a nonlinear periodization training program. This information aids in the design of a program that meets the specific goals and training needs for a specific sport or activity. Changes in workout variables, such as the number of sets performed or choice of exercise, may occur at various points in the training season for a specific sport. Emphasizing power development during the late preseason and performing fewer sets because of the need to perform a greater volume of other types of training during in-season are just two examples. Each mesocycle in a nonlinear training program (typically 12-16 weeks) needs to be carefully planned in order to meet the goals and needs determined for each athlete.

CHAPTER 4

Practical Considerations

A case for the use of a nonlinear periodization training method can be made from two very practical perspectives. Foremost is the ability to deal with schedule demands of athletes as well as fitness enthusiasts; the secondary concern is readiness to train optimally in a workout. With a nonlinear program, athletes can make dramatic changes in the workouts they perform day to day. In addition, with the use of a flexible nonlinear periodization model, trainees can respond rapidly to the events of the day. This is important in situations such as training and competition for sports, demanding work schedules, and fitness, where boredom is a major factor in lack of adherence. These daily variations are much greater than can be seen in a classic linear periodization model (Plisk & Stone, 2003).

In a nonlinear periodization training program, dramatic changes can occur day to day in a week of training with changes in the intensity and volume of exercise used. Typically a trainee periodizes large-muscle-group exercises. However, variation schemes can also be created for smaller muscle groups. Furthermore, the use of periodization in resistance training has been shown to be superior to constant training methods. Therefore coaches, trainers, and trainees are faced with choosing the type of periodization model that will best fit their training goals (Fleck & Kraemer, 2004). In many cases the nonlinear approach provides greater versatility in the development of various mesocycles if not for the entire macrocycle.

Both classic strength and power programs and nonlinear periodization programs result in greater fitness gains than nonvaried programs can provide. However, practical differences between classic strength and power periodization and nonlinear periodization demonstrate that the nonlinear model is more appropriate in various training situations where scheduling of weight training sessions as well as other types of training and fatigue affect the readiness to train. Some basic physiology concepts, such as order of recruitment of muscle fiber types, also indicate that the nonlinear model may be more appropriate when fatigue is a factor affecting whether or not a trainee is ready to train for a specific outcome, such as increased maximal power.

COMPARISON OF PERIODIZATION MODELS

In terms of training volume and intensity, the differences between strength and power periodization and nonlinear periodization are presented in chapter 1. The areas of focus here are understanding how these two methods of periodization differ in their practical implementation and understanding the many manipulations that can be made when using the nonlinear approach, including flexible nonlinear periodization.

Classic Strength and Power Periodization

Classic strength and power periodization methods use a progressive increase in the intensity and decrease in volume with small variations in each 1- to 4-week microcycle. An example of a 4-microcycle strength and power periodization program is shown in the sidebar.

There is some variation within each microcycle because of the repetition range of each cycle. Still, the general trend for the 16-week program is a steady linear increase in the training intensity. Concomitantly, there is a decrease in the volume of exercise. For advanced athletes who can tolerate higher volumes of exercise during the heavy and very

---

SAMPLE PROTOCOL
Classic Linear Periodization Program

Microcycle 1
3 to 5 sets of 10- to 12RM

Microcycle 2
4 or 5 sets of 8- to 10RM

Microcycle 3
3 or 4 sets of 4- to 6RM

Microcycle 4
3 to 5 sets of 1- to 3RM

Active Rest
Cycle 2 to 4 weeks

heavy microcycles, the decrease in volume may not be as apparent. Because of the straight-line increase in the intensity of the program, classic strength and power periodization has also been termed *linear* periodization training. Two to four mesocycles are normally combined to produce a macrocycle with a definite peaking phase at the end of the macrocycle. An active rest cycle is used after the peaking phase. This basic sequence has been the essence of the classic strength and power periodization model of physical training.

One outcome of the strength and power periodization program is the increase in the intensity develops the necessary nervous system adaptations for enhanced motor unit recruitment. One of the nervous system adaptations is as intensity increases, the high-threshold motor units become more involved in the mechanisms of force and power production. Thus the goal of the peaking phase is to maximize neural adaptations in all of the muscles involved in an exercise, including any muscle that was developed during the earlier training phase.

Variations of the 16-week mesocycle would be repeated several times within a year to produce a yearlong macrocycle. Each mesocycle functions to increase the body's muscle hypertrophy and strength and power toward a trainee's genetic maximum as the training year progresses. Strength and power periodization programs appear to be easier for a beginner because the exercises are not heavily loaded (high percentage of 1RM) until later in a training cycle. They start with light weights and low volumes for 3 to 6 weeks (see chapter 5).

Nonlinear Periodization

As previously pointed out, one reason nonlinear periodization training programs have been developed is to produce greater day-to-day variation in the training stimuli. This makes implementation of a nonlinear periodization training program easier when travel, illness, or competitive game schedules are factors to consider. These factors place demands on the resistance training program that do not allow the long sequences of the same type of training used in the strength and power training model. With the nonlinear model, if training sessions are missed, the trainee simply begins training at the point of the missed sessions and there is no need to increase the length of the mesocycle in which the missed session occurs.

The nonlinear program allows for substantial variation in the intensity and volume within each week over a mesocycle (typically 12-16 weeks). Because of the large variations in intensity and volume that occur with the nonlinear approach, a base resistance training program is performed for 3 to 6 weeks to allow an individual to learn the exercises and recover from any initial muscle soreness. This is important because heavy days (3- to 6RM) are prescribed much sooner in a nonlinear program than in the classic strength and power program. In addition to the large variations in training volume and intensity during a microcycle of nonlinear training, any training variable of interest (e.g., length of rest period, order of exercise) can be varied if it relates to the training goals of the individual. Therefore the question of toleration of the workout must always be addressed and appropriate starting points used for all workout styles in a nonlinear program (e.g., if rest between sets and exercises is shortened, a trainee would start with a 2- to 3-minute rest period between sets and repetitions and gradually shorten the rest periods). An example of a nonlinear periodization training program over a 16-week mesocycle is shown below. For the beginner the potential weakness of the nonlinear program is that heavy loads are implemented in the first week of workouts. Thus, the beginner needs to perform a base program for 4 to 6 weeks using lighter weights, allowing the individual to gain toleration to the resistance training program. Then one starts a nonlinear progression of varying intensities as shown. An active rest or recovery period of 2 to 3 weeks in length could be placed after the 16-week cycle. Active rest allows the trainee to get away from resistance training and remain active with other sporting activities (e.g., swimming, walking, or cycling).

SAMPLE PROTOCOL
Nonlinear Periodization in a 16-Week Mesocycle

This protocol uses a 6-day rotation.

Monday	*Monday*
4 sets of 12- to 15RM	4 or 5 sets of 1- to 3RM
Wednesday	*Wednesday*
4 sets of 8- to 10RM	Power day
Friday	*Friday*
3 or 4 sets of 4- to 6RM	2 sets of 12- to 15RM

Active Rest

For 2 to 3 weeks after the 16-week mesocycle is completed

An active rest period could also be simply a reduction in the intensity and volume of resistance training.

It is apparent that intensity varies widely in terms of percentage of 1RM in a week of nonlinear periodization training. In addition to the training intensity zones used in the example protocol on page 68, mechanical power training days (where loads vary from 30 to 65% of 1RM depending on the exercises used in the program) can be added. One important factor in any power exercise day is to limit the amount of deceleration at the end of the range of motion in an exercise. Trainees can accomplish this by performing exercises that minimize the deceleration phase (e.g., power clean and power snatch). Medicine ball plyometrics and other lower-body plyometrics can also be substituted and performed on a power training day. The key factor in power development is that the exercise used does not allow a deceleration to take place when holding on to the bar. For example, a bench press performed at a high velocity while holding on to the bar will only create a large deceleration over the range of motion compared to a bench throw, where the weight is released into the air allowing acceleration to take place over the range of motion. Thus, exercises used on a power day are those in which little or no deceleration exists in the joint range of motion except after the exercise is completed (e.g., hang pull where the weight decelerates after the highest point in the range of motion is achieved and the weight decelerates due to gravity) (Newton et al., 1996).

The major practical difference between strength and power periodization programs and nonlinear programs is that an individual trains the various trainable components of the neuromuscular system (e.g., power, local muscular endurance, strength) within the same week or so with the nonlinear model. This is accomplished with the use of the varied-intensity training zones used within the same microcycle with nonlinear programs.

Flexible Nonlinear Periodization

The concept of flexible nonlinear periodization came about because of the challenges of training athletes during the in-season. This has also been called *unplanned nonlinear periodization,* but in this book we refer to it as *flexible nonlinear periodization* because an overall plan must be devised for a particular 7- to 10-day cycle along with a 12-week mesocycle, but its implementation is dependent on the ability of the athlete to perform the workout. In other words, readiness to train is an important feature of this type of periodization.

The first flexible nonlinear periodization program came about with the challenges of training basketball players and tennis players.

© University of Connecticut Office of Athletic Communications.

Strength coaches at the University of Connecticut (head strength and conditioning coach Gerard Martin and associate head strength and conditioning coach Andrea Hudy consulting with W.J. Kraemer, PhD) were faced with the challenge of meeting highly variable physical and psychological demands on basketball players over the off-season and in-season programs. The nonlinear approach had been used for a couple of years at the University of Connecticut and was effective. However, in the nonlinear approach, when a player came in on a given day and was fatigued from a hard practice the previous day, could a trainer successfully implement a planned power workout if the athlete's physical capacity was not sufficient? Probably not, and when it was attempted, the quality of the training session was poor and it did little to improve the athlete's power potential. To overcome this problem of lack of physical readiness to train, the flexible non-linear program was developed. The 2004 University of Connecticut

Huskies basketball teams were very successful: They won both the men's and the women's NCAA Division I National Championships in the same year—a first in basketball history.

Comparison of 4 years of using the classic strength and power model and 4 years of using the nonlinear periodization model in female basketball players at the University of Connecticut shows very few differences in strength and power gains, although one difference did arise that may be of significance. The rate of increase for a variable was more rapid with the nonlinear method (unpublished data). More rapid gains with nonlinear periodization might be due to greater changes in training volume and intensity over a mesocycle.

Flexible nonlinear periodization results in dramatic and highly varied interaction patterns between volume and intensity (figure 4.1). The volume of exercise in a resistance training program must be reduced when other conditioning activities (e.g., practice, agility drills) and frequency of competitive games increase. The flexible

Using the flexible nonlinear periodization approach, both 2004 University of Connecticut basketball teams were peaking physically as March Madness started and championship games were played.

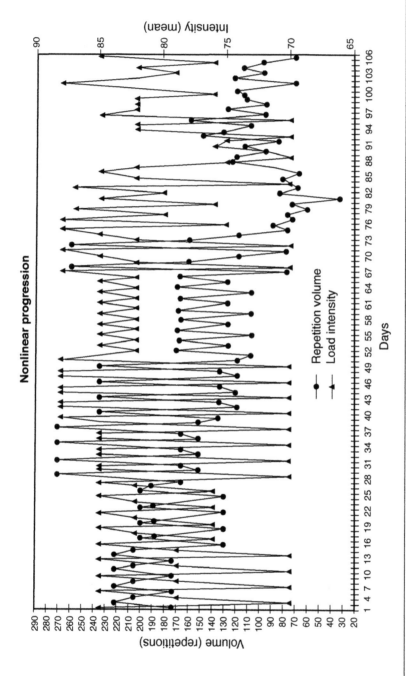

Figure 4.1 Load and repetitions (volume) graphed over workouts for the University of Connecticut women's basketball team. Each day is represented by a load, or intensity (triangle), mean, and a repetition volume (diamond). The intensity (load) and the volume are depicted on separate vertical axes. Volume was reduced as the competitive season and championship tournaments took place starting at about workout 73. Prior to that, time volume and intensity were differentially modulated using the nonlinear periodization approach.

nonlinear model allows adjustment in training intensity and volume in relation to these other physical and psychological stresses.

PHYSIOLOGY OF NONLINEAR PERIODIZATION WORKOUTS

To understand nonlinear periodization, it is necessary to appreciate the importance of the size principle of motor unit activation or, in other words, how muscle is stimulated as it relates to the amount of resistance lifted. While the neurological aspects of this topic are beyond the scope of this text, a few important concepts are addressed that will cement an understanding of the differential use of the neuromuscular system with various resistance loads or training intensities.

The physiological basis of muscle activation starts with the motor unit, which is composed of the alpha motor neuron and all the muscle fibers it stimulates. One of the most important concepts to understand in regard to strength training is the concept of how muscle is recruited or stimulated. The size principle states that motor units are recruited to meet the demands of a task (Clamann & Henneman, 1976; Henneman et al., 1974; Luscher et al., 1979). The size effect relates to the fact that recruitment is based on physiological factors that go from small to big, low to high, or few to many. In other words, muscle is recruited from fibers with low to high electrical thresholds, from small- to large-sized muscle fibers, and from a few Type I (slow-twitch) muscle fibers to many Type II (fast-twitch) muscle fibers that make up the motor unit. Ultimately it is the task of the neuromuscular system to most efficiently recruit the needed muscle tissue to produce the exact force for a given demand (e.g., lift a 50 lb, or 23 kg, weight or a 500 lb, or 227 kg, weight). This all happens in a progressive manner, starting from small motor units to larger motor units of recruitment—thus the term *size principle.*

With the size principle, as more and more force is needed, more and more motor units are recruited. A motor unit is generally composed of either all Type I (slow-twitch) or Type II (fast-twitch IIA or IIX) muscle fibers. Type I fibers make up the smaller motor units and are normally recruited first in a muscle action followed by the recruitment of the Type II muscle fibers (IIA and IIX), which make up the larger motor units. Thus the order of recruitment is normally Type I first and then Type II fibers as the demands for more force increase up to maximal force production (see figure 4.2).

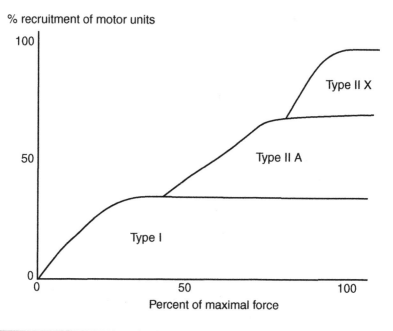

% recruitment of motor units

Figure 4.2 Recruitment of motor units containing the various types of muscle fibers is related to the amount of force that is needed for performing the exercise with a given resistance. More and more motor units are recruited as the force demands increase to maximal levels. The higher-threshold motor units contain the fast-twitch, or Type II, muscle fibers, which are recruited to produce the needed force at high percentages of the maximal force a muscle can develop.

In addition, the muscle fibers in a motor unit are not all located adjacent to one another, but they are spread out in the muscle in microbundles of about 3 to 15 fibers. Thus, adjacent muscle fibers are not necessarily from the same motor unit. With this spreading out of the fibers in a motor unit, the whole muscle appears to be activated when motor units are activated. Spread, or disbursement, of muscle fibers in a motor unit throughout the muscle allows the whole muscle to appear to be activated rather than just segments of the whole muscle. Thus, an athlete might move an arm up and down to lift a submaximal weight, but the whole muscle appears to be activated even though not all motor units in the muscle are activated. If the weight lifted is gradually increased, more and more motor units will be activated until all motor units are activated at maximal force (see figure 4.2). Motor units and their associated muscle fibers that are not activated during an exercise do not generate force and move only passively through the range of motion; in the nonlinear periodization paradigm they are essentially rested during a training session in which they are not recruited.

Only the motor units that are actively recruited during an exercise to produce force will subsequently adapt to the resistance training. Therefore, motor unit recruitment is of primary importance in the effectiveness and specificity of resistance exercise programs. In resistance exercise it is the load, or training intensity, that determines how many motor units are recruited. Heavier loads (higher intensities) recruit more motor units than lighter loads (lower intensities). Motor units and their associated muscle fibers that are not activated during an exercise do not generate force and move only passively through the range of motion. In the nonlinear periodization model, motor units (i.e, an alpha motor neuron and the associated muscle

Not every individual has the same absolute potential for gains in muscular strength and size.

fibers) that are not recruited (e.g., high threshold Type II motor units) during a training session when using a light training intensity (e.g., 12- to 15RM) are essentially rested during the training session. This is the key to nonlinear periodization in that some lighter intensity training sessions rest the motor units that are used in the higher intensity workouts, providing for recovery. Continued day-to-day use of high intensity loads without rest or recovery can lead to overtraining or plateaus in training adaptations, thus the genius of nonlinear periodization.

OPTIMAL PROGRAM SEQUENCING

Optimal program sequencing is a matter of making proper choices based on evaluation of the training load over the various training cycles. Optimal sequencing is dependent on the recovery of the body's musculature from the stress of the resistance exercise, practice, physical labor, or mental state that occurs prior to the workout. As shown in figure 4.3, the stress of resistance exercise can be depicted in a pyramid of volumes and intensities that lead to higher and higher levels of physical stress. Each of the acute program variables can be combined to create exercise stimuli that span a continuum of stress from low to high. Volume and intensity are only two noteworthy variables, but others can be interfaced with them (e.g., going from long to short rest periods between sets and exercises). The higher the stress of the workout, the greater the recruitment of a muscle's motor units, the greater the potential tissue damage, and the longer the recovery may take after a given workout. Optimal sequencing is really a coaching or clinical art of assessment and understanding the science behind the design of a workout and its ramifications.

In general, workouts from a resistance loading perspective can go from very light to very heavy. We use this in our subsequent examples of workouts. This essentially addresses the variation that can be achieved from using the perspective of size principle. With this type of load sequencing, a trainee keeps some of the other program variables in line with optimizing this particular feature. Exercise order is chosen to support the appropriate exercises—from large-group to small-group exercises. The number of sets is consistent with the necessary decreases in volume to accommodate increases in load. Finally, lengths of rest periods are positioned to allow for the necessary force production or augment the endurance

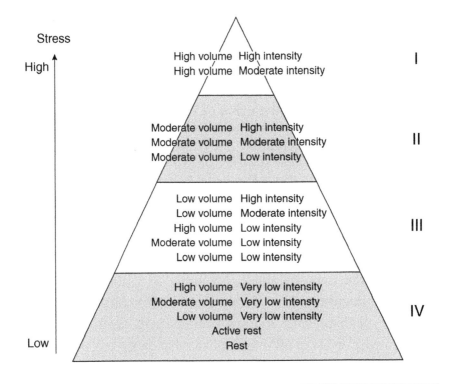

Figure 4.3 Pyramid of physical intensity for resistance workout stresses related to the recruitment of motor units (muscle tissue activation). Zone I is the highest level of physical stress and zone IV is the lowest. This model assumes that acute training variable conditions are constant over the zones (e.g., rest between sets and exercises).

aspects of the lighter loads. Thus, the programs are created with a loading variable as the primary feature to be varied over the workout sequence.

Other acute program variables can be set as a focus of the workout sequences as well. For example, if there were a need for the trainee to develop the ability to buffer high acidic conditions and perform under these demanding physiological conditions (e.g., wrestler, 800-meter sprinter), rest periods could be the primary acute program variable in a mesocycle. Therefore the exercise sequences would all be related to a reduction in length of rest periods. In this case the rest periods would be progressively lowered even when using the heavier RM loads despite the resulting use of lower resistances caused by fatigue. With training, the resistances used with the shorter rest periods would increase, representing the adaptation for this type of priority in the workout sequence (Kraemer et al., 1987).

Each of the acute program variables can therefore be used in some type of prioritization of the workout sequences. Even order of exercises may be the priority because of a complex training design. Whatever the goal, the interaction of the various effects caused by the variety of combinations of the acute program variables is evident and needs to be considered.

In a *scheduled nonlinear sequence program*, a trainee simply rotates through the various workout protocols (varied training volumes and intensities) in a preplanned format. This has been termed a *planned daily rotation* of workouts. For example, the training sessions rotate through the following sequence of training sessions:

1. Light intensity and high volume (12- to 15RM)
2. Moderate intensity and high volume (8- to 10RM)
3. High intensity and moderate volume (4- to 6RM)
4. Very high intensity and low volume (1- to 3RM)
5. Power day (1- to 6RM with power exercises)
6. Very low intensity and very low volume (20- to 23RM for 1 set)
7. Active rest microcycle

The primary core exercises are typically periodized, but a trainee can also use a protocol of 2 or 3 training sessions to vary the small-muscle-group exercises. For example, in the hamstring curl, the trainee could rotate between the moderate (8- to 10RM) and the heavy (4- to 6RM) cycle intensities. This would provide the hypertrophy needed for isolated muscles of a joint and also provide the strength needed to support heavier resistances of the large-muscle-group or multijoint exercises. The key in any nonlinear workout day is to keep the stimuli to the muscle unique for that training day by using various types of training sessions.

Practically speaking, if a trainee misses a workout on Monday, she could perform it on Wednesday and continue the rotation or even skip it and make it up later in the rotation of sessions. Specifically, if the light 12- to 15RM workout was scheduled for Monday and the trainee missed it, she would just perform it on Wednesday and continue on with the rotation sequence. In this way no workout stimulus is missed in the training program. A mesocycle can be set for a given number of weeks or when a certain number of workouts is completed (e.g., 36).

MASTER SCHEDULES

It is important to develop a master schedule for the macrocycle even when using either a scheduled or flexible nonlinear program. With the flexible nonlinear approach, a trainee checks off a workout when it is completed. Schedules can be created for any number of workouts per week. Three or four weight training days a week are typical for most athletes, especially considering other conditioning demands. It is also important after each mesocycle to have a period of 1 to 2 weeks of active rest. On a given weight training day, an active rest day may be required even if it is not planned for, especially within the context of various sports during the in-season (see tables 4.1 to 4.4).

Ultimately, it is important to have a master plan for each mesocycle and determine the priorities for the workout that must be performed. In a planned nonlinear program, a trainer or trainee can intentionally place the workout sequence on the calendar.

Table 4.1   Sample Mesocycle With Emphasis on Power

Week		1	2	3	4	5	6	7	8	9	10	11	12
Workout sequence	Day 1	H	L	H	H	P	P	P	L	P	H	P	P
	Day 2	P	P	P	P	H	VH	P	P	P	P	H	P
	Day 3	VH	P	P	H	VL	L	VL	H	L	L	P	VH

VL = Very light intensity workout.
L = Light intensity workout.
M = Moderate intensity workout.
H = Heavy intensity workout.
VH = Very heavy intensity workout.
P = Power workout.
An active rest day can be used for any workout if needed.

Table 4.2   Sample Mesocycle With Emphasis on Strength

Week		1	2	3	4	5	6	7	8	9	10	11	12
Workout sequence	Day 1	H	L	H	H	L	P	P	L	H	H	L	H
	Day 2	L	VH	M	P	H	VH	H	VH	H	VH	H	L
	Day 3	VH	M	M	H	VL	L	VL	H	L	L	P	VH

VL = Very light intensity workout.
L = Light intensity workout.
M = Moderate intensity workout.
H = Heavy intensity workout.
VH = Very heavy intensity workout.
P = Power workout.
An active rest day can be used for any workout if needed.

Table 4.3   Sample Mesocycle With Emphasis on Hypertrophy and Strength

Week		1	2	3	4	5	6	7	8	9	10	11	12
Workout sequence	Day 1	H	L	M	M	M	L	H	L	H	M	L	M
	Day 2	M	M	H	H	H	M	M	L	L	M	M	M
	Day 3	M	H	L	L	VH	H	VL	M	VH	H	VH	L

VL = Very light intensity workout.   H = Heavy intensity workout.
L = Light intensity workout.   VH = Very heavy intensity workout.
M = Moderate intensity workout.   P = Power workout.
An active rest day can be used for any workout if needed.

Table 4.4   Sample Mesocycle With Emphasis on Endurance and General Preparation

Week		1	2	3	4	5	6	7	8	9	10	11	12
Workout sequence	Day 1	L	L	M	VL	M	L	VL	H	L	M	L	VL
	Day 2	M	VL	H	H	M	M	M	VL	L	M	M	H
	Day 3	L	H	L	L	L	H	L	M	VH	VL	VL	L

VL = Very light intensity workout.   H = Heavy intensity workout.
L = Light intensity workout.   VH = Very heavy intensity workout.
M = Moderate intensity workout.   P = Power workout.
An active rest day can be used for any workout if needed.

In the flexible nonlinear periodization model, the athlete has to have a plan. But the days on which specific sessions will take place are only tentative; each type of session is dependent on the ability of the athlete to do the workout. The flexible nonlinear periodization is more dynamic and may be more effective in getting the best out of the trainee during a given training session. Again, each mesocycle will have a priority element that may dominate the workout number (e.g., power workouts), or in fitness sequences the trainee may balance the workouts among all of the training elements (e.g., strength, local muscular endurance). Trainers and athletes must consider what acute program variables are to be periodized over a mesocycle and macrocycle and then use the microcycles to define them.

A master plan functions as a guide for the goals of the training cycle. With the scheduled nonlinear program, the type of session to be performed on a given training day is predetermined. However, with the flexible nonlinear program, the type of workout to be performed is decided on the day of the training session. Thus, the concept of flexible nonlinear periodization really refers to waiting until the day of the workout to make the decision about the type of training session to perform. Flexible nonlinear periodization does not mean there is no overall training plan or goals of the training cycle. It actually means having a training plan for a given microcycle in order to understand if an athlete is able to meet the demands for adaptations needed. For example, if, because of other circumstances, an athlete cannot perform two power training sessions a week that emphasize power development, it is doubtful that the athlete will be able to make any progress on power development. So, in the subsequent microcycles, the athlete would have to compensate for the decrease in power development over the mesocycle by picking up those missed power sessions later in the mesocycle because the athlete must train a muscle group with a particular stimulus at least twice a week over a 12-week mesocycle. Thus, extenuating circumstances can affect a well-planned training program despite good intentions.

The decision about when to administer the workouts is the key factor in the flexible nonlinear program. There needs to be some level of confidence that the quality of the workout will be adequate to produce a training effect. Using both the art and science of conditioning helps in the challenge of making such decisions. For the strength and conditioning coach, personal trainer, and trainee, this requires some preliminary assessment and information immediately before the workout. During the workout the trainer and trainee can observe how the session is performed. And, using the workout log, they can determine how the performance progresses compared to prior workouts in the training cycle for a given workout type. If a decrease in performance or quality of the training session is seen, rest or an alternative workout is indicated.

INDIVIDUALIZATION

Another factor that comes into play with the nonlinear approach is the individualization process for each workout. Individualized workouts are the gold standard for any training program. With a nonlinear as well as a flexible nonlinear periodization approach, a trainer can carefully address the needs of each player or trainee. It has become obvious through both scientific studies and anecdotal information from personal trainers and strength coaches that each person will respond uniquely to a given workout. Not all people will be ready to perform the same workout effectively on a given day. This underscores the problems with quality for a training session and also supports the use of a flexible nonlinear approach. Obviously individualization of workouts does present logistical problems from assessment demands and workout assignments that must be solved, particularly with large teams that train at the same time of the day. With the flexible nonlinear program, readiness to perform a certain type of session is tested and, if a trainee is not physically ready to perform the planned session, another type of session (i.e., an alternative session) is performed. The benefits of the flexible nonlinear approach are great when trainees are allowed to follow their own pattern of workouts toward a given training goal for a particular mesocycle.

Readiness to train on a given day is especially important in the flexible nonlinear approach to periodization training. Each athlete must perform a training program that is directed toward his or her own goals. While the overall requirements for the various trainable characteristics of muscle may be the same, the progression, timing, and approach of achieving them will differ individually because of the inherent genetic differences among athletes.

In nonlinear periodization, individualization of workouts becomes the cornerstone in determining what an athlete is capable of on a given day for optimal training.

READINESS TO TRAIN

The key to any workout is an athlete's readiness to train. Coaches, trainers, and athletes can determine this by paying attention to signs of fatigue, testing before starting the session, and monitoring the workout performances. For example, if a 6- to 8RM training zone is used and the athlete had performed 8 repetitions of the squat with 425 pounds (~193 kg) on the previous Monday and Friday, but today the athlete can complete only 2 reps with 425 pounds, it demonstrates a deficit from the previous identical workout. Acute overtraining is a possibility, and continuing with the 6- to 8RM zone during this training session would be ineffective. At this point the athlete might need to switch to a lighter training session. The strength and conditioning coach and personal trainer might also want to determine what caused the performance deficit—perhaps hard practices, psychological stress, or physical stress. Whatever it is, a reduction in resistance stress and close monitoring of the other exercises in the session might be warranted to determine whether it is a whole-body problem or a problem with a specific muscle group or body part (such as the legs or lower back in the previous example of squatting). Thus, the workout continues with a modification of the squat protocol and monitoring to see if other exercises have to be modified to accommodate recovery.

Preworkout evaluations can consist of a host of items, but an action as a result of the test results must be in place. As noted previously, what is the alternative workout if an athlete cannot perform the planned session effectively? This is where coach–athlete interactions come into play. A coach must first have a good sense of the athlete's capabilities, habits, and personality. Next, the coach and athlete can quantify fatigue with the use of a simple fatigue scale. A scale from 0 to 10 (shown in figure 4.4) can be used in assessing physical and mental fatigue (Kraemer et al., 2000). It is important to note that mental fatigue can be present when the body is physically able to perform. This has been seen in female tennis players who, after a weekend of match play, were mentally fatigued, yet their physical performances were not affected after a 24-hour recovery period (Kraemer et al., 2000). Thus, getting a handle on the athlete's mental fatigue may be as important as determining physical capacity to train. This is easy to accomplish at the beginning of every workout, along with evaluations of body mass to evaluate hydration status, which is important in many scenarios, especially when heat stress is involved in the training environment.

•

10	Very, very heavy, almost maximum feelings of physical fatigue
9	
7	Very heavy feelings of physical fatigue
5	Heavy (strong) feelings of physical fatigue
3	Moderate physical fatigue
2	Very light physical fatigue
0.5	Physical fatigue that is just noticeable
0	No fatigue

Figure 4.4 Basic fatigue scale with anchors to relate the magnitude of fatigue. The symbol • indicates magnitude estimation, which allows the athlete to pick any number above 10 to express stronger feelings of physical fatigue. Another scale for mental fatigue simply replaces the word *physical* with *mental* and creates another scale rating.

Adapted from Kraemer, et al., 2000.

When an athlete goes into a workout 2 to 3% under his or her normal body mass, the athlete might be hypohydrated from a prior workout or even chronically dehydrated over longer periods. The potential then exists for a loss of performance and workout quality and an increased susceptibility to heat illness. This performance decrement during the workout is especially apparent in the smaller muscle groups, which appear to be more sensitive to the effects of hypohydration and dehydration. When an athlete has a weight loss of 2% or more from one workout to the next, unless the athlete is in a prescribed and monitored weight-loss diet program, it is likely that the athlete is hypohydrated or, even worse, chronically dehydrated. In this case a rest day is warranted for recovery to normal body mass. The key is to rest and ingest adequate water and food over the next 24 hours to be ready for the next workout. Chronic dehydration is a problem with many athletes caused by poor drinking and eating behaviors. This can negatively affect workout quality, sport performance, health, susceptibility to heat illness, and overall well-being.

In chapter 6 some of the basic assessments are discussed. The assessments determine the functional ability of the individual going into a training session as well as the progress of the individual in relation to the resistance training goals for a particular mesocycle or macrocycle. Many times coaches, trainers, and even athletes think, *I don't feel like training, but I still can.* That may be why the workout goes forward as planned if the physical performance markers in the preworkout session are not decreased as the initial exercise performances in the session will dictate if there is a true physical decrement. The beauty of the flexible nonlinear periodization approach is that a session can be altered if warranted, and therefore more flexibility is allowed in the recovery process.

The typical preworkout check-off might involve the following points in order to determine readiness to train at the beginning of a workout:

1. Coach–athlete interactions
2. Injury check, especially in combative sports
3. Body weight check, hydration, and fluid intakes, especially in athletes who may be chronically dehydrated, such as weight-class athletes
4. Mental and physical fatigue ratings
5. Vertical jump power
6. First- and second-set performances in comparison to the recent workout performances for the same workout (is the athlete handling the workout as well or better than previously?)

Switching to an alternative workout if the trainee is not ready to perform the planned workout is an important strategy. In chapter 8, case studies help in determining when alternative workouts might be needed. This is a judgment call that combines both testing and working with trainees in the context of the overall needed number of specific workouts in the mesocycle. The overall training plan and priorities of the mesocycle come into play in the decision-making process concerning whether or not a certain type of session should or should not be performed. However, the optimization of the athlete's training determines progress. It is also important to keep the use of a rest day as an option when cycling through the various workouts both in the scheduled and flexible nonlinear periodization models.

SUMMARY

Scheduled periodization and flexible nonlinear periodization were developed with the use of the concepts of training variation found in classic strength and power periodization. With nonlinear periodization, determining the order of recruitment of muscle fiber types and motor units aids in planning the sequence of training sessions to allow adequate recovery between sessions. The practical implementation of a planned nonlinear periodization training program is done with the use of a planned sequence of training sessions. A flexible nonlinear periodization program involves using a master plan of training session types for mesocycles and macrocycles as in a scheduled model, but the exact day of implementation of a given workout type is dependent on the athlete's ability to optimally perform the workout that day. This optimization is determined from interactions among coaches, athletes, and personnel trainers; limited testing before a workout; and monitoring of the workout as it proceeds. Rest and recovery of each aspect of the neuromuscular system as well as mental capacities to train are monitored and are important elements in the flexible nonlinear model for resistance training periodization.

CHAPTER 5

Workout Design

The acute program variables discussed in chapter 3 provide the tools to design an infinite number of workouts. Variation between days in a microcycle is the key to the nonlinear periodization approach to training. One of the goals is to create workouts that are very different in their force production demands, thereby training varying percentages of the motor unit pool of a muscle. Typically this means variations among workouts with very light to very heavy resistance loads. The light resistance day essentially allows for recovery as many of the fast-twitch (Type II) motor units are not used in performing the exercise and the physical demands can be decreased. For example, a trainer might plan a light day, a moderate day, and a heavy day, each of which would use various amounts of muscle tissue to perform the exercises with a particular resistance. The light day would require less tissue, and on each successive day in this sequence, more and more tissue would be needed in order to complete the workout with the chosen resistance loads. The variation of the workouts over the 3 days would provide a dramatic difference in neuromuscular demands, which is characteristic of nonlinear periodization methods. Figure 5.1 reflects this theory and how it might work with various resistance loads requiring a range of muscle tissue to perform the exercise.

BASE PROGRAM PHASE

A base program is a beginning program using relatively light resistances (12- to 15RM) and lower training volumes. The trainee slowly increases the training intensity and volume. A trainee would need to follow a base program before initiating a nonlinear program, because heavier loads will be used more quickly in a program sequence. Typically a beginning base program is made up of only one exercise for

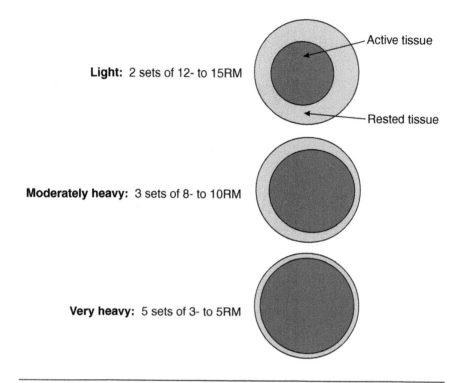

Light: 2 sets of 12- to 15RM

Moderately heavy: 3 sets of 8- to 10RM

Very heavy: 5 sets of 3- to 5RM

Figure 5.1 The amount of tissue needed for performing the exercise will vary depending on the resistance load and volume of exercise. This is a theoretical paradigm for tissue used with various resistance loads and volume of exercise.

each muscle group and only one set of each exercise. Then additional exercises are added so that more than one exercise for each muscle group is performed and the number of sets is increased. This phase of a training program is typically used for beginners or after a long layoff from resistance training in order to introduce or reintroduce the body to resistance exercise. With muscle memory, those who have had extensive experience in resistance training may need a much shorter base program to get into the periodized array of workouts used in nonlinear formats because their muscles are much more responsive to the exercise stimuli than the muscles of individuals just beginning to perform resistance exercise (Staron et al., 1991). A base program typically is 3 to 6 weeks in length with 3 training sessions a week and 48 hours between workouts. If too much soreness develops, an extra day or two of rest between sessions is allowed and the base program phase may be extended by 1 week.

Following are the three primary goals of a base program:

1. Learning the basic principles of resistance training
2. Learning the exercise techniques
3. Developing initial physical toleration to the stress of the resistance workout

EXERCISE STIMULI

Each workout in a nonlinear program should create a "fingerprint" for the specific exercise stimuli a trainee tries to create. This allows the session to result in a unique training stimulus and ideally allows the body to respond to a very specific stressor. This is a key to nonlinear periodization training protocols. Not all muscle is stimulated with every workout (see figure 5.1). Thus, rest of muscle tissue occurs during some workouts that are not using resistances heavy enough to recruit all the motor units. Again, understanding this concept is vital to understanding the theoretical basis of any periodization training program, especially the nonlinear method of workout design and presentation.

In these sample templates are suggestions for each of the acute workout program variables. These sample protocols have the acute program variable of intensity as a primary prioritization. Percentage of 1RM ranges for this intensity are presented in addition to the RM zone. It is also important to understand that not all sets need to be taken to failure, because that may cause greater joint compression and soreness. It will also produce higher rates of breath holding resulting in a Valsalva maneuver, causing excess amounts of blood pressure increases and dizziness.

SAMPLE PROTOCOL
Base Program

Exercise Choice and Order

Squat or leg press
Bench press
Seated row
Abdominal exercise
Low back machine or deadlift
Leg curl
Calf raise
Military press
Upright row
Arm curl

Number of Sets

Start with 1 set and progress to 2 or 3 sets for each exercise

Training Intensity

Warm-up set: None needed
Resistance: 12- to 15RM zone

Length of Rest Period

As needed (2 to 4 minutes)

Older individuals or those with joints that have been injured need to recognize that not all sets need to be taken to failure.

© Bananastock

STANDARD WORKOUTS

Using the nonlinear periodization process allows the art to meet the science of conditioning as there are many possible workouts that can be used based on the goals of the individual and the manipulation of the acute program variables. The goal of any training program is to maximize the workout in some manner so that the adaptations to the training program are optimized. In some cases this means that rest is needed; in other cases the individual is ready for a maximal workout; in other cases it means a light recovery day is warranted.

Power Training Workouts

Many coaches and athletes focus only on the force component of the power equation and hope that the velocity component (time) will be dragged along. In fact, a false adage is that all you need to do is train heavy and practice the sport and power will be taken care of.

$$\text{Power (watts)} = \frac{\text{Force} \times \text{Distance}}{\text{Time}}$$

Unfortunately it is not as simple as the old saying suggests, and the research related to the force–time curve has shown this not to be true. With conventional heavy resistance training, maximal force is developed, but the whole force–time curve is not affected. Forces such as 100 and 200 milliseconds are changed only when power training is performed. In many sports and daily functional activities, power becomes a much greater limiting factor in performance than absolute strength. Thus the ability to produce force in very small amounts of time is vital to success in many sport skills (e.g., throwing a ball or

Popular power resistance exercises are Olympic-type lifts (e.g., power clean, pull, snatch) and plyometrics, which provide the power needed in sport skills such as pitching.

spiking in volleyball) and crucial survival reactions (e.g., a person catching oneself before falling) and needs to be trained for optimal performance.

Power training requires explosive exercises, which require rapid rates of force production and reduce or eliminate the deceleration of the mass over the range of motion to emphasize acceleration. More recently the use of modified Smith machines to allow for squat jumps and bench throws that allow the bar to be released and landings to be softened by having either manual (e.g., ropes or cords used with spotters to catch or hold the bar in place) or computerized systems (mechanical breaking systems) help to catch the bar during the eccentric phase (downward movement of the bar or on landing). Typically, optimal amounts of resistance are used to train the maximal mechanical power output in the bench throw and squat jump movement (typically 30-45% of the 1RM). However, each exercise may have a different peak power as a function of a percentage of the 1RM, ranging from 30 to 65% of the 1RM in most cases. Again, training with only heavy weights will not augment the rate of force production or power development beyond what force can contribute to the equation. In some cases, the concept of the intent to move explosively has been used to augment the rate of force development when using resistances that do not allow such velocities needed for power development with high levels of acceleration.

Plyometrics and associated medicine ball training programs have been used on power days to allow for training of the velocity component of the power equation emphasizing the stretch-shortening cycle. The underlying principle of plyometric training is the stretch-shortening cycle, which is essentially the eccentric phase immediately followed by a concentric phase of muscle actions. The elastic energy in the muscle (thought to be due to the connective tissue component) provides the stored energy that, after the forced lengthening, is realized in the rapid forceful shortening as seen in a jump. Plyometric exercises can help to fully train all aspects of the power equation, specifically velocity.

The goal on power training days in the nonlinear periodization model is to increase maximal power output and improve rate of force development. This requires appropriate exercise movements, optimal loading of the exercises, and high velocities of explosive movement. It also requires that the trainee be rested and ready to train at maximal levels of explosiveness in order to improve.

Resistance Load Workouts

The following is a set of workouts that can be used in the nonlinear periodization model, which is focused on the resistance load as the priority for this workout sequence.

Very Heavy Workout

In this workout, resistances are very heavy. These workouts are directed to the skill component of physical performance and may not be used for all individuals, such as people who do not need to enhance maximal strength and power. A warm-up set of 10 repetitions at about a 12RM or 65% of the 1RM is used as the first set. Then the loads are increased to near-maximal resistances. This is what many people call *skill lifting* because technique is vital to optimal safety and performance. This type of training is needed in certain time periods, such as before maximal strength or power testing or before competitive events for athletes dependent on maximal strength for success. In this type of session, large-muscle-group exercises are typically performed, such as the squat, bench press, deadlift, and variations of Olympic lifts. Resistances range from 1 to 3 reps using a 1- to 3RM or 95 to 100% of the 1RM resistances. Volume is varied by doing 2 to 5 sets, depending on the training cycle or experience of the individual. Rest between sets and exercises should be about 5 to 7 minutes because sufficient rest is necessary in order to ensure near-maximal efforts in successive exercises in the session. This type of session is a low-volume, high-intensity workout focusing on the primary lifts being trained.

SAMPLE PROTOCOL

Very Heavy Workout

Exercise Choice and Order

Clean pull

Squat

Bench press

Deadlift

Number of Sets

2 to 5

Training Intensity

Warm-up set: 6 to 10 repetitions at a 12- to 15RM load or 65% of the 1RM

Resistance: 1- to 3RM or 95 to 100% of the 1RM

Length of Rest Period

5 to 7 minutes

Heavy Workout

The heavy workout is more appropriate than the very heavy workout for a greater number of people interested in making optimal strength

SAMPLE PROTOCOL
Heavy Workout

Exercise Choice and Order
Squat or leg press
Bench press
Seated row
Abdominals
Low back machine or deadlift
Hamstring curl
Calf raise
Military press
Upright row
Arm curl

Number of Sets
2 to 4

Training Intensity
Warm-up set: 6 to 10 repetitions at a 12- to 15RM load or 65% of the 1RM

Resistance: 3- to 5RM or 90 to 95% of the 1RM

Length of Rest Period
3 to 4 minutes

gains and increasing the force component of the power equation. With this workout, more exercises can be used to stimulate strength development. A warm-up set of 6 to 10 repetitions at about a 12RM or 65% of the 1RM is used as the first set. Resistances range from 3- to 5RM or from 90 to 95% of the 1RM. Typically 2 to 4 sets are used with 3 to 4 minutes of rest between sets and exercises.

Power Workout

This type of session can consist of many types of workouts, including lifting for maximal mechanical power, performing plyometrics, using various medicine ball workouts or a combination of all of these. The key is to focus on the resistance used and the velocity of the movement. High-speed movements incorporating the stretch-shortening cycle are vital for development of muscular power. Many elite power and speed athletes need motor unit recruitment related to the rapid force development demands of an exercise. In the nonlinear set of workouts, power development is important not only to athletes but also to older individuals, where power and rate of force development of a muscle apply to the majority of daily physical demands.

It has long been known that the key to these types of workouts is that the trainee must be completely rested and capable of performing at 90 to 100% of maximal effort. If the individual cannot perform at this level, then it is better to use another workout protocol as previously discussed. Such workouts should not be performed in any sequence in which prior exercise has been done (e.g., sport practice, cardio exercise) that results in significant fatigue. Also the number of exercises in the workout should be minimized in order to optimize the

Power and speed athletes, as well as individuals who have limited motor unit pools, can benefit from various types of power training days.

Power Workout

Exercise Choice and Order

Power snatch   Power clean

Number of Sets

3 to 8 sets of 3-repetition sets performed maximally

Training Intensity

Warm-up set: None needed

Resistance: Maximal mechanical power training using 30 to 45% of the 1RM or conventional loading using 60 to 70% of 1RM for loading ranges

Length of Rest Period

4 to 5 minutes or when completely rested so that successive sets can be done at near-maximal power

Alternative Protocols

Other power development workouts can be used for this day, such as typical plyometric training or medicine ball training performance of each set. Adding too many exercises to this workout routine will limit the development of power due to fatigue as the session progresses. In power training the goal is maximal velocity and power output in each of the training sets. This necessitates a greater number of sets, few repetitions, more rest between sets to enhance recovery, and fewer total exercises.

Hypertrophy Workout

This workout is the typical body-building workout used for developing muscle size and definition. It provides a high anabolic hormonal response as well as a significant cardiovascular stress. This protocol also can result in large increases in lactic acid because of the shorter rest periods, which results in a significant drop in pH in the muscle and blood. However, this may aid in developing the trainee's acid–base buffering system to improve toleration of reductions in pH that come with intense anaerobic exercise. It is a moderate workout day from an RM loading perspective. This workout uses shorter rest periods. However, the length of the rest period must be carefully progressed from a longer (2- to 3-minute) rest period down to a 1-minute rest period to eliminate any adverse symptoms of dizziness, nausea, or vomiting, which are *not* signs of a good

SAMPLE PROTOCOL

Hypertrophy Workout

Exercise Choice and Order

Squat or leg press
Bench press
Seated row
Abdominals
Low back machine or deadlift
Hamstring curl
Calf raise
Military press
Upright row
Arm curl

Number of Sets

3

Training Intensity

Warm-up set: None needed
Resistance: 8- to 10RM or 75 to 85% of the 1RM

Length of Rest Period

1 to 2 minutes

workout but rather signs of intolerance of the demands placed on the acid–base system. If these signs appear, the workout should be stopped, and rest periods should be increased when using this workout in a future training session. Too much too soon, in any workout protocol, can be problematic and care should be taken to progress changes in length of rest period in a tolerable manner. No warm-up set is needed and the resistance is in the 8- to 10RM zone or 75 to 85% of the 1RM with the larger muscles using the higher percentages. Three sets should be performed and progression in length of rest periods from 3 minutes down to 1 minute should be part of the protocol.

Light Workout

The light workout is part of the recovery series of workouts for motor units that are used for the heavier and power workouts. The light workout is especially good for the development of local muscular endurance. Thus, more sets can be used to optimize this trainable feature of muscle. However, care should be taken so that the volume is not too high; high volume may promote glycogen depletion in the lower-threshold motor units, resulting in the use of higher-threshold motor units that are supposed to rest during such a training day. No warm-up set is needed and the resistance is relatively light (a 13- to 15RM zone or 50 to 60% of the 1RM for 2 sets) with a progression from 2-minute to 1-minute rest periods.

Very Light Workout

The very light workout is truly a recovery day and may in fact function as an active rest day. The

---

SAMPLE PROTOCOL

Light Workout

Exercise Choice and Order

Lunge

Incline bench press

Seated row

Abdominals

Lat pull-down

Stiff-leg deadlift

Hamstring curl

Calf raise

Military press

Upright row

Arm curl

Number of Sets

2

Training Intensity

Warm-up set: None needed

Resistance: 13- to 15RM or 50 to 60% of the 1RM

Length of Rest Period

1 to 2 minutes

---

goal of the training session is to allow for recovery of motor units higher in the recruitment threshold by lifting relatively light weights. Many times this type of workout can be used after a hard day, after a heavy practice before the weight room workout, or after too much cardiorespiratory conditioning. No warm-up set is needed and the resistance is very light (a 16- to 20RM zone or 40 to 55% of the 1RM for 1 set with 1-minute rest periods between exercises).

Very Light Workout

Exercise Choice and Order

Squat or leg press
Bench press
Seated row
Abdominals
Low back machine or deadlift
Hamstring curl
Calf raise
Military press
Upright row
Arm curl

Number of Sets

1

Training Intensity

Warm-up set: None needed
Resistance: 16- to 20RM or 40 to 55% of the 1RM

Length of Rest Period

1 minute

ACTIVE AND TOTAL REST DAYS

As pointed out previously, there are days when active rest can help an individual recover from the physical demands of a conditioning or sport training program. In a classic sense, active rest has meant undertaking exercise activities that are not related to the weight room. So games, hiking, and swimming can provide some recovery for the neuromuscular system. It is vital that the active rest activities do not have a high injury potential. For example, it has often been seen that athletes playing basketball for fun get injured and this sets them back in their training program. Pick activities that have a low risk of injury and promote safe active rest physical activity.

Total rest days can also be very important to allow needed recovery of the neuromuscular system and prevent overtraining. In our research on the topic of overtraining, it has been demonstrated that one day of rest will reduce the chance of overtraining from heavy lifting days. In addition, athletes many times are physically and emotionally challenged by the total amount of stress from the sport competition or total training volume (weight room, conditioning, skill practice), and a complete day of rest is vital for restoration. Thus a complete day of rest in the nonlinear cycle of training involves no activity and adequate nutritional intake.

These sample workouts demonstrate the variety of possible sessions that can make up training in a nonlinear program. Many other combinations of acute training variables can be prioritized in a sequence of workouts.

Safe games, hiking, swimming, and other similar activities provide some recovery for the neuromuscular system on active rest days.

SUMMARY

The types of workouts that can be used in nonlinear periodization are as limitless as they are for any other workout progression (ACSM, 2002). The choice of workout sequence is the determining factor in this type of periodization model. Learning how to choose the right workout for the trainee or for the muscle group at the right time is a vital issue in the flexible nonlinear program approach.

CHAPTER 6

Assessment

A ssessments need to be made in two primary areas. First (as discussed in chapters 3 and 4) is the determination of the individual's ability to physically perform a given workout, also known as readiness to train. The second is the determination of the resistance training program's success in meeting the goals established for a particular mesocycle or macrocycle. Both aid in the decision-making process regarding the program emphasis as well as the daily workout routines.

PREEXERCISE ASSESSMENTS

Training readiness is dependent on several factors, which can be assessed using a combination of preexercise tests and evaluation of exercise performance during a training session. Preexercise assessments can be made in these areas:

1. Physical and mental fatigue and stress level
2. Injury status
3. Physical performance capacity

Exercise performance during a training session is also an important part of determining training readiness and can be assessed by observing whether a trainee achieves the desired number of repetitions with a certain resistance or is not able to achieve the minimum number of repetitions of an RM training zone. Information concerning training readiness can also be obtained through evaluation of training logs. Both of these methods of determining training readiness are discussed in chapter 7. With nonlinear periodization and flexible nonlinear periodization, testing can be performed in order to track changes in a variable over time, such as maximal strength or local muscular endurance. Additionally, with flexible nonlinear periodization, testing is used in determining whether an individual should perform a particular type of training session or should use another type of training session. The use of another type of training session is the flexible aspect or flexible nonlinear periodization.

Physical and Mental Fatigue and Stress Level

As described in chapter 4, having interactions between the coach, trainer, and trainee is the best method of determining how the individual feels and what is happening in his or her life. Even with large teams, coaches and trainers can get a general sense of the emotional environment that is affecting the players. Standard mental and physical scales as shown in chapter 4 can be used in quantifying such feelings and tracking them over various training cycles. Trainees need to be educated about the seriousness of this information in order to make it an effective tool. If done correctly, cut-off scores for certain workouts (e.g., no greater than an 8 on both the physical and mental basic fatigue scales to allow a power training day to proceed) can also indicate that an alternative workout is needed. Documentation of fatigue should not be disregarded as a tool because psychological staleness and fatigue can accumulate in any individual because of the stress of competition or the daily stresses of work and school.

It is important to track prior physical and emotional stressors (e.g., practice schedules and what was done, big business meetings, personal stresses) outside of the weight room or fitness facility, especially the ones that are within a 24-hour period before a workout. This can be difficult without help and a good relationship with the athlete, sport coach, or trainee. This initial information (gathered from direct questioning of the trainee or from direct observations of behavior) will help in gauging whether an individual is ready to perform a training session at the desired intensity and volume.

Injury Status

Physical injury can result in an inability to perform a training session. Assessment of physical injury can be done in part by observation, such as merely noticing that the person is limping or has difficulty with a particular bodily movement. However, if possible, part of injury assessment also involves having an open dialogue with athletic trainers, physicians, and other health professionals. In some situations it is possible to have the training session work around contraindicated exercises. For example, an individual with a knee injury would avoid lower-body exercises but that person could perform seated upper-body exercises. Performing exercises that are not contraindicated is important in maintaining strength, power, and local muscular endurance in noninjured areas of the body. This will allow the individual to return to normal physical activity as quickly as possible after recovering from an injury and aid in preventing injury to a different area of the body upon returning to normal physical activity. Whenever a trainee is recovering from an injury, he or she should work closely with health care professionals in order to recover as quickly as possible as well as to avoid further injury.

Preexercise Testing to Determine Performance Capacity

Testing before a training session in the flexible nonlinear training model aids in determining whether a particular type of training session should be performed. Tests used for this purpose should not result in significant fatigue that would affect performance of the upcoming training session and should not take a great deal of time to administer. So many tests that are typically used to track changes caused by training, such as 1RM testing or a set to failure to test local muscular endurance or body composition changes, cannot be used for this purpose. To date, tests that determine some measure of power are used in deciding whether an alternative type of training session should be performed. The acceptable level for determining whether a particular type of training session can be performed is typically 90% of the individual's score on a maximal test.

Another consideration for testing before a training session is whether several testing stations can be set up and used simultaneously so that all members of an athletic team or a large group can be tested in a short period of time. Another way to minimize testing time before a training session is to break up the group into several smaller groups that train at different times of the day. New technologies allow a trainer to see the power output on a test immediately on test completion, which allows for an immediate decision concerning whether an alternative session should be performed.

The following tests have been used in deciding whether an individual is ready to perform the planned session in the flexible nonlinear model:

- Maximal vertical jump
- Maximal standing long jump
- Medicine ball throw
- Power development during an exercise

The most sensitive parameter to fatigue is power; therefore it is important to test for power before any power training sessions. With other workout styles, a trainer can use the actual performance within the first few sets to determine if the workout can be performed. (This is discussed further in chapter 8.) For example, on a heavy day (3- to 5RM zone) an athlete lifted 300 pounds (136 kg) for 5 repetitions in the bench during the first set. A week later, for the same exercise with the same resistance, the athlete could perform only 2 repetitions in the first set. In this case, it is possible that the lifter is not ready to undertake a heavy 3- to 5RM workout. The trainer might want to have the athlete try another set; if the performance is still not within the 3- to 5RM range, the trainer must use a lighter lifting day and determine why the athlete's physical performance is reduced. It might be that an overtraining situation is developing. At best, a trainer can alternate to a moderate or light day of training and see how the athlete's performance compares to that of prior workouts of similar intensity. It is also important to know whether fatigue is a problem for just the first exercise in the session or if it is apparent in other exercises in the session. If it appears to be a general phenomenon, an active rest day or complete rest day is indicated. As discussed in chapter 4, determining when to use another workout from the master schedule is an important feature of flexible nonlinear programming.

Even if an individual does achieve an acceptable score in one of the tests, an unacceptable level of performance of the overall training session would override the test result in terms of deciding whether to continue with a particular type of training session. For example, if a person's test score indicated that she was ready to perform a power training session, but she was able to perform only 3 repetitions of the clean pull to chest height instead of 5 repetitions, as she had done previously, a switch to a strength training day would take place. Once a lifter gets into a workout, it is important to use and compare performances from prior workouts to see if the lifter has maintained her level of performance. If she has not maintained the level of performance of the session, the quality of the training session will not be optimal. A decrease in performance is expected when performing an intentional overreaching protocol. However, unintentional drops in performance and increases in fatigue are indications of something else going on in the individual's life or total exercise program. It is important to catch these situations and provide an alternative training session option to maximize the training performed on a given day. In some cases this means switching to a session of reduced intensity or volume.

Not all of the previously mentioned tests would be performed before each training session in the flexible nonlinear model. Typically only one or at most two tests would be performed before a training session. Abilities in both the maximal vertical jump and maximal standing long jump are measures of lower-body power. Therefore only one of these tests would be performed immediately before a training session to evaluate lower-body power. The seated medicine ball throw evaluates upper-body power. Therefore, to evaluate both upper- and lower-body power, one jump test and the seated medicine ball test could be performed. Power during exercises, such as variations of the power clean or power snatch, is determined by most of the major muscle groups of the body. Therefore if such exercises are used immediately before a training session, the athlete does not need to undergo other tests to evaluate total-body power. With the use of various systems to measure power, a trainer or coach can also directly measure the power output in a given power-type lift (e.g., hang pull) to determine what training weight to use in a certain workout (e.g., 60% of the 1RM).

Regardless of whether testing is used to evaluate training progress or to decide on a particular type of training session, the first priority for any test is safety of the trainee. Therefore, all safety precautions, such as spotters where needed, should be employed during all testing sessions.

ALTERNATIVE WORKOUTS

As discussed in chapter 5, many situations exist in which the planned workout in a flexible nonlinear program may not be appropriate. When using the flexible approach, the typical alternative is to use an easier workout to provide rest and recovery. However, in some cases an opportunity exists to get in a higher-intensity workout as the alternative workout. Alternative workouts are all about the scenarios and circumstances that surround the workout planned for a particular day. The strength and conditioning specialist or personal trainer determines the best alternative workout based on the trainee's history, understanding of the situation, testing data, and reflective insight.

When a preexercise test is used for determining whether a particular type of training session should be performed, an acceptable score on the test indicates the trainee should perform the planned training session. An unacceptable score indicates the individual should alternate to another type of training session. For example, an unacceptable score in a power test would result in switching to a maximal-strength training session or to a lighter workout to provide more time for muscle recovery (typically the high-threshold motor units need more recovery time).

EVALUATING TRAINING PROGRESS

Any test that is typically used for tracking changes in a variable, such as body composition or local muscular endurance, can be applied to nonlinear periodization. These types of tests are typically performed no more frequently than every several months. Often these types of tests are performed before beginning a training program, in the middle of the program, and at the end of the training program. For athletes, testing might occur at the beginning of preseason, at the end of the preseason, during the midseason, and at the end of the season.

Tests used for tracking changes in a variable indicate individual and group progress in the training program. These types of tests also evaluate whether the training program results in the desired physiological changes. If the desired physiological changes occur, the program is deemed successful. If the desired changes do not occur, the program is evaluated and changes are made so that the desired changes occur in subsequent performances of the program.

The following are tests that are often used for evaluating training progress:

- One-repetition maximum (1RM) testing
- Prediction of 1RM strength
- Local muscular endurance
- Body composition, such as percentage of body fat and fat-free mass

- Body and limb circumferences
- Maximal vertical jump
- Maximal standing long jump
- Medicine ball throw
- Power development during an exercise

One-Repetition Maximum Testing

Testing of one-repetition maximum (1RM testing) can be performed for any exercise in which a coach or trainer wants to track strength and power gains due to a training program. Normally 1RM testing is performed on multijoint or large-muscle-group exercises and not on single-joint or small-muscle-group exercises. For some exercises in which speed of movement is relatively slow when lifting heavy resistances, such as the bench press and back squat, determination of the 1RM is a measure of maximal strength. However, for other exercises in which speed of movement is fast even when lifting heavy resistances, such as the power clean and power snatch, determination of the 1RM is a measure of power as well as strength. So whether maximal strength or a measure of power is being tested depends on the exercises for which the 1RM is determined.

Regardless of what exercise is tested for 1RM, trainers and coaches need to consider several factors to ensure accuracy and safety of testing. The starting position of the exercise needs to be defined and held constant for all testing. In a squat or leg press, the width of the feet should be measured and recorded. Correct starting and finishing positions of a repetition need to be defined. For example, in the bench press and overhead press, the elbows need to be straight at the end of the concentric repetition phase. In the lat pull-down, the bar must touch the top of the sternum at the end of the concentric repetition phase. In the squat the thighs need to be parallel to the floor at the end of the eccentric repetition phase. The starting and finishing positions define the range of motion of the exercise. Normally if the complete range of motion as defined by the starting and finishing positions is not achieved, the repetition is not counted as a successful 1RM attempt. Other factors in exercise technique may result in an unsuccessful 1RM attempt. So incorrect exercise technique needs to be defined for each exercise tested. For example, bouncing the bar off of the chest in the bench press, bridging or raising the buttocks off of the bench in the bench press, or raising the buttocks off of the seat during a machine

To track strength and power gains, 1RM testing is typically performed on exercises such as the bench press, overhead press, squat, leg press, power clean, power snatch, or lat pull-down.

overhead press would be considered incorrect exercise technique. Whether free-weight or machine 1RM testing is performed, the complete range of motion and incorrect exercise technique need to be defined and explained to the individuals being tested.

All lifters performing 1RM testing should have good exercise technique in all lifts before they are tested on them. Correct exercise technique should be stressed when lifters are learning to perform exercises and in all training sessions to ensure correct technique not only during training but also during testing. Correct exercise technique also is necessary for safety reasons. Another aspect of correct exercise technique is whether a weight training belt will be allowed during testing in some lifts such as the squat, power clean, and deadlift. The lifters being tested should know whether a weight training belt is allowed. The rules should not change after the first testing; that is, if a belt cannot be used on the first test, then the lifter should not be allowed to use a belt on any subsequent occurrences of testing.

One-repetition maximum testing involves lifting very heavy resistances, and all possible safety precautions for each exercise tested should be used. Exercises such as the squat should be performed in a power rack with the pins set slightly lower than the bar will go during the eccentric phase of a repetition, spotters should be used in many exercises, and collars should be used at all times. It is also necessary to have an emergency plan in place in case injury does occur. The person being tested should be sufficiently rested to allow true maximal efforts during the 1RM testing procedure. No matter what exercises are tested, to help prevent injury during testing, all safety precautions should be used during the entire testing protocol.

All aspects of the testing protocol (including warm-up sets, rest between 1RM attempts, and increases in resistance) need to be established and followed during all testing. The following is a test protocol applicable to all 1RM testing that has been used successfully in both research projects and testing of athletic teams. One difficulty associated with 1RM testing, especially for the initial test, is estimating what is termed the *perceived 1RM*. Some estimate of the 1RM is needed in order to define warm-up sets and the first resistance to be used as a 1RM attempt. During the first 1RM testing session, data from training logs should be used along with interaction with the person being tested to help establish the perceived 1RM. After the first 1RM testing session, the results from that session can be used along with training log information in establishing the perceived 1RM for the second testing session.

If the 1RM is to be tested for more than one exercise in one testing session, allow at least 5 minutes between exercises to ensure adequate recovery between determining 1RMs for successive exercises. If the 1RM for more than one exercise is to be determined, always use the same exercise order in all testing sessions. Using this protocol and all safety precautions in a 1RM testing session will ensure accuracy of the results and safety of the lifter.

Following is a list of common exercises tested for 1RM and some typical guidelines for starting and finishing positions, complete range of motion, and faults in exercise technique that would result in the 1RM attempt not being counted as successful. For many exercises, the foot or hand positioning in the starting position needs to be controlled and recorded in order to ensure testing accuracy. Close attention to all aspects of exercise technique ensure testing accuracy as well as safety of the lifter. This is not a complete description of

Warm-Up Sets

1. A warm-up set of 5 to 10 repetitions using 40 to 60% of the perceived 1RM

2. After 1 minute of rest, a second warm-up set of 3 to 5 repetitions using 60 to 80% of the perceived 1RM

1RM Attempts

1. Instruct the lifter on what will be counted as a successful 1RM attempt, including complete range of motion and the faults in exercise technique that will result in an unsuccessful repetition.

2. After the last warm-up set, 3 to 5 minutes of rest are allowed and then the perceived 1RM is used to perform 1 repetition.

3. If the first 1RM attempt is successful, after 3 to 5 minutes of rest another 1RM attempt is made using a heavier resistance. If the first 1RM attempt was not successful, after 3 to 5 minutes of rest another 1RM attempt is made using a lighter resistance. The resistance used for subsegent attempts is typically increased or decreased in small (2.5-5%) increments depending on the amount of effort used during the previous 1RM attempt.

4. Step 3 is repeated no more than 5 times to determine the 1RM.

5. If step 3 is repeated 5 times and the 1RM has not been successfully determined, schedule another testing session and use the results of the testing session to establish the perceived 1RM for the next testing section.

correct exercise technique and range of motion (see Kraemer & Fleck, 2005, for complete descriptions of exercise technique), but it presents factors that are sometimes overlooked when performing testing. Additionally, when resistance training machines are used, correct exercise technique may vary from one manufacturer's machine to another.

Predictions of 1RM

At times it may be more convenient to predict the 1RM than to actually test to determine the true 1RM. Prediction of the 1RM can be done by using either a table or a formula; both methods predict

Bench Press

Whether a machine or free weight is used in determining the 1RM starting and finishing position, complete range of motion and exercise technique need to be stressed during all testing.

Positioning and Range of Motion

1. Buttocks and upper back are in contact with the bench or seat and seat back.
2. A complete range of motion in a repetition goes from a chesttouch position to a straight-elbow position.

Faults in Exercise Technique or Testing

1. The back bridges (buttocks rise off the bench or seat).
2. The bar bounces off the chest or the weight stack bounces off its rubber stoppers at the end of the eccentric repetition phase.

Squat

The most common squat used for testing is the back squat. However, the front squat can also be used.

Positioning and Range of Motion

1. The bar positioning on the back needs to be standardized. Normally the bar is placed on the spines of the scapula. Whether a high-bar or low-bar squat is to be performed needs to be clearly defined.
2. Range of motion is from an upright standing position to the point at which the thighs are parallel to the floor.

Faults in Exercise Technique or Testing

1. Lifter has excessive forward lean, which should not be allowed because it places the lifter in an injurious position.
2. Lifter is not told whether a weight training belt is allowed.

1RM based on the number of repetitions in a set to failure with a submaximal resistance. Whichever method is used, several factors should be considered in order to enhance the accuracy of the 1RM prediction. First, the tables and formulas were developed for the multijoint exercises of bench press, back squat, and in some cases the power clean. Thus the prediction of 1RM is most accurate for

Leg Press or Hip Sled

Positioning and Range of Motion

1. Foot position on the foot plate needs to be held constant.
2. Normally a complete range of motion requires a 90° knee angle at the beginning of the concentric repetition phase and the knees to be straight at the end of the concentric repetition phase.
3. The seat or sled position needs to be held constant. This can normally be done by recording the seat or sled position used.

Faults in Exercise Technique or Testing

The weight stack or sled bounces off all its rubber stops at the end of the eccentric repetition phase.

Lat Pull-Down

Positioning and Range of Motion

1. In the starting position the elbows are completely straight and the lifter is positioned so that the bar can be pulled straight down to the top of the sternum.
2. At the end of the concentric repetition phase the bar touches the top of the sternum or breastbone.
3. The position of the thigh pad should be held constant.
4. Grip width needs to be held constant.

Faults in Exercise Technique or Testing

1. Lifter leans backward or uses a back extension movement to get the weight moving at the start of the concentric repetition phase.
2. Lifter does not achieve a position in which the bar touches the top of the sternum at the end of the concentric repetition phase.

these exercises. The tables and formulas were not developed with the use of data from other multijoint exercises and not from data on single-joint exercises. The prediction of 1RM is most accurate when a resistance that allows 10 or fewer repetitions is used. The prediction accuracy actually increases with the use of a heavier resistance, which allows performance of fewer repetitions to failure. This means that the prediction based on a resistance that allows 5

Power Clean

Positioning and Range of Motion

1. Hand and foot positions in the starting position need to be held constant.

2. The bar must be caught in a shoulder-height position.

3. When the lifter catches the bar, the knees cannot bend past a 90° angle.

Faults in Exercise Technique or Testing

1. Lifter steps forward after catching the bar.

2. Lifter has excessive forward lean, which places him or her in an injurious position.

3. Lifter is not told whether wrist straps and a weight training belt are allowed.

Power Snatch

Positioning and Range of Motion

1. Hand and foot positions in the starting position need to be held constant.

2. The bar must be caught overhead with the elbows completely straight.

3. When lifter catches the bar, the knees cannot bend past a 90° angle.

Faults in Exercise Technique or Testing

1. Lifter steps forward after catching the bar.

2. Lifter is not told whether wrist straps and a weight training belt are allowed.

repetitions to failure will be more accurate than a prediction based on a resistance that allows 10 repetitions to failure. Accuracy of the prediction is also enhanced if individuals have been training for several months using relatively heavy resistances allowing 10 repetitions per set or fewer. Prediction of a 1RM does require the performance of a set of the exercise to failure. Generally, unless the prediction is based on training log data of sets to failure, even though a prediction is made a testing protocol needs to be performed. Prediction of 1RM does have a large amount of individual variation. (See chapter 3 for a discussion of the amount of individual variation in the number of repetitions that can be performed to failure at a specific resistance.) This means that the table or equation may predict 1RM very accurately for some individuals and inaccurately for other individuals.

Some of the limitations of using a 1RM prediction equation are shown by the use of four different equations (described in the following pages) to predict bench press 1RM of American football players (Ware et al., 1995). The 1RM was predicted by having the players perform a set to failure at an average of 71% of their 1RM in the squat and bench press.

The actual bench press 1RM was 273.5 pounds (124 kg). The predicted bench press 1RM with the four formulas ranged from 266.6 to 307.5 pounds (120.9 to 139.5 kg). The mean 1RM predictions range from a 2.5% underestimation to 12.4% overestimation of the true bench press 1RM. The actual squat 1RM was 394.2 pounds (178.8 kg). The predicted squat 1 RM with the four formulas ranged from 420.0 to 500.9 pounds (190.5 to 227.2 kg). All of the formulas overpredicted the squat 1RM with a range of overprediction of 6.5 to 27.1%

Despite these limitations, prediction of 1RM can be performed and used in tracking strength increases. However, prediction of 1RM is an estimate, and use of different tables or formulas does result in variations in 1RM prediction. Thus the same formula or table should always be used in predicting 1RM of an individual when tracking strength increases. Following is a protocol that can be used in testing the number of repetitions to failure in order to predict 1RM.

Several formulas can be used to predict 1RM. The following calculations using four commonly used formulas demonstrate several important points concerning prediction of 1RM. All of the sample calculations are based on using 250 pounds ($\sim$ 113.6 kg) to perform 6 repetitions in a set to failure. These four equations predict 1RMs varying from 290.36 to 303.77 pounds ($\sim$ 131.9 to $\sim$ 138.1 kg) or an approximate range of 13 pounds ($\sim$ 6.0 kg). All but one of the equations has been used to predict 1RM of the bench press and squat. The Mayhew, Ball, and Bowen equation (1992) was developed specifically for the bench press exercise and therefore probably should be used only for predictions of bench press 1RM. The range does indicate, however, that the same equation should always be used when predicting the 1RM of an individual or group.

Warm-Up Set

A light warm-up set of 5 or 6 repetitions at approximately 50% of the perceived 1RM can be performed, especially if a resistance that will allow a very few number of repetitions (6 or fewer) is used to predict 1RM. If approximately 10 repetitions per set are used to predict the 1RM, no warm-up set is necessary.

Set to Failure

1. Choose a resistance that allows for 10 or fewer repetitions per set to failure. If this is the first time 1RM will be predicted, the resistance used should be based on training log data.
2. The resistance used in subsequent 1RM predictions can be based on a combination of the previous 1RM prediction and training log data.
3. Perform 1 set to failure, following all the safety precautions that should be used when actually determining a true 1RM.
4. The set should be terminated if exercise technique deterioration places the lifter in an injurious position.

Brzycki, 1993

$$\% \ 1RM = 102.78 - 2.78 \ \text{(repetitions)}$$
$$\% \ 1RM = 102.78 - 2.78 \ \text{(6 repetitions)}$$
$$\% \ 1RM = 102.78 - 16.68$$
$$\% \ 1RM = 86.10$$
$$86.10 \times 100 = 0.8610 \ \text{of 1 RM}$$
$$1RM = 250 \ \text{pounds} / 0.8610$$
$$1RM = 290.36 \ \text{pounds}$$
$$1RM = 113.6 \ \text{kilograms} / 0.8610 = 131.9 \ \text{kilograms}$$

Lander, 1985

$$\% \ 1RM = 101.3 - 2.67123 \ \text{(repetitions)}$$
$$\% \ 1RM = 101.3 - 2.67123 \ \text{(6 repetitions)}$$
$$\% \ 1RM = 101.3 - 16.03$$
$$\% \ 1RM = 85.22$$
$$85.22 \times 100 = 0.8522 \ \text{of 1RM}$$
$$1RM = 250 \ \text{pounds} / 0.8522$$
$$1RM = 293.36 \ \text{pounds}$$
$$1RM = 113.6 \ \text{kilograms} / 0.8522 = 133.3 \ \text{kilograms}$$

Mayhew, Ball, and Bowen, 1992

This equation requires the use of the exponent function on a calculator.

$$\% \ 1RM = 52.2 + 41.9^{-0.0555 \ (\text{repetitions})}$$

$$\% \ 1RM = 52.2 + 41.9^{-0.0555 \ (6 \ \text{repetitions})}$$

$$\% \ 1RM = 52.2 + 41.9^{-0.33}$$

$$\% \ 1RM = 52.2 + 30.12$$

$$\% \ 1RM = 82.3$$

$$82.3 \times 100 = 0.823$$

$$1RM = 250 \text{ pounds} / 0.823$$

$$1RM = 303.77 \text{ pounds}$$

$$1RM = 113.6 \text{ kilograms} / 0.823 = 138.0 \text{ kilograms}$$

Epley, 1985

$$1RM = ([0.033 \times \text{repetition weight}] \times \text{repetitions}) + \text{repetition weight}$$

$$1RM = ([0.033 \times 250 \text{ pounds}] \times 6 \text{ repetitions}) + 250 \text{ pounds}$$

$$1RM = ([8.25] \times 6 \text{ repetitions}) + 250 \text{ pounds}$$

$$1RM = 49.5 + 250 \text{ pounds}$$

$$1RM = 299.5 \text{ pounds}$$

$$1RM = ([0.033 \times \text{repetition weight}] \times \text{repetitions}) + \text{repetition weight}$$

$$1RM = ([0.033 \times 113.6 \text{ kilograms}] \times 6 \text{ repetitions}) + 113.6 \text{ kilograms}$$

$$1RM = ([3.75] \times 6 \text{ repetitions}) + 113.6 \text{ kilograms}$$

$$1RM = 22.5 + 113.6 \text{ kilograms}$$

$$1RM = 136.1 \text{ kilograms}$$

Tables used for predicting 1RM based on the number of repetitions performed in a set to failure are based on an equation or a combination of equations. Therefore they suffer the same limitations as equation predictions of 1RM. However, tables are no less accurate than

NFL 225-Pound Bench Press Test

The NFL 225-pound bench press test has gained popularity, especially among American football teams, as a way of predicting 1RM bench press ability. This test uses the performance of repetitions to failure at an absolute resistance of 225 pounds (~102.3 kg) to predict 1RM. Similar to the previous prediction equations and table to predict 1RM, this test has all the limitations of a submaximal prediction of 1RM. This equation has been shown to be valid in the prediction of bench press 1RM in American football players (Chapman, Whitehead, & Binkert, 1998; Mayhew et al., 1999). Similar to other predictions of 1RM, using a submaximal resistance for the prediction has been shown to be most accurate when 10 repetitions or fewer are performed.

Warm-Up Set

A light warm-up set of 5 or 6 repetitions at 135 to 175 pounds (~61.4-79.5 kg) can be performed depending on the strength level of the individual being tested.

Set to Failure

1. Perform 1 set to failure at a resistance of 225 pounds (~102.3 kg), following all the safety precautions that should be used when actually determining a true 1RM.
2. The set should be terminated if deterioration in exercise technique places the lifter in an injurious position.

equations. A sample prediction table is presented in table 6.1. This table gives not only the predicted 1RM but also the approximate 1RM percentage of the weight used for predicting the 1RM. For example, if 216 pounds ($\sim$ 98.2 kg) were used and 8 repetitions were performed to failure, the predicted 1RM is 270 pounds ($\sim$ 122.7 kg) and 216 pounds ($\sim$ 98.1 kg) is 80% of the 1RM.

The 1RM equation used with the NFL 225-pound bench press prediction is as follows:

1RM pounds = 226.7 + 7.1 (repetitions at 225 pounds)

Table 6.1 1RM Prediction Table

Resistance (lb or kg)	MAXIMUM REPS (RM)											
	1	2	3	4	5	6	7	8	9	10	12	15
	% 1RM											
	100	95	93	90	87	85	83	80	77	75	67	65
10	10	9	9	9	9	8	8	8	8	7	7	
20	19	19	18	17	17	17	16	15	15	13	13	
30	29	28	27	26	26	25	24	23	23	20	20	
40	38	37	36	35	34	33	32	31	30	27	26	
50	48	47	45	44	43	42	40	39	38	34	33	
60	57	56	54	52	51	50	48	46	45	40	39	
70	67	65	63	61	60	58	56	54	53	47	46	
80	76	74	72	70	68	66	64	62	60	54	52	
90	86	84	81	78	77	75	72	69	68	60	59	
100	95	93	90	87	85	83	80	77	75	67	65	
110	105	102	99	96	94	91	88	85	83	74	72	
120	114	112	108	104	102	100	96	92	90	80	78	
130	124	121	117	113	111	108	104	100	98	87	85	
140	133	130	126	122	119	116	112	108	105	94	91	
150	143	140	135	131	128	125	120	116	113	101	98	
160	152	149	144	139	136	133	128	123	120	107	104	
170	162	158	153	148	145	141	136	131	128	114	111	
180	171	167	162	157	153	149	144	139	135	121	117	
190	181	177	171	165	162	158	152	146	143	127	124	
200	190	186	180	174	170	166	160	154	150	134	130	
210	200	195	189	183	179	174	168	162	158	141	137	
220	209	205	198	191	187	183	176	169	165	147	143	
230	219	214	207	200	196	191	184	177	173	154	150	
240	228	223	216	209	204	199	192	185	180	161	156	
250	238	233	225	218	213	208	200	193	188	168	163	
260	247	242	234	226	221	206	208	200	195	174	169	
270	257	251	243	235	230	224	216	208	203	181	176	
280	266	260	252	244	238	232	224	216	210	188	182	
290	276	270	261	252	247	241	232	223	218	194	189	
300	285	279	270	261	255	249	240	231	225	201	195	

MAXIMUM REPS (RM)											
1	2	3	4	5	6	7	8	9	10	12	15
% 1RM											
100	95	93	90	87	85	83	80	77	75	67	65
310	295	288	279	270	264	257	248	239	233	208	202
320	304	298	288	278	272	266	256	246	240	214	208
330	314	307	297	287	281	274	264	254	248	221	215
340	323	316	306	296	289	282	272	262	255	228	221
350	333	326	315	305	298	291	280	270	263	235	228
360	342	335	324	313	306	299	288	277	270	241	234
370	352	344	333	322	315	307	296	285	278	248	241
380	361	353	342	331	323	315	304	293	285	255	247
390	371	363	351	339	332	324	312	300	293	261	254
400	380	372	360	348	340	332	320	308	300	268	260
410	390	381	369	357	349	340	328	316	308	274	267
420	399	391	378	365	357	349	336	323	315	281	273
430	409	400	387	374	366	357	344	331	323	288	280
440	418	409	396	383	374	365	352	339	330	295	286
450	428	419	405	392	383	374	360	347	338	302	293
460	437	428	414	400	391	382	368	354	345	308	299
470	447	437	423	409	400	390	376	362	353	315	306
480	456	446	432	418	408	398	384	370	360	322	312
490	466	456	441	426	417	407	392	377	368	328	319
500	475	465	450	435	425	415	400	385	375	335	325
510	485	474	459	444	434	423	408	393	383	342	332
520	494	484	468	452	442	432	416	400	390	348	338
530	504	493	477	461	451	440	424	408	398	355	345
540	513	502	486	470	459	448	432	416	405	362	351
550	523	512	495	479	468	457	440	424	413	369	358
560	532	521	504	487	476	465	448	431	420	375	364
570	542	530	513	496	485	473	456	439	428	382	371
580	551	539	522	505	493	481	464	447	435	389	377
590	561	549	531	513	502	490	472	454	443	395	384
600	570	558	540	522	510	498	480	462	450	402	390

Resistance (lb or kg)

Reprinted, by permission, from T.R. Baechle, R.W. Earle and D. Wathen, 2000, Resistance training.
In *Essentials of strength training and conditioning,* 2nd ed., edited by T.R. Baechle and R.W. Earle
(Champaign, IL: Human Kinetics), 410-411.

For example, if 8 repetitions are performed, the following calculations would be used to predict the bench press 1RM.

$$1RM \text{ pounds} = 226.7 + 7.1 \ (8)$$
$$1RM \text{ pounds} = 226.7 + 56.8$$
$$1RM \text{ pounds} = 283.5$$

It is important to note that this equation has been validated only for bench press ability. It is not meant to be used for the 1RM prediction of any other exercise.

Local Muscular Endurance

Local muscular endurance is defined as the number of repetitions to failure of a certain exercise performed using a specific resistance. The specific resistance can be an absolute amount of resistance, such as 200 pounds ($\sim$ 90.9 kg). However, normally the specific resistance used for testing is determined as a specific percentage of the 1RM of an exercise, for example, number of repetitions performed to failure using more than 80% of 1RM in the leg press. Local muscular endurance can be determined for any exercise. Similar to 1RM testing, local muscular endurance is normally determined using a multijoint or multimuscle-group exercise, such as the leg press or bench press. Also similar to 1RM testing, local muscular endurance can be determined using either free-weight or machine exercises.

As in 1RM testing, safety and exercise technique are concerns when performing local muscular endurance testing. The range of motion needed for a successful repetition must be defined, and repetitions not meeting that definition should not be counted. For example, the elbows must be straight at the end of the concentric repetition phase and the bar must touch the chest at the end of the eccentric repetition phase in the bench press. Proper exercise technique must also be defined. The bar should not bounce off the chest during the free-weight bench press; during the machine leg press, the sled should not bounce off the machine's rubber stops to aid in initiating the concentric phase of the next repetition. Whether free-weight or machine exercises are used in testing local muscular endurance, proper exercise technique and a complete range of motion for the exercise being tested must be defined and followed for accuracy of the test results as well as for safety reasons. The same definitions for complete range of motion and faults in exercise technique, as described previously in the exercises tested for 1RM, can be used when performing testing for local muscular endurance. And as in 1RM testing, all lifters should know and follow safety precautions and proper exercise technique for all exercises being tested, such as the use of spotters. Performance of appropriate exercises inside of a power rack should be followed during all local muscular endurance testing.

Normally 80 to 90% of 1RM of an exercise is used as resistance when testing local muscular endurance. Resistances in this range are used because a sufficient number of repetitions can be performed so that local muscular endurance is indeed being tested. However, with these resistances not so many repetitions can be performed so that the test becomes boring. The number of repetitions possible at a specific percentage of 1RM is quite different from exercise to exercise. One factor unique to local muscular endurance testing is that if the resistance used is not adjusted as the lifter becomes stronger (1RM increases), what was once 80% of 1RM is now less than 80% of 1RM. This is an important consideration because generally large increases in the number of repetitions possible at a specific absolute resistance occur as a result of the resistance training program because a specific absolute resistance becomes a smaller percentage of the 1RM as the lifter becomes stronger. The number of repetitions possible at a specific percentage of 1RM is relatively stable, even as strength increases as a result of the resistance training program. Generally performance of sport or daily life activities is determined by the ability to repetitively move a specific absolute resistance, such as body weight when climbing stairs or sprinting up a hill. So progress in local muscular endurance is normally measured over the course of a sport's season or a year or months of training using a specified resistance of the pretraining or initial 1RM. If the resistance is adjusted to represent a certain percentage of the ever-increasing 1RM due to training, the number of repetitions possible at that percentage will remain relatively constant. This is not to say that the resistance used for local muscular endurance testing should never be adjusted to represent a new 1RM, but it should not be done too frequently. For athletes, normally the specified percentage of the initial or pretraining 1RM is used for an entire season and is then adjusted at the start of the next season.

The following is a protocol that can be used in testing local muscular endurance of any exercise:

Warm-Up Sets

Normally no warm-up sets are used because although the resistance is relatively heavy, multiple repetitions can be performed.

Repetitions for Local Muscular Endurance

1. Choose the percentage of the 1RM to be used. Typically 70 to 85% of the 1RM is used.
2. Instruct the lifter on what will be counted as a successful repetition during the testing and what faults in exercise technique will result in an unsuccessful repetition.
3. During testing, explain to the lifter why a repetition has been counted as successful or a repetition has not been counted as successful.
4. Count the total number of successful repetitions.

If local muscular endurance is to be tested in more than one exercise, allow at least 5 minutes between exercises. Generally local muscular endurance would not be determined for two exercises using the same muscle groups, such as the bench press and overhead press, in the same testing session. When the 1RM and local muscular endurance are to be determined in the same exercise during the same testing session, the 1RM test should be performed first so that fatigue caused by the local muscular endurance test does not affect the 1RM testing. Allow at least 5 minutes between the tests.

Body Composition

Physical training, including resistance training, does bring about changes in body composition. The desired changes in body composition are a decrease in fat mass or percentage of fat and an increase in muscle mass. When determining body composition, the body is divided into two major components. The first component is fat mass, or fat weight. Fat mass is the weight of all adipose (fat) tissue in the body. The second component is termed fat-free mass (FFM) and is the weight of all other tissues in the body except fat. FFM is calculated by subtracting fat mass from total body weight. Another term that is sometimes used in relation to body composition is lean body mass (LBM). LBM is sometimes used interchangeably with FFM, but really these two terms have different meanings. FFM refers to all tissues except fat tissue, and LBM refers to FFM plus essential fat. Essential fat is the adipose tissue that is necessary for normal functioning of the body. Essential fat is found in many places in the body. For example, some fat exists in cell membranes, some exists as fat pads to protect internal organs, and some fat is stored in cells as a metabolic fuel and eventually metabolized to generate energy. A person cannot have 0% fat. Essential fat levels for males are 5 to 6% and essential fat levels for females may be as low as 8%. Because LBM includes essential fat and FFM includes no fat, LBM is always greater in mass than FFM. No methods of determining body composition can distinguish between essential fat and other fat tissue. Therefore all methods of determining body composition determine FFM and not LBM.

The following illustrates the difference between FFM and LBM:

A male athlete's total body weight = 200 pounds (90.9 kilograms)

% fat = 12%

Fat mass = 200 pounds × 0.12 = 24 pounds

FFM = 200 pounds – 24 pounds = 176 pounds (80.0 kilograms)

Assuming essential fat = 6%

Essential fat = 200 pounds × 0.06 = 12 pounds

LBM = FFM + essential fat

LBM = 176 pounds + 12 pounds = 188 pounds (85.5 kilograms)

The average college-age male is 14 to 16% fat and the average college-age female is 24 to 26% fat. Highly conditioned athletes can approach essential fat levels. For example, male weight-class athletes, such as wrestlers and boxers (but not including heavyweights), may have fat levels that approach essential fat levels of 6 to 8%. Male and female bodybuilders may have fat levels as low as 5% and 9%, respectively, which also approach essential fat levels. On the other end of the spectrum are athletes such as American football lineman, where a high body mass is desirable so their percentage of fat is typically greater than the average college-age male and may be as high as 30%.

One of the typical goals of a resistance training program is to increase FFM. However, unrealistic goals in FFM increases are sometimes established. The largest increases in FFM consistently reported with drug-free resistance training are a little greater than 6.6 pounds (3 kg) in approximately 10 weeks (Fleck & Kraemer, 2004). This translates into approximately an increase of 0.66 pound (0.3 kg) per week. Weight gains greater than this normally involve an increase in fat mass and percentage of fat rather than an increase in FFM. Normally during short-term drug-free training periods (less than 20 weeks), resistance training causes a decrease in percentage of fat not by decreasing fat mass but by increasing FFM (Fleck & Kraemer, 2004). In setting goals for FFM during training, a realistic gain in FFM needs to be considered.

Several methods are commonly used in determining body composition. Hydrostatic weighing and dual-energy X-ray absorptiometry (DEXA) are considered the most accurate ways to determine body composition. However, the use of skinfold testing is also a very accurate, convenient, and inexpensive method of determining body composition. Therefore many athletic teams and fitness enthusiasts use skinfolds to track changes in body composition caused by training.

Many possible skinfold sites exist, and many formulas use skinfolds in determining body composition. Formulas have been developed for specific athletic groups. However, the Jackson/Pollock formulas have gained popularity and are accurate over a wide range of groups (Jackson & Pollock, 1978; Jackson, Pollock, & Ward, 1980). These formulas use the thigh, chest, and abdomen sites for males and the thigh, triceps, and suprailium (near the top of the hip bone) sites for females. Following are descriptions of how to determine skinfold thickness at these sites. If another formula uses other skinfold sites in determining body composition, it is imperative to have a protocol for locating and determining the other sites.

The Jackson/Pollock equations, as do many skinfold equations, estimate body density. Because FFM is denser than fat mass, the greater the body density, the lower the fat mass or percentage of body fat. After body density has been estimated, another equation, called the Siri equation (1961) is normally used to determine percentage of fat. After percentage of fat is known, FFM and fat mass can be calculated. The following are the Jackson/Pollock equations for both males and females:

Male body density g/ml = $1.1093800 - (0.0008267 \times \text{SSF}) + (0.0000016 \times \text{SSF}^2) - (0.0002574 \times \text{age in years})$

Female body density g/ml = $1.0994921 - (0.0009929 \times \text{SSF}) + (0.0000023 \times \text{SSF}^2) - (0.0001392 \times \text{age in years})$

General Procedures for Measuring Skinfolds

Although measuring skinfolds looks relatively easy, it is an acquired skill that needs to be practiced before it can be used in accurately determining body composition. The following is a list of general procedures to use when measuring any skinfold:

1. Use a good skinfold caliper, such as the Lange or Harpenden caliper.
2. Use a tape measure to determine skinfold locations. After determining the skinfold site, mark it using an erasable pen.
3. Generally all skinfold sites are located on the right side of the body, even if the individual is left handed.
4. Generally the skinfold is pinched approximately 0.5 inch (1 cm) toward the front of the marked skinfold site using the tips of the index finger and thumb.
5. Place the jaws of the calipers on the marked site about halfway between the base and top of the skinfold. The calipers are placed so that the jaws of the calipers are at a right angle to the skinfold.
6. Allow the jaws of the calipers to compress the skinfold for no more than 4 seconds and then determine the skinfold thickness to the nearest 0.5 millimeter when using a Lange caliper or to the nearest 0.1 millimeter when using a Harpenden caliper.
7. Release the skinfold.
8. When multiple skinfolds are determined, all skinfold sites are marked and then each site is measured one time and the circuit of the sites is repeated 3 times so that three measurements at each skinfold site are made.
9. The mean value of the skinfold site is used in determining body composition.
10. With practice, multiple measurements of a skinfold should not differ by more than 1 millimeter.
11. The subject should wear clothing that allows easy access to the skinfold sites. No clothing should be included in the measurement of the skinfold.

SSF is the sum of the three skinfolds used for males and females. For males, the three skinfolds used are the chest, abdomen, and thigh. For females the three skinfolds used are the suprailium, triceps, and thigh.

Chest Skinfold Site

1. The subject is standing.
2. This skinfold is located midway between the anterior axillary fold (front of the armpit) and the nipple.
3. Grasp the chest skinfold about 0.5 inch (1 cm) above or toward the armpit of the marked skinfold site.
4. The skinfold is raised in line with the line between the anterior axillary fold and the nipple.
5. Place the jaws of the calipers inferior (toward the nipple) at the marked skinfold site from where the skinfold is grasped.

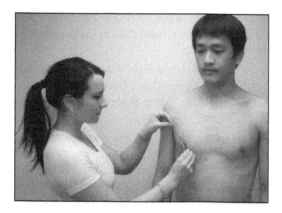

Chest skinfold location using a tape measure.

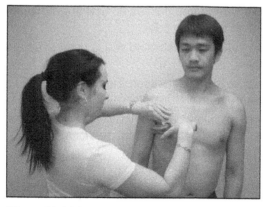

Chest skinfold measurement with a caliper.

Abdomen Skinfold Site

1. The subject is standing.
2. This skinfold is located slightly less than 1 inch (2 cm) to the right of the navel.
3. Grasp the abdomen skinfold about 0.5 inch (1 cm) laterally from the marked skinfold site.
4. The skinfold is raised in a vertical direction.
5. Place the jaws at the marked skinfold site.

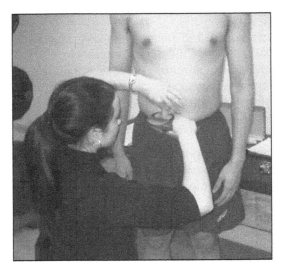

Abdomen skinfold measurement with a caliper.

To calculate body density for a female athlete who is 20 years old and weighs 130 pounds (58.1 kg) and whose skinfold thicknesses for the suprailium, triceps, and thigh skinfolds are 20, 15, and 20 millimeters, respectively, the following calculations would be made:

$$SSF = 20 \text{ mm} + 15 \text{ mm} + 20 \text{ mm} = 55 \text{ millmeters}$$

$$\text{Female body density} = 1.0994921 - (0.0009929 \times 55) + (0.0000023 \times 55^2) - (0.0001392 \times 20 \text{ years})$$

Whenever a calculation is in parentheses, it needs to be performed before other calculations. So the previous equation results in the following:

Female body density = 1.0994921 – (0.0546) + (0.0069) – (0.0028)
Female body density = 1.0448826 + (0.0069) – (0.0028)
Female body density = 1.0490 g/ml

Small changes in body density result in relatively large changes in percentage of fat; therefore the calculation of body density should be carried out to no fewer than 3 decimal places.

Triceps Skinfold Site

1. The subject is standing.
2. This skinfold is located in the middle of the back of the upper arm halfway between the acromion process of the scapula and the olecranon. The acromion process is the bony protuberance located at the top outside portion of the shoulder. The olecranon is the bony protuberance of the ulna, a bone in the forearm at the back of the elbow. To help locate the olecranon, the subject may bend the elbow to a 90° angle.
3. With the elbow straight, the upper arm relaxed, and the arm hanging straight down at the subject's side, grasp a vertical skinfold at the back of the arm, 0.5 inch (1 cm) above the marked skinfold site.
4. This skinfold is raised in a vertical direction about 0.5 inch (1 cm) above the marked site.
5. The jaws of the calipers are placed at the marked skinfold site.

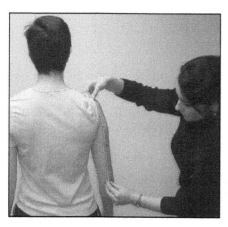

Triceps skinfold location using a tape measure.

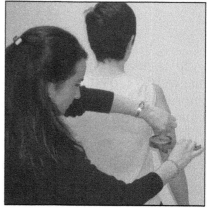

Triceps skinfold measurement with a caliper.

Thigh Skinfold Site

1. The subject is standing with the right heel in line with the left foot's arch. Most of the subject's weight is on the left foot.
2. This skinfold is located halfway between the inguinal crease (the crease between the torso and the thigh, also known as the groin) and the top of the patella (kneecap) and in the center of the front of the thigh.
3. To help locate the inguinal crease, the subject can be seated or flex the right hip.
4. The subject relaxes the muscles of the right thigh.
5. The skinfold is raised in the vertical direction 0.5 inch (1 cm) above the marked skinfold site.
6. The jaws of the calipers are placed on the skinfold at the marked skinfold site.

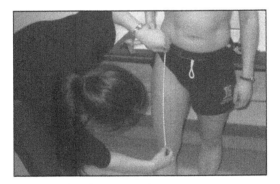

Thigh skinfold location using a tape measure.

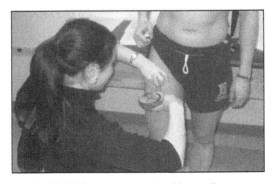

Thigh skinfold measurement with a caliper.

Suprailium Skinfold Site

1. The subject is standing.
2. This skinfold is located at the most superior aspect of the iliac crest, the bony protuberance of the top of the hip bone.
3. Grasp the skinfold slightly above and to the front of the marked site. Generally there is a natural fold of this skinfold that runs diagonally from the crest of the ilium toward the navel.
4. This skinfold is raised in line with the long axis of the natural fold of this skinfold.
5. The jaws of the calipers are placed 0.5 inch (1 cm) toward the front of where the skinfold is grasped.

Suprailium skinfold site measurement with a caliper.

The Siri equation (1961) is used in calculating percentage of fat using body density. Continuing with the previous example, percentage of fat for a female athlete would be calculated as follows:

$$\% \text{ fat} = (495/\text{Body density}) - 450$$
$$\% \text{ fat} = (495/1.049 \text{ g/ml}) - 450$$
$$\% \text{ fat} = 471.8 - 450$$
$$\% \text{ fat} = 21.8, \text{ which can be rounded to } 22\%$$

People of African descent have a higher body density than their Caucasian counterparts. Therefore, some experts (Clark, Kuta, & Sullivan, 1994; Thorland, Johnson, & Housh, 1993) believe that a slightly different equation should be used in calculating percentage of fat for people of African descent. Some experts also believe that a slightly different equation should be used for women instead of the original Siri equation (Lohman, 1981). If either of these equations is used, all other calculations to determine body composition are the same.

Equation for people of African descent

$$\% \text{ fat} = (437.4/\text{Body density}) - 392.8$$
$$\text{Body density} = 1.049 \text{ g/ml}$$
$$\% \text{ fat} = (437.4/1.049 \text{ g/ml}) - 392.8$$
$$\% \text{ fat} = 416.96 - 392.8$$
$$\% \text{ fat} = 24.16\%$$

Equation for Women

$$\% \text{ fat} = (503/\text{Body density}) - 457$$
$$\% \text{ fat} = (503/1.049 \text{ g/ml}) - 457$$
$$\% \text{ fat} = 479.5 - 457$$
$$\% \text{ fat} = 22.50\%$$

Once percentage of fat is known, calculation of fat-free mass (FFM) and fat mass can be done. Continuing with the previous example, the female athlete's FFM and fat mass would be calculated as follows:

$$\text{Fat mass} = \text{body weight} \times \% \text{ fat}$$
$$\text{Fat mass} = 130 \text{ pounds (59.1 kilograms)} \times 0.22$$
$$\text{Fat mass} = 28.6 \text{ pounds (13.0 kilograms)}$$
$$\text{FFM} = \text{total body weight} - \text{fat mass}$$
$$\text{FFM} = 130 \text{ pounds} - 28.6 \text{ pounds}$$
$$\text{FFM} = 101.4 \text{ pounds (46.1 kilograms)}$$

Similar calculations and equations would be made to determine the FFM and fat mass for anyone. The accuracy of skinfolds in measuring percentage of fat is, at best, approximately 3%. This means that small changes in percentage of fat may be due to measurement error. In order for real changes in body composition to take place, sufficient time must be allowed. Therefore body composition is not determined more often than once every several months.

Body and Limb Circumferences

Body and limb circumferences are typically thought of as representing muscle size. However, changes in some circumferences may indicate not just changes in muscle size but also loss of body fat. Perhaps the most representative of the possible loss of body fat resulting in a change in a circumference is the waist measurement. For changes in circumferences to occur similar to those found with skinfold measurements, sufficient time must be allowed. Therefore normally circumferences are not determined more frequently than every several months.

A body or limb circumference can be taken at virtually any location on the body. The following is a list of common circumference sites. Using the definition of the site and the general procedures for measuring circumferences given on page 133, an accurate measure of circumference should be achieved. Limb circumferences can be taken on both the right and left side of the body. In many situations, however, to save time only the right-side or dominant-side circumference is determined. As with all measurements, following an established protocol is necessary in order to ensure an accurate measurement.

Upper Thigh

Body Position

1. Person is standing with the feet hip-width apart and weight evenly distributed over both feet.
2. The muscles of the legs are not contracted.

Circumference Site

The tape is placed directly around the upper thigh with the tape at the level of the gluteal fold. The gluteal fold is the natural skinfold where the buttocks meet the back of the upper thighs.

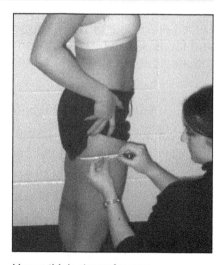

Upper-thigh circumference.

General Procedures for Measuring Circumferences

Determination of all body and limb circumferences has several procedural factors in common. These procedures ensure accurate and repeatable determination of circumference.

1. The body position during measurement must be held constant.
2. The anatomical location of the measurement must be clearly defined.
3. An anatomical measuring tape with a spring-loaded handle, such as the Gulick tape, should be used.
4. The tape needs to be positioned so that it is perpendicular to the body part for which a circumference is being measured. This tape position will result in the smallest circumference. If the tape does not go directly around the body part for which a circumference is being determined, the measurement will be greater than what it actually is.
5. When determining a circumference, the spring-loaded handle of the anatomical tape should be in the midrange of its tension position. The spring-loaded handle ensures a constant tension on the tape as a circumference is being measured. This results in the same amount of tissue compression while a circumference is being determined and therefore aids in accuracy of measurement.
6. Circumferences are normally determined to the nearest millimeter.
7. Normally three measurements are taken and they should not differ by more than 0.5 centimeters.
8. The person being measured should wear appropriate clothing. Clothing should not cover any portion of the body or limb over which the tape must pass.

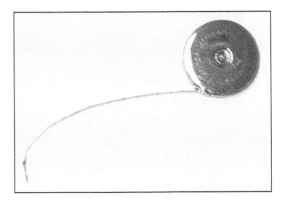

The spring-loaded handle of an anatomical measurement tape.

Upper Arm

Body Position
1. Person is standing.
2. Upper arm is pointing directly out to the side and parallel to the floor.
3. The elbow is at a 90° angle and the fist is clenched.

Circumference Site
1. The subject contracts the biceps but maintains a 90° elbow angle.
2. The tape is placed directly around the greatest circumference of the upper arm; typically this will be at the maximum height of the biceps.

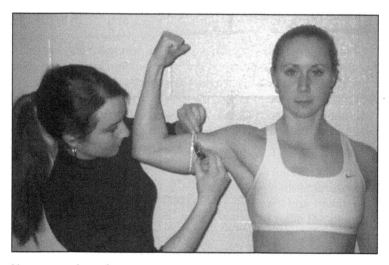

Upper-arm circumference.

Calf

Body Position

1. Person is seated with the feet flat on the floor and the knee at a 90° angle.
2. Calf muscles are not contracted.

Circumference Site

The tape is placed around the greatest circumference of the calf musculature.

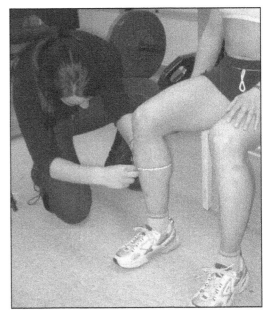

Calf circumference.

Waist

Body Position

1. Person is standing.
2. The abdominal muscles are not contracted.

Circumference Site

The tape is placed directly around the narrowest abdominal point above the navel.

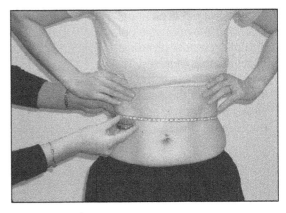

Waist circumference.

Midabdomen

Body Position

1. Person is standing.
2. The abdominal muscles are not contracted.

Circumference Site

Tape is placed directly around the abdomen at the level of the center of the navel.

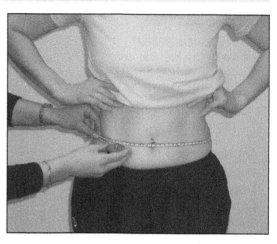

Midabdominal circumference.

Hip

Body Position

1. Person is standing.
2. The gluteal and thigh muscles are not contracted.

Circumference Site

Tape is placed directly around the hip area at the level of the symphysis pubis and the greatest protrusion of the gluteal muscles. The symphysis pubis is the area in the front of the pelvis where the two bones of the pubis meet.

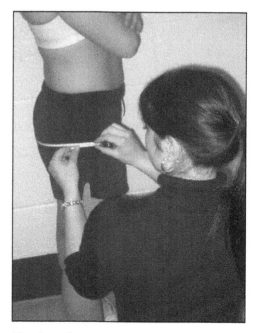

Hip circumference.

Maximal Vertical Jump

Maximal vertical jump ability is a measure of lower-body power because the velocity of movement is very high. Although height and power in the maximal vertical jump can be determined in several manners, such as using a force platform or a chalkboard hung high on a wall, use of a Vertec is quite simple and accurate. The Vertec is a piece of equipment with vanes (slats) that can be raised or lowered depending on the subject's vertical jump ability. Although several types of vertical jumps can be measured using a Vertec, a no-step countermovement jump and a three-step countermovement jump are perhaps the most common types of vertical jumps measured. Following is a brief description of how to perform vertical jump tests of these two types using a Vertec (a more complete description of how to perform tests using the Vertec is supplied by the manufacturer).

Warm-Up

Allow the subject to perform several minutes of warm-up activity, including several vertical jumps. Only ballistic or dynamic stretching should be performed before the workout.

Standing Reach Height

1. Standing reach height refers to the maximal height that can be reached with the dominant hand while standing flat footed with the feet approximately hip-width apart.
2. Adjust the height of the Vertec so that the lowest vane is lower than the subject's standing reach height.
3. The subject stands directly below the Vertec's vanes with the feet approximately hip-width apart. The subject then reaches as high as possible with the dominant hand and pushes aside as many of the Vertec's vanes as possible while keeping both feet flat on the floor.
4. Determine the highest height reached.

Whether a no-step countermovement jump or a three-step countermovement jump is performed, the procedure for determining maximal vertical jump ability is the same except for the starting position.

Starting Position and Jump for No-Step Countermovement Jump

1. The subject stands directly below the Vertec's vanes with the feet approximately hip-width apart.
2. Subject then performs a maximal vertical jump by bending at the knees and hips and using the arms in a normal jumping motion.
3. Subject reaches as high as possible with the dominant hand and pushes aside as many vanes as possible.

Starting Position and Jump for Three-Step Countermovement Jump

1. Subject stands three steps away from the Vertec. If the subject is right-hand dominant, he or she stands slightly to the left of the Vertec. If the subject is left-hand dominant, he or she stands slightly to the right of the Vertec.
2. Subject then takes a three-step approach starting with either foot and then performs a maximal vertical jump off of both feet at the same time. The arms can swing as if performing a normal jump. A three-step approach means stepping first with the left foot, then the right foot, then the left foot again and then bringing the right foot even with the left foot and jumping.
3. Subject reaches as high as possible with the dominant hand and pushes aside as many vanes as possible.

Maximal vertical jump height is determined by subtracting the standing reach height from the maximal vertical jump height. Typically measurement of maximal reach height needs to be performed only once per testing session. Maximal reach height can also be used for successive testing sessions if the subject did not grow taller. Normally three maximal vertical jumps are performed with a rest of at least 30 seconds between attempts. Because the goal is determining maximal vertical jump height, once the subject has reached a certain height, the vanes up to that height can be pushed aside. If more vanes are reached on successive attempts, more vanes will be pushed aside. However, if on successive jumps no more vanes are pushed aside you still have determined the subject's maximal vertical jump.

For testing before a training session to determine whether a particular type of training session can be performed on a particular day, measurement of maximal vertical jump height is all that is necessary.

For testing to determine progress during a training program, it is also possible to determine not just maximal vertical jump height but power during the jumping motion using the following equation.

Whenever a vertical jump is performed on earth, the acceleration of the pull of gravity on the jump is the same. So mean power during a vertical jump can be calculated with the use of an equation with constants that account for the acceleration of gravity. Other equations are also available for calculating peak power (Johnson & Bahamonde, 1996). However, mean power and peak power will both increase when vertical jump ability increases. So it is not really necessary to calculate both mean power and peak power to track changes in vertical jump power.

Power equals force times vertical distance moved divided by time. In the case of a vertical jump the force moved equals body weight and the vertical distance equals the height of the jump. So power in the case of a vertical jump includes a force (kilograms), a vertical distance (meters) as well as time (seconds) resulting in power being measured in kilogram-meters per second.

$$\text{Mean power (kgm·s}^{-1}) = 2.21 \times \text{body mass in kilograms} \times \sqrt{\text{maximal vertical jump in meters}}$$

For example, if a person weighs 220 pounds ($\sim$ 100 kilograms) and has a maximal vertical jump of 24 inches (60.96 centimeters), the person's mean power would be calculated as follows.

$$2.2 \text{ pounds} = 1 \text{ kilogram}$$

$$1.0 \text{ in} = 2.54 \text{ centimeters}$$

$$220 \text{ pounds divided by } 2.2 \text{ pounds/kilogram} = 100 \text{ kilograms}$$

$$24 \text{ divided by } 2.54 \text{ cetimeters/inch} = 60.96 \text{ centimeters}$$

$$100 \text{ centimeters} = 1 \text{ meter}$$

$$60.96 \text{ cm} \times 100 = 0.6096 \text{ meters}$$

$$\text{Mean power (kgm·s}^{-1}) = 2.21 \times 100 \text{ kg} \times \sqrt{0.6096} \text{ m}$$

$$\text{Mean power (kgm·s}^{-1}) = 2.21 \times 100 \text{ kilograms} \times 0.781 \text{ meters}$$

$$\text{Mean power (kgm·s}^{-1}) = 172.60$$

Changes in mean power can be brought about by either a change in body weight or a change in vertical jump ability. An increase in body weight and no change in vertical jump ability will increase mean power. A decrease in body weight and no change in vertical jump ability will decrease mean power. An increase in vertical jump

For many athletes, including shot putters, an increase in vertical jump ability would be desirable.

ability and no change in body weight will result in an increase in mean power. For some training programs, such as those for high jumpers and long jumpers, an increase in vertical jump ability and an increase in mean vertical jump power brought about by an increase in vertical jump ability would be desirable. In other activities, such as those for American football players and shot putters, an increase in vertical jump ability would also be desirable. However, if these athletes maintained their vertical jump ability and increased their body weight, which would result in an increase in vertical jump power, this also would be a desirable change. So depending on the activity being trained, how an increase in mean vertical jump power occurred might be important when considering adaptations the training program brought about.

Maximal Standing Long Jump

Maximal standing long jump ability is a measure of lower-body power because the movement is very fast. Vertical jump ability and standing long jump ability are both measures of lower-body power, so in most situations it is not necessary to test both types of jumping ability. Standing long jump ability may be more important in testing certain types of athletes, such as long jumpers, American football players, and ski jumpers. Standing long jump ability can be assessed with the use of a specially designed standing long jump test mat made of rubber and marked with the distance from the start line. However, it can also be determined by using tape to mark the closest heel to the start line after a jump and then using a tape measure to measure the distance jumped.

Warm-Up

Allow the subject to perform several minutes of warm-up activity, including several standing long jumps.

Standing Long Jump

1. Subject stands with both feet just behind the starting line. Feet are approximately hip-width apart or whatever distance at which the subject feels comfortable.
2. Subject bends the knees and hips and uses the arms and jumps forward as far as possible. No step or movements of the feet are allowed in preparation for the jump.
3. The back of the heel closest to the start line is marked. If using a jump mat, the heel can be marked with a finger and the distance recorded. If not using a jump mat, the heel can be marked with a piece of tape and the distance measured with a standard tape measure.
4. The subject should step forward after the jump. If the subject falls backward, and a hand or the buttocks touch the floor, the distance from the start line to whatever body part touched the floor is measured.
5. Normally the subject is given three jump attempts with a rest of at least 30 seconds between jumps.
6. If the subject falls backward during one of the attempts, a substitute attempt is allowed. However, if the subject falls backward in more than one attempt, only one substitute attempt is allowed. So the greatest number of jumps allowed per testing session is four.
7. Typically the longest of the attempts is recorded and used for evaluation.

Medicine Ball Throw

Because of the fast velocity at which it is performed and the relatively light resistance supplied by the ball, the medicine ball throw is a measure of power. Many types of medicine ball throws are possible. Standing-type throws are measures of not just upper-body power but also lower-body power because the lower body can be used in the throwing motion. In the flexible nonlinear training program, when testing before a training session to determine if a trainee is ready for a particular type of training session, the goal of using a medicine ball throw is to isolate upper-body power. Therefore, the seated medicine ball throw is used when testing for this purpose because it minimizes the use of the lower body in the throwing motion. Following are general guidelines for all medicine ball throw tests and a description of the seated two-hand chest pass medicine ball throw.

Any medicine ball throw could be used for tracking changes in power brought about by a training program.

General Procedures for Medicine Ball Throws

1. Medicine balls ranging in weight from 5 to 15 pounds (~2.3 to 6.8 kg) can be used, depending on the strength and power of the person tested.
2. The same medicine ball should be used for successive tests on the same person.
3. The throwing motion needs to be standardized for any medicine ball throw test.
4. Distance thrown should be measured from where the back of the ball hits the floor.
5. Typically three throws are allowed when testing for training progress, and the best throw is used for evaluation of progress.

Seated Two-Hand Chest Pass Medicine Ball Throw

1. Thrower sits on the floor with the back flat against a wall.
2. The legs are comfortably spread apart.
3. Thrower holds medicine ball with both hands as if performing a basketball chest pass.
4. The thrower's thumbs are touching the chest.
5. Thrower then uses a two-hand chest pass to throw the medicine ball as far as possible straight forward.
6. In the attempt to throw the ball as far as possible, the thrower can lean forward, and the back may lose contact with the wall during the throwing motion.
7. The spot where the back of the ball hits the floor is marked.
8. The distance from where the thrower is sitting against the wall to where the back of the ball hit the floor is measured. Although the goal is to throw the ball straight forward, the thrower is not penalized if the ball goes slightly to the left or right. This measuring procedure is similar to that used in the shot put or discus throw.

When testing before a training session to determine if the trainee is ready for a particular type of training session, typically only one throw is needed. If the thrower's hands slip off the ball or there is some other major flaw in technique, such as throwing the ball predominantly with one arm, a second throw may be allowed. As with all tests, once a testing protocol has been established, it must be followed in order to ensure testing accuracy.

Power Development During an Exercise

Determination of a power measurement during some exercises no longer requires expensive laboratory equipment. Pieces of equipment attach to the end of a free-weight bar or to a machine's weight stack that measure the velocity of movement and then use the resistance, velocity of movement, and range of motion (e.g., FITROdyne Sports Powerlizer, Tendo sport machines, Trencin, Slovak Republic) to calculate a measure of power. These pieces of equipment measure only vertical movement. Therefore any horizontal movement in a free-weight exercise does not enter into the power calculation. If horizontal movement is less than 7% from vertical, this effect is minimized. Horizontal movement does, however, introduce some error into the calculation. Therefore it is best to use these pieces of equipment in exercises where the predominant movement is vertical, such as the bench press, vertical jump, and squat. Even with these exercises, some error in the power calculation will occur. The error, however, will be relatively constant for each individual. Therefore, a comparison of the power measurement from day to day for each individual will show if power is increasing or decreasing. The use of a Smith machine, in which only vertical movement is allowed, does enhance the accuracy of the power measurement. Many of these instruments give only the average power over the range of motion, while more advanced models give the peak power.

Another factor that needs to be considered when calculating power during exercises is whether the resistance or bar must be decelerated at the end of the range of motion of an exercise. For exercises such as the bench press and squat, unless the bar in the bench press or the bar and lifter's mass can be accelerated and then launched into space, deceleration of the bar must occur at the end of the range of motion. The need for a deceleration phase at the end of the repetition can be eliminated only when launching the bar into space is allowed. The need for a deceleration phase can be eliminated by choosing specific exercises, such as the power clean, clean pull, power snatch, or snatch pull. However, these types of exercises have a significant amount of horizontal movement and therefore the calculation of power will be affected. It can be assumed that the amount of horizontal movement for each individual will be relatively constant. So changes in calculated power, even though error is introduced, will reflect actual changes in power during the exercise. The following protocol can be used in calculating power during exercises:

Warm-Up

1. One warm-up set of 4 to 6 repetitions using 30 to 45% of the 1RM is performed.
2. The eccentric portion of each repetition is performed at a controlled velocity. However, the concentric portion is performed at 80 to 90% of maximal velocity.

Power Repetition Attempts

1. All safety precautions as presented for 1RM testing should be in place and followed.
2. The lifter performs 3 repetitions in succession. If there is an eccentric portion to the exercise, it is performed in a controlled manner. However, the concentric portion is performed in an explosive manner at as high a velocity as possible.
3. Controlling the eccentric portion of some exercises is necessary for safety reasons. For example, the lifter cannot be allowed to bounce the bar off the chest to initiate the concentric portion of the repetition in the bench press, and the lifter should not be allowed to perform the eccentric portion of a squat repetition at a fast velocity because undue stress to the knees and low back will occur when the lifter attempts to reverse direction to initiate the concentric portion of the repetition.
3. Controlling the eccentric portion of the exercise is not needed in some exercises, such as variations of the power clean or snatch pull.

Using the equipment's software, the mean, or peak power, is calculated. The software varies from manufacturer to manufacturer. Most equipment will indicate the average power, and other higher-level models will give the peak power for the range of motion. Peak power is ideal for use in determining the small changes that may occur from workout to workout when using the flexible nonlinear approach.

SUMMARY

Some of the tests described in this chapter can be used either in evaluating training progress over time or in evaluating whether a trainee is ready to perform a certain type of training session when using a flexible nonlinear program. Other tests, such as skinfolds for evaluating body composition and 1RM testing, would be used only in evaluating training progress over time. Whether a trainer is testing to evaluate training progress or testing immediately before a training session using the flexible nonlinear model, safety is the primary concern. The unique aspects of the flexible nonlinear training model are testing before a training session and the use of exercise performance at the start of a training session to make the clinical judgment that the individual is or is not prepared to perform a particular type of training session. The ability to make the judgment to continue with a particular type of training session or to switch to another type of training session is critical to the success of the flexible nonlinear training model.

CHAPTER 7

Training Tips and Tools

In implementing a training program using the nonlinear method, many habits must be developed. Not only should a master schedule be planned for the program, but the lifter also needs to be able to respond to the workout and to any testing information, whether it is on the day of the workout or a planned evaluation time after each mesocycle. Testing protocols and training logs are vital for this process. As discussed in chapter 3, exercise choice is an important part of the development of a nonlinear program. However, it is also necessary to have basic knowledge of the muscles trained with a particular exercise and the role of muscle soreness in helping to modify a nonlinear program so that continued gains in fitness occur. If a nonlinear program is being developed for older individuals, for young people, or for women, some considerations are unique to these populations. The goal of the nonlinear resistance training program is to maximize the individual's ability to optimally perform appropriate training on a given day.

TRAINING LOGS

A training log must adhere to the five acute program variables of a resistance workout protocol. In a good training log, the exercises to be performed need to be noted, the exercises need to be placed in the proper order, the number of sets should be noted, the length of rest period should be noted, and the intensity or resistance to be used for a particular exercise needs to be noted. A training log must be properly constructed to reflect the planned workout for the day and to record the actual performances.

A common sight in a weight room involves people trying to remember what weights they used the last time they performed certain exercises. This is one of the basic reasons for maintaining a good training log. The nonlinear training program is impossible to implement without a good training log. The following are several reasons to use a training log:

- To know what has been done in previous training sessions
- To note the progress as the program advances
- To know when to increase the resistance for a specific exercise
- To have a record of the program so that a very successful program can be repeated
- To have a record of the program so that changes can be made to an ineffective program
- To note any change in the acute program variables based on testing before a training session
- To give an immediate indication of the quality of performance in a particular exercise

Keeping a training log is especially important when using nonlinear and flexible nonlinear programs, because the acute program variables will change regularly. With nonlinear plans, some acute program variables, such as the exercises performed and resistance used, can change on a session-by-session basis. Table 7.1 gives an example of a specific training log that can be used in both paper and computerized formats. A blank copy of this training log is provided in the appendix.

Many types of training logs are being used in the field today. Some weight rooms even have a computer interface to resistance training machines or LCD displays at training stations that automatically track training and create training logs. With some of these systems, however, exercise choice is limited to the exercise machines that are interfaced to the computer. Newer concepts are using logs that are tied to a training station, and each person can access it by typing in a code number. The person's program pops up on an LCD screen, ready for him or her to enter training data, which then go to a computer server that keeps track of their individual workouts. The key is to retrieve and have the information from prior workouts available and to chart comparative progress in the current workout. Documentation of the workout can take many forms, such as a spiral notebook, a printed workout card, a computer, or a palm pilot.

Table 7.1 Training Log of a Periodized 6-Week Nonlinear Training Program

WEEK 1

Monday (heavy): EXERCISES	Rest	Resistance/Reps for each set	RM Zone	Wednesday (light w/short rests): EXERCISES	Rest	Resistance/Reps for each set	RM Zone	Friday (explosive): POWER Assistance Exercises Moderate EXERCISES	Rest	Resistance/Reps for each set	RM Zone
Squat	3	/ / / /	3-5	Hyperextension	1	/ / / /	12-15	Hang cleans	3	/ / /	30-45% 1RM
Bench press	3	/ / / /	3-5	Stiff-leg deadlift	1	/ / / /	12-15	Jump squats	3	/ / /	30-45% 1RM
Leg press (sled)	3	/ / / /	3-5	Squat	1	/ / / /	12-15	Bench throws	3	/ / /	30-45% 1RM
Seated row	3	/ / / /	3-5	Pec fly	1	/ / / /	12-15	Cable row	2	/ / /	8-10
Dumbbell incline press	3	/ / / /	3-5	Wide pull-down	1	/ / / /	12-15	Seated row	2	/ / /	8-10
Narrow-grip pull-down	3	/ / / /	3-5	Triceps push-down	1	/ / / /	12-15	Dumbbell shoulder press	2	/ / /	8-10
Shoulder press	3	/ / / /	3-5	E-Z Bar curl	1	/ / / /	12-15	Dumbbell curl	2	/ / /	8-10
Sit-ups	1.5	/ / / /	12-15	Calf raise	1	/ / / /	12-15	Abdominal crunch	1	/ / /	25-30

WEEK 2

Monday (moderate): EXERCISES	Rest	Resistance/Reps for each set	RM Zone	Wednesday (light w/short rests): EXERCISES	Rest	Resistance/Reps for each set	RM Zone	Friday (heavy): EXERCISES	Rest	Resistance/Reps for each set	RM Zone
Squat	2	/ / / /	8-10	Squats	1	/ / / /	12-15	Squat	3	/ / / /	3-5
Bench press	2	/ / / /	8-10	Leg extension	1	/ / / /	12-15	Bench press	3	/ / / /	3-5
Leg press (sled)	2	/ / / /	8-10	Leg curl	1	/ / / /	12-15	Leg press (sled)	3	/ / / /	3-5
Seated row	2	/ / / /	8-10	Pec fly	1	/ / / /	12-15	Seated row	3	/ / / /	3-5

(continued)

Table 7.1 (continued)

WEEK 2 (continued)

Monday (moderate): EXERCISES	Rest	Resistance/Reps for each set	RM Zone	Wednesday (light w/short rests): EXERCISES	Rest	Resistance/Reps for each set	RM Zone	Friday (heavy): EXERCISES	Rest	Resistance/Reps for each set	RM Zone
Dumbbell incline press	2	/ / /	8-10	Wide pull-down	1	/ / /	12-15	Dumbbell incline press	3	/ / /	3-5
Narrow-grip pull-down	2	/ / /	8-10	Triceps push-down	1	/ / /	12-15	Narrow-grip pull-down	3	/ / /	3-5
Shoulder press	2	/ / /	8-10	E-Z Bar curl	1	/ / /	12-15	Shoulder press	3	/ / /	3-5
Sit-ups	1.5	/ / /	15-20	Calf raise	1	/ / /	20-25	Sit-ups	1	/ / /	12-15

WEEK 3

Monday (Moderate): EXERCISES	Rest	Resistance/Reps for each set	RM Zone	Wednesday (explosive): POWER Assistance Exercises Moderate EXERCISES	Rest	Resistance/Reps for each set	RM Zone	Friday (heavy): EXERCISES	Rest	Resistance/Reps for each set	RM Zone
Squat	2	/ / /	8-10	Hang cleans	3	/ / /	30-45% 1RM	Squat	3	/ / /	3-5
Bench press	2	/ / /	8-10	Jump squats	3	/ / /	30-45% 1RM	Bench press	3	/ / /	3-5
Leg press (sled)	2	/ / /	8-10	Bench throws	3	/ / /	30-45% 1RM	Leg press (sled)	3	/ / /	3-5
Cable row	2	/ / /	8-10	Cable row	2	/ / /	8-10	Seated row	3	/ / /	3-5
Dumbbell incline press	2	/ / /	8-10	Seated row	2	/ / /	8-10	Dumbbell incline press	3	/ / /	3-5
Narrow-grip pull-down	2	/ / /	8-10	Dumbbell shoulder press	2	/ / /	8-10	Narrow-grip pull-down	3	/ / /	3-5
Shoulder press	2	/ / /	8-10	Dumbbell curl	2	/ / /	8-10	Shoulder press	3	/ / /	3-5
Sit-ups	1.5	/ / /	15-20	Abdominal crunch	1	/ / /	25-30	Sit-ups	1.5	/ / /	12-15

WEEK 4

Monday (explosive): POWER Assistance Exercises Moderate

EXERCISES	Rest	Resistance/Reps for each set	RM Zone
Hang cleans	3	/ / / /	30-45% 1RM
Jump squats	3	/ / / /	30-45% 1RM
Bench throws	3	/ / / /	30-45% 1RM
Cable row	2	/ / / /	8-10
Seated row	2	/ / / /	8-10
Dumbbell shoulder press	2	/ / / /	8-10
Dumbbell curl	2	/ / / /	8-10
Abdominal crunch	1	/ / / /	25-30

Wednesday (light): EXERCISES

EXERCISES	Rest	Resistance/Reps for each set	RM Zone
Hyperextension	2	/ / /	12-15
Leg extension	2	/ / /	12-15
Stiff-leg deadlift	2	/ / /	12-15
Pec fly	2	/ / /	12-15
Wide pull-down	2	/ / /	12-15
Triceps push-down	2	/ / /	12-15
E-Z Bar curl	2	/ / /	12-15
Calf raise	1.5	/ / /	12-15

Friday (very light): EXERCISES

EXERCISES	Rest	Resistance/Reps for each set	RM Zone
Squat	1	/ / X	16-18
Bench press	1	/ / X	16-18
Leg press (sled)	1	/ / X	16-18
Cable row	1	/ / X	16-18
Dumbbell incline press	1	/ / X	16-18
Narrow-grip pull-down	1	/ / X	16-18
Shoulder press	1	/ / X	16-18
Sit-ups	1	/ X X	30-40

WEEK 5

Monday (heavy): EXERCISES

EXERCISES	Rest	Resistance/Reps for each set	RM Zone
Squat	3	/ / / / /	3-5
Bench press	3	/ / / / /	3-5
Leg press (sled)	3	/ / / / /	3-5
Cable row	3	/ / / / /	3-5

Wednesday (moderate w/short rests): EXERCISES

EXERCISES	Rest	Resistance/Reps for each set	RM Zone
Hyperextension	1	/ / /	8-10
Leg extension	1	/ / /	8-10
Leg curl	1	/ / /	8-10
Pec fly	1	/ / /	8-10

Friday (explosive): POWER Assistance Heavy Exercises

EXERCISES	Rest	Resistance/Reps for each set	RM Zone
Hang cleans	3	/ / / /	30-45% 1RM
Jump squats	3	/ / / /	30-45% 1RM
Bench throws	3	/ / / /	30-45% 1RM
Cable row	3	/ / / /	3-5

(continued)

151

Table 7.1 *(continued)*

WEEK 5 (continued)

Monday (heavy): EXERCISES	Rest	Resistance/Reps for each set				RM Zone
Dumbbell incline press	3	/	/	/	/	3-5
Narrow-grip pull-down	3	/	/	/	/	3-5
Shoulder press	3	/	/	/		3-5
Sit-ups	1.5	/	/	X		12-15

Wednesday (moderate w/short rests): EXERCISES	Rest	Resistance/Reps for each set				RM Zone
Wide pull-down	1	/	/	/	/	8-10
Triceps push-down	1	/	/	/		8-10
E-Z Bar curl	1	/	/	/		8-10
Calf raise	1	/	/	/		8-10

Friday (explosive): POWER Assistance Heavy Exercises EXERCISES	Rest	Resistance/Reps for each set				RM Zone
Seated row	3	/	/	/	/	3-5
Dumbbell shoulder press	3	/	/	/		3-5
Dumbbell curl	3	/	/	/		3-5
Abdominal crunch	1	/	/	/		10-15

Week 6

Monday (very heavy): EXERCISE	Rest	Resistance/Reps for each set				RM Zone
Squat	3	/	/	/	/	2-3
Bench press	3	/	/	/	/	2-3
Leg press (sled)	3	/	/	/	/	2-3
Seated row	3	/	/	/		2-3
Dumbbell incline press	3	/	/	/		2-3
Narrow-grip pull-down	3	/	/	/		2-3
Dumbbell press	3	/	/	/		2-3
Sit-ups	1.5	/	/	X	X	10-15

Wednesday (moderate w/short rests): EXERCISES	Rest	Resistance/Reps for each set			RM Zone
Low back machine	1	/	/	/	8-10
Leg extension	1	/	/	/	8-10
Stiff-leg deadlift	1	/	/	/	8-10
Pec fly	1	/	/	/	8-10
Wide pull-down	1	/	/	/	8-10
Triceps push-down	1	/	/	/	8-10
E-Z Bar curl	1	/	/	/	8-10
Calf raise	1	/	/	/	8-10

Friday (explosive): POWER Assistance Heavy Exercises EXERCISES	Rest	Resistance/Reps for each set			RM Zone
Hang cleans	3	/	/	/	30-45% 1RM
Jump squats	3	/	/	/	30-45% 1RM
Bench throws	3	/	/	/	30-45% 1RM
Cable row	3	/	/	/	3-5
Seated row	3	/	/	/	3-5
Dumbbell shoulder press	3	/	/	/	3-5
Dumbbell curl	3	/	/	/	3-5
Abdominal crunch	1	/	/	/	10-15

X = the set is not performed; sled = leg sled exercise; pec = pectorals (pec deck); high pull = no clean; jumping = maximal vertical jump; rest is in minutes.

For optimal progress in all training situations,
some type of written training log must be used in
order to keep track of workouts.

Some abbreviations make keeping a log quick and easy. For example, in your workout plan you might have the bench press scheduled as "bench press, 3 × 8- to 10RM × 250 × 2 minutes." This would mean the bench press exercise should be performed for 3 sets of 8 to 10 repetitions per set (the 8- to 10RM zone), using 250 pounds (~ 113.4 kg) with a 2-minute rest between sets. When using an RM zone, it is not necessary to go to complete failure but the external resistance should be kept within that rep range. Some sets will go to failure if the load is too heavy or if you want to get a sense of where you are in the RM zone. In a training log it is also important not just to note what was supposed to be performed but also what was actually performed. For example, 3 × 10, 10, 7 means that in the third set only 7 repetitions could be completed. This is vital information that can be used in altering the current workout or for changing a future workout when using this loading range or RM zone. The following are some examples.

EXAMPLE 1

Using the Log to Adjust a Current Workout

You had planned to do 3 sets of 8 to 10 repetitions using 250 pounds (~113.4 kg) in the bench press exercise, which you have previously been able to do. On the first set, you are able to do only 4 repetitions. In this case, you would need to make an immediate decision about whether to continue with the subsequent sets using the same load. It is obvious that you are not at the same level of strength for this workout as you were in previous workouts when you were able to perform all of the RM zone reps using the 250 pounds. This could indicate many possible situations:

- You may be fatigued from a prior day's workout or practice.
- You may have had a rough day at work or school, which created psychological stress that does not allow you to concentrate on the training session.
- You may have an injury.
- You may be training at a different time of day than you normally train.
- You may be suffering from the first signs of acute overtraining.
- It may be that you just did not put forth a solid effort in the first set and want to try again.
- The length of rest periods between sets was too short to provide sufficient recovery.

The workout performance on each set is an important indicator of current physical state of readiness. If you were to try the same resistance again and the number of repetitions did not improve, this would give you solid evidence that one or more of the situations described in the list may exist. If, however, you do succeed in performing 8 to 10 repetitions, you would continue with the training session as planned.

It is important that you react to the performance of a training session. If you are using the flexible nonlinear approach, you should switch to another workout style for that exercise or, if possible, for all upper-body exercises or for the entire training session. Most important is that if you continue not reaching the desired number of repetitions for a major lower-body exercise or a structural exercise, then you need to switch to a different workout style for all of the primary exercises. Ultimately, trainers, coaches, and athletes need to become "workout detectives" to determine the root cause of the drop in performance and then work to modify the current workout and the subsequent workout using that specific workout style.

In the first example, the first set is used to determine what the loading should be for the next sets and possible subsequent workouts. As discussed, you need to determine whether this is just a function of a particular exercise or all of the exercises in the workout protocol for that day. Therefore you need to evaluate the performance level in any prior large-muscle-group exercise or in the next large-muscle-group exercise in order to optimize the workout for that day. If an 8- to 10RM zone was planned for the squat and each of the sets was done in this repetition range using the planned load, then the problem would appear to be isolated to the upper body. Typically, in a flexible nonlinear program, all of the major exercises are performed using the same resistance loading pattern. However, it is possible that in some advanced programs the loading zone may be varied on an exercise-by-exercise basis.

Exercises performed in a session must allow for appropriate rest for the muscle tissue that is not to be trained due to a need for recovery. For example, if you switched to a lighter weight because of your inability to complete the reps at a scheduled load of an 8- to 10RM zone for the squat exercise, you would not want to continue to use the heavier load for the power clean exercise that involves the use of virtually the same muscle groups. This would not allow you to rest the muscle groups that are not ready to perform the squat at the planned training load. Unless the squat exercise was dramatically miscalculated in its load, you would then decrease the training intensity in the power clean exercise as well. If you were capable of performing the power clean with a high intensity, then it may well be that you overestimated the resistance for the squat. It becomes a complicated trial-and-error process, where the loading and the response to training must be continually evaluated in order to optimize the exercise performance while allowing enough planned recovery with lighter-load days without continually defaulting to lighter-load sessions. The potential mistake with switching to an alternative workout with lower intensities is minimizing the needed stimulation needed for power and maximal strength when using very heavy and heavy workouts.

Conversely, you may be undertraining if you do not increase the load of a particular exercise when you find you are stronger as a result of normal physiological adaptations. For instance, imagine that you had been scheduled to perform the bench press for 8 to 10 repetitions at 250 pounds, but in the first set you perform 15 repetitions. This is outside of the planned 8- to 10RM zone. In this case you would want to immediately increase the load in the next set so that only 8 to 10 repetitions can be performed. In the workout log you need to be able to change the resistances and the repetition numbers as they are performed in your workout to meet the training goals of the entire program.

EXAMPLE 2

Using the Log to Adjust a Future Workout

On completion of a workout, you can use the data to develop the volumes and resistances to be used in future workouts. For example, you can record the load used for an 8- to 10RM zone and use it the next time for the same exercise. If you are able to complete 2 sets with 250 pounds for 10 repetitions, but the third set for only 7 repetitions, this would mean that for a future workout you may want to start with 250 pounds but understand that your strength level or the amount of rest between the sets does not allow you to complete the entire scheduled training protocol. When this style of workout comes up in the training zone rotation, whether it is a planned or flexible nonlinear program, you will know what load was appropriate for the 8- to 10RM zone.

Keeping track of progress is a function of the training log because it functions as a living diary. In the nonlinear training approach it is a vital component to success. Knowing what you did the previous time when performing a heavy workout or a light workout is important for comparison to any current workout performance. This will tell you whether the workout is producing the same results or if a change needs to be made in the resistances used for the current workout or as you develop a future workout for this RM zone. When using the flexible nonlinear approach, you may want to switch to a completely different RM zone during the current workout if the resistances are just too light or too heavy and not placing you into the correct RM training zone. When using the planned nonlinear approach, you may want to perform the workout and see how you perform the entire session, but then use the training log data to develop the next workout for that RM zone.

You can make many manipulations when developing a future workout. In the case of the nonlinear program approach, you must have a variety of workouts ready to go. This is especially important when using the flexible nonlinear method. After each workout it is important to develop the next workout to be used for that workout style (i.e., heavy, light). The place to start is the resistance used. If you performed more repetitions than planned, then you must increase the resistance for the next workout to get back into the correct RM zone. You must also look at the length of the rest period because it will affect the performance. If you reduce rest periods for the next session using the same training zone, then the resistance should stay the same, and you should evaluate the session to see if you performed the planned number of repetitions. Shorter rest periods would be used only if you were trying to develop local muscular endurance. Reductions in rest will affect the number of repetitions that can be used for a given load and must be quantified in order to understand its effect on the loads for the different exercises.

The next variable to look at is the number of sets, because this dictates the volume of exercise. Increasing the volume by adding sets may also require you to maintain the resistance at its current level in order to see whether the higher volume has any effect on exercise performance. Finally, if you make changes to the order of the exercises or add exercises to the workout, you should keep the resistances the same in order to observe the effect on actual performance.

In the following section is a workout plan for a heavy day after evaluating the actual performance of a heavy-day workout that was just completed. In this case, looking at the mesocycle and the overall plan, no changes in any of the other acute program variables are needed. Therefore you have to focus only on the resistances used in order to keep the number of repetitions in the desired RM zone. For the power clean, the resistance is kept the same because the performance was within the planned RM zone. In the back squat, the resistance is increased to 325 pounds ($\sim$ 147.4 kg) because the repetitions performed were greater than the RM zone. For the incline bench press, the resistance is maintained because it resulted in performances that were within the RM zone. For the leg press, the resistance is increased in the hope that it will put the next performance within the heavy RM zone.

It is not always possible to do more. When your body stops adapting to a particular exercise stimulus, it may be due to fatigue or that you are close to your genetic maximum for gains in a specific adaptive ability in strength or size. It is also possible that you have reached a training plateau in your physical development for that particular exercise. In such cases other workout sequences or reevaluation of a

---

EXAMPLE 3
Heavy-Day Workout Plan

May 1, 2007: Heavy Day

Power clean: 3 × 4 to 6 @ 225, 4-minute rest, actual 6, 6, 4

Back squat: 4 × 4 to 6 @ 315, 4-minute rest, actual 6, 5, 4

Incline bench press: 3 × 4 to 6 @ 200, 4-minute rest, actual 5, 5, 5

Leg press: 3 × 4 to 6 @ 450, 4-minute rest, actual 8, 7, 7

Next Planned Heavy-Day Workout

Power clean: 3 × 4 to 6 @ 225, 4-minute rest, keep the same

Back squat: 4 × 4 to 6 @ 315, 4-minute rest, increase the load to 325

Incline bench press: 3 × 4 to 6 @ 200, 4-minute rest, keep the same

Leg press: 3 × 4 to 6 @ 450, 4-minute rest, increase the load to 475

---

program's goals needs to be addressed. In this case you will have to reevaluate the overall master plan of the macrocycle.

The information from the training log must be compared to the master plan for a particular mesocycle (see chapter 4). In the nonlinear training approach, you need to make check-offs for a particular workout style (i.e., light, moderate, heavy, very heavy, active rest, etc.) or achieve a certain number of each workout style in order to meet the desired training goals. Whether it is in the planned approach (in which the cycle of workouts is already determined) or whether it is the flexible approach (in which check-offs are made based on the trainability of the individual on a given day), the training log functions as a diary for the overall plan. When planning a future workout, you will need to evaluate each of the acute program variables (i.e., choice of exercises, order of exercises, number of sets, rests between sets of exercises, and resistances used). The training log will help determine each of these specific variables for future workouts. The design of future workouts will be based upon the success of the prior workouts in meeting the goals of each mesocycle.

CHOICE OF EXERCISES

Many exercise choices can be made for an exercise program. These have been extensively described for technique and spotting in a previous text (Kraemer & Fleck, 2005). However, it is good to have a basic understanding of the exercise possibilities in order to be more confident in the exercise prescription used in a nonlinear program.

Core, multijoint, or structural exercises are typically periodized across the full array of loadings (i.e., very heavy to very light including power), and assistance exercises (small-muscle-group exercises) are varied across a few loading schemes, typically from moderate to very light. Table 7.2 presents some basic exercises that can be of help when designing a program. Each exercise must be taught and proper technique learned before it should be performed with resistance. In addition, understanding of proper spotting techniques associated with the exercise is vital for safety of the lifter. Many exercises have variations that can be performed with free weights (dumbbells or barbells), a Smith machine, and specific exercise machines. In addition, unilateral (single-limb) and bilateral (two-limb) exercises should be included in the program progression for each body part. The roles each type of exercise plays in a program can vary from a primary power-type exercise to a primary strength exercise, to a secondary strength or power exercise. While all exercise movements are directed toward improving strength, not all exercises are used for this primary role in a program. Many exercises play an assistance role and are not targeted for maximal loading under typical training circumstances. In addition, it is important to remember the general rule for exercises: Every time you change an angle, you change the exercise. Although it is not an exhaustive list of all possible resistance training exercises, some basic exercises are noted in table 7.2. The techniques of many of the exercises are described in one of our previous works (Kraemer & Fleck, 2005).

MUSCLES EXERCISED

You need to understand the muscles used in each exercise. Table 7.3 overviews the muscles used in each of the exercise choices presented in table 7.1. These muscles are depicted in figure 7.1. Multijoint exercises stimulate a host of muscles in a general body area, such as the lower body or in some cases almost all major muscle groups of the body. When single-joint exercises are used, each exercise focuses more on a specific muscle group and becomes an isolated exercise movement. The use of multijoint exercises, including structural exercises, is important for all programs because these exercises are very efficient in stimulating several muscles with a single exercise and developing total-body power and strength. Multijoint exercises

Table 7.2 Basic Exercise Choices for a Resistance Exercise Program

Primary core lifts	Alternative exercises	Primary role
Clean and jerk	Hang pull, hang clean, high pull, squat jump, shrug jump, pull from the knees and thighs	Power
Snatch	Hang snatch from the knees or thighs, pull from the knees and thighs	Power
Squat	Front squat, lunge, split squat	Strength
Leg press	45° angle leg press, inverted leg press, leg extension	Strength
Standing calf raise	Leg press calf raise, machine calf raise, calf raise with various foot positions, calf raise on a 2-inch (5 cm) block	Strength
Seated calf raise	Machine calf raise and calf raise with various foot positions	Strength
Reverse calf	(Front of lower-leg muscles) Toe raise for tibialis anterior	Assistance
Deadlift	Low back machine, Smith machine	Strength
Good morning	Back extension	Assistance
Stiff-leg deadlift	Seated, supine, standing leg curl	Assistance
Abduction and adduction exercises	Seated machine	Assistance
Abdominal exercises	Sit-up, twisting sit-up, knee-up, incline sit-up, crunch, stability ball sit-up, abdominal machine crunch	Assistance
Bench press	Incline bench press, decline bench press, fly exercises, machine bench press, various grip widths	Strength
Seated row	T-bar row, bent-over row	Strength
Lat pull-down	Barbell pull-over, pull-up	Strength
Push press	Machine jammer	Power
Standing close-grip push-down	Triceps machine, kickback, dip	Assistance
Arm curl	E-Z bar curl, preacher curl, concentration curl, machine curl	Assistance
Shoulder press	Upright row, machine upright row	Strength
Reverse arm curl	Machine reverse curl, hammer curl	Assistance
Wrist curl	Wrist roller, machine wrist curl	Assistance
Neck exercises	Self-resisted, machine	Assistance
Medicine ball exercises	Throw, twisting throw	Power
Plyometric exercises	Jump, jump onto boxes, drop jump, push-up with a clap	Power

also allow for the integration of motor patterns across the various joints used, and such intramuscular coordination is important for daily activities and sport skills. When focusing on developing muscle size, you would choose single-muscle-group exercises because they isolate a particular area and therefore emphasize a specific body part or muscle group. Such exercises are important for bodybuilding, in strengthening the weak muscle group in a multijoint exercise, and rehabilitating from injury.

Table 7.3 Basic Muscle Groups Stimulated by an Exercise

Lift	Primary muscle areas stimulated	Type of exercise
Clean and jerk	Upper and lower body	Multijoint, structural
Snatch	Upper and lower body	Multijoint, structural
Squat	Low back and lower body: 14, 15, 16	Multijoint, structural
Leg press	Lower body: 14, 15	Multijoint, structural
Standing calf raise	Lower body: 18	Single joint, isolated
Seated calf raise	Lower body: 18	Single joint, isolated
Reverse calf raise	Lower body: 19	Single joint, isolated
Deadlift	Upper and lower body	Multijoint, structural
Good morning	Upper body, low back	Single joint, structural
Stiff-leg deadlift	Upper body, low back and lower body: 16	Multijoint, structural
Abduction and adduction exercises	Lower body: 17	Single joint, isolated
Abdominal exercises	Upper body: 12, 13, 20	Single joint, isolated
Bench press	Upper body: 6, 7, 8	Multijoint
Seated row	Upper body: 9, 10	Multijoint
Lat pull-down	Upper body: 9, 10	Multijoint
Push press	Upper body: 6, 7	Multijoint, structural
Standing close-grip push-down	Upper body: 6	Single joint, isolated
Arm curl	Upper body: 5	Single joint, isolated
Shoulder press	Upper body: 6, 7	Multijoint
Reverse arm curl	Upper body: 3, 4, 5	Single joint, isolated
Wrist curl	Upper body: 3, 4	Single joint, isolated
Neck exercises	Upper body: 1, 2	Single joint, isolated
Medicine ball exercises	Upper and lower body	Multijoint, structural
Plyometric exercises	Upper and lower body	Multijoint, structural

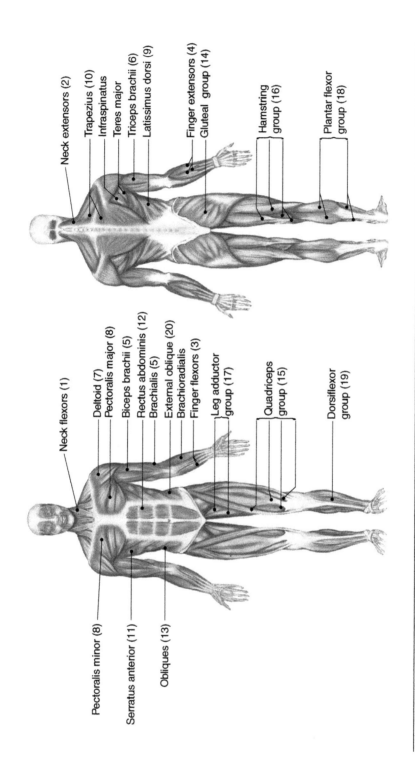

Figure 7.1 Basic muscle chart of the body. Specific exercises will stimulate specific muscle groups.

Adapted, by permission, from E. Harman, 2000, The biomechanics of resistance of exercise. In *Essentials of strength training and conditioning*, 2nd ed., edited by T.R. Baechle and R.W. Earle (Champaign, IL: Human Kinetics), 29.

MUSCLE SORENESS, TISSUE DAMAGE, AND RECOVERY

Two major factors create muscle soreness. First is the acute muscle damage created by the loading of the muscle fibers themselves, predominantly the eccentric loading stress. The higher the eccentric load, the greater the stress. Remember that when a person is at his or her maximal dynamic concentric strength level, it represents only about 80% of eccentric maximal strength. As the speed of eccentric movement increases, the forces on the muscle increase. The second factor in muscle damage arises from the chemical damage that follows the mechanical events and hypoxia of the tissue when exercising under anaerobic conditions. This can cause continuous tissue breakdown, soreness, and delays in recovery for up to 10 days. This is typically called delayed-onset muscle soreness, or DOMS, and normally peaks at 24 to 48 hours postexercise. The greater the DOMS, the longer the delay in the ability to perform optimal training because rest is needed in order to allow the muscle to repair the damage caused by the training.

The first rule in the recovery from a resistance exercise workout is proper planning and refraining from doing too much too soon. Once injury or significant muscle damage occurs, a lifter has to deal with it. So the best strategy for avoiding excessive DOMS is sound planning of the training program. Many common treatments (e.g., ice, hydrotherapy, massage) have not been effective in treating DOMS. However, compression has been shown to limit the amount of swelling and loss of force production over a 24- to 72-hour postexercise time frame (Kraemer et al., 2001). Therefore the best treatment is an ounce of prevention. This resides in proper program progression in a nonlinear format using part of the mesocycle as a preparation phase as well as a gradual progression to any very heavy, power, or heavy eccentric training (see Base Program, chapter 5).

With a nonlinear program a trainee cannot jump right into the heavier loading schemes, which by their nature also have a high eccentric component and therefore can cause significant muscle damage. Muscle damage will be more dramatic in beginners or in those who have taken a long break from training. In these situations a type of general preparation phase is necessary before the heavier training zones or cycles. This means that the first 4 weeks of a mesocycle's workouts are in the very light-intensity to moderate-intensity range, the volume of exercise starts with one set and progresses to

2 or 3, rest periods last from 2 to 4 minutes, and exercise technique is stressed. Each time a new exercise is added or the resistance is increased, a trainer or coach needs to check the exercise technique. Remember that toleration of the exercise stress is vital to optimal progress. With prior exposure to moderately heavy resistances, a natural protection against eccentric damage will be developed. Essentially this is a *base program*.

No heavy protocols should be done in the early phases of a training program. Use of eccentric-only workout protocols is not typical in the nonlinear program approach; these protocols would be used only in some advanced training techniques typically targeted at breaking through a plateau in performance. However, the efficacy of this approach has not been validated by scientific studies.

AGING CONSIDERATIONS

Resistance training has been shown to be effective across every age group, including seniors. Nevertheless, as a person grows older, changes in the physiological system occur that make the person less adaptive to an exercise stimulus. As a person ages, reductions in water content in cells, hormonal releases, and other physiological functions occur. In other words, the adaptive processes that allow a person to repair and remodel tissues are not as robust as they were in younger years. It is very common to hear an older person say, "I used to be able to get in shape in a matter of weeks, but now it seems to take months." The perception of a delayed response to exercise training is simply a function of aging.

One of the major considerations when training as we age is the toleration of a particular workout. Individuals over the age of 50 many times have joint soreness and muscle soreness in response to heavy and very heavy workouts. Therefore, the frequency for these particular workout intensities must be carefully prescribed. As a general rule, as a person ages the frequency of such high intensities over the course of a mesocycle should be reduced. In addition, training zones may be adapted for older lifters. In other words, a very heavy day may mean a 6- to 8RM zone, a heavy day could be a 9- to 11RM zone, a moderate day a 12- to 14RM zone, and a light day a 15- to 17RM zone. It has been shown that older men and women can tolerate typical heavy-loading days, but the recovery and responses to the workouts need to be carefully monitored for everyone, especially in people over the age of 50 years. If joint soreness or stiffness occurs, then you must reduce the frequency of heavy-loading days or redefine the RM training zones. The latter should definitely occur if symptoms persist.

Another effect of aging is the inability to tolerate decreases in muscle and blood pH or challenges to the buffering capacity of the body in dealing with acidity. When reducing lengths of rest periods, pay a great deal of attention to any adverse symptoms (e.g., nausea, dizziness) in all trainees, but especially in individuals over the age of 50 due to a reduction in buffering capacity. If you reduce lengths of rest periods between sets and exercises during a program for individuals over the age of 50, do so slowly over a mesocycle.

Finally, older individuals need to be very careful when completing a set to failure. The natural breath holding (Valsalva maneuver) that occurs can cause undue increases in blood pressure. This is of particular concern in individuals who have a history of cardiac problems, a family history of cardiac problems, or unstable left-ventricular function. In general, older lifters should avoid or at least minimize the use of the Valsalva maneuver. Another precaution is that the RM zone indicates repetitions that are typically not done to absolute failure, but rather with a keen perception that more than the prescribed repetitions cannot be performed. Therefore, inform each lifter that an RM zone is a load that typically allows a person to complete a set without going to complete failure. Teach each lifter to breathe properly: Exhale during the concentric (lifting or pushing) phase and inhale during the eccentric (lowering or releasing) phase. While failure in a repetition may occur, breathing during each repetition needs to occur and breath holding should be eliminated. Going to failure will cause greater joint compression and potential joint soreness due to shearing forces. The loads for each RM zone should be found without going to complete failure in a repetition, as one can typically know what a resistance will allow for a repetition in a 3RM zone. As is standard, older individuals (over the age of 45 years) should have a physician's approval to engage in a vigorous exercise program.

YOUTH CONSIDERATIONS

When designing a resistance training program for children, all the safety factors normally associated with an adult program apply. However, there are several other considerations that uniquely apply to children. One of these factors is the possibility of damage to the epiphyseal plates, or growth plates, of bones caused by the lifting of heavy resistances by children whose skeletal systems have not matured. Although this type of injury can occur, it is very rare and typically occurs when children attempt to lift close to 1RM resistances in an unsupervised setting. To prevent damage to epiphyseal plates, children should not lift resistances heavier than 6RM. When using the nonlinear periodization training approach with children, this simply means that the training zones need to be adjusted accordingly. For example, for children, heavy, moderate, and light training zones might be 6- to 8RM, 8- to 12RM, and 12- to 15RM, respectively. In general, a progression in training occurs with age as many young men and women start to enter adult programs at 15 or 16 years of age depending upon their prior training experience. Extensive guidelines for young athletes at different ages have been presented in our book *Strength Training for Young Athletes, Second Edition,* (see Kraemer & Fleck, 2005).

Another consideration when you are training children is establishing realistic training goals. Here one major difference between an

The difference in program goals should be made clear to children, perhaps especially to young boys, who want the large muscles they see in older boys and adult males.

© DAJ/Getty Images

adult's program goals and the goals for children is that, in children, it is unrealistic to expect large gains in muscle size. After a child has reached puberty, gains in muscle size become a more realistic goal. Other training goals, such as increased strength and injury prevention when participating in other sporting activities, are achievable for children.

The following are other considerations that uniquely apply to children and should be considered when children perform weight training:

- Is the child psychologically and physically ready to participate in weight training?
- Do the child and the weight training supervisor understand proper lifting techniques for each exercise being performed?
- Do the child and the weight training supervisor understand proper safety and spotting techniques for each exercise being performed?
- If resistance training machines are used, does each piece of equipment fit the child's body?
- Does the child have a balanced physical exercise program that includes not only resistance training but also cardiorespiratory and flexibility training?
- Have any fears or misconceptions the child has about weight training been discussed with the child and dispelled?
- Is there a sufficient number of adult supervisors to ensure the practice of safe lifting habits, proper exercise technique, and all safety precautions?

All of these factors and others that uniquely apply to resistance training for children have been discussed in great detail (Kraemer & Fleck, 2005). The bottom line is that children can safely perform resistance training, and resistance training can be effective in bringing about strength and fitness gains in children, but some program design and performance considerations are unique to this age group.

GENDER CONSIDERATIONS

When designing a resistance training program for women, including a nonlinear program, on the surface there may seem as though there should be a lot of differences between a program designed for males and a program for females. But in reality there are very few differences between programs designed for men and those designed for women. Skeletal muscle, whether it is in a male or a female, responds to a resistance training program with similar adaptations.

Generally adult males are stronger than adult females. However, much of this difference is because adult males are simply larger and have greater fat-free mass than their female counterparts. If maximal lower-body strength (1RM) is equated relative to body weight, males and females are very similar, and the similarity increases if maximal strength is expressed relative to fat-free mass or muscle mass. In fact, some studies report females to be stronger than males when lower-body maximal strength is expressed relative to fat-free mass (for review, see Fleck & Kraemer, 2004). This, however, is probably because women have a greater percentage of their fat-free mass in their lower bodies than their male counterparts. This means that men have a higher percentage of their fat-free mass in their upper bodies compared to women and so have stronger upper bodies. Although total fat-free mass and distribution of fat-free mass may explain strength differences between the sexes, it does not mean that male muscle and female muscle respond differently to training. This will, however, affect the training resistance required in order to stay within a training zone. This simply means that males, especially for upper-body exercises, will need a heavier resistance for any particular training zone. It does not mean that women need to use different training zones when using a nonlinear periodization training program. In fact, the majority of long-term training studies using a nonlinear periodization training model have had women as participants (for review, see Fleck & Kraemer, 2004).

The differences between the genders in terms of distribution of fat-free mass (i.e., men have a greater percentage of their fat-free mass in their upper bodies) does, however, lead to a possible difference in resistance training programs between the sexes. Upper-body strength and power are very important for success in many sports and activities. With a smaller percentage of fat-free mass in their upper bodies, women are at a disadvantage when performing sports or activities dependent on upper-body strength and power. So to optimize physical performance, upper-body strength and power exercises may be emphasized in a training program slightly more in women than in men. The need for upper-body strength and power to optimize physical performance can be demonstrated quite clearly even in activities that you might not think are dependent on upper-body strength. For

The same training zones in the nonlinear periodization training model are used for both genders.

example, many people, including women, can increase 1RM squat strength by performing only upper-body training. Here the increase in squat 1RM is because the lower body is already capable of performing the squat with more resistance. However, the ability for the lower body to express its maximal strength is limited by the upper body's ability to support more weight in the squat. Thus for female athletes who are dependent on upper-body strength and power for success, emphasizing upper-body exercises may be appropriate. This can be accomplished by adding one or two more exercises for the upper body or, after the individual is moderately trained, adding one set to some of the upper-body exercises already included in the program.

Generally women increase their fat-free mass or muscle mass to a lesser degree in both absolute terms (pounds or kilograms) and relative terms (percentage of increase) when performing the same weight training program as males. Again, this does not mean that the muscle of males and females responds differently to training. It merely means that when establishing a training goal concerning increases in fat-free mass or muscle mass, the goal should be lower in women than in men.

So there are relatively very few differences between nonlinear periodization programs designed for men and for women. None of the differences causes a significant change in the total design of the program. The differences between men's and women's responses to resistance training have been more extensively discussed (Fleck & Kraemer 2004).

SUMMARY

A well-kept training log is vital in monitoring training progress and in making modifications to the training sessions in a nonlinear resistance training program. Use of the nonlinear program can be applied in almost any situation, including the training of older adults, children, and women. Optimal sequencing, correct exercise choices, monitoring recovery, and appropriate training goals are the keys to an effective nonlinear program. Reductions in the boredom brought about by a resistance training program as well as a higher quality of training will be realized with the nonlinear approach. The variations possible in nonlinear programming make it ideal for all athletes as well as average people interested in health and fitness goals. Understanding how to evaluate effectiveness of programs and determine the amount of fatigue is also vital for making logical and effective changes in the program used for each mesocycle.

CHAPTER 8

Case Studies

Understanding how to implement a program is the most important aspect of using the science and the art of nonlinear periodization. This chapter presents examples in which decisions have to be made on what to do on a given day of a workout. Using the flexible nonlinear approach is the most challenging but also the most satisfying for strength and conditioning professionals because it puts professional skills and insights to the test. It is important to understand that each case study presents a concept that can be used for a variety of situations even when the example is for a specific sport. Use these studies to challenge yourself in thinking of situations and cases in which you were in a similar situation. The case studies do not appear in any particular order because they should be viewed individually as concepts of application for use of the flexible nonlinear method of resistance exercise prescription. This chapter brings to life the application of the science of nonlinear periodization. So in your own experiences, see where principles of application can be used.

To see how the flexible nonlinear program approach works, you need to see how it looks when it is implemented. These case studies are derived from real-life situations and will give you a sense of how you can manipulate workouts to optimize the daily workout plan.

CASE STUDY 1

Scenario

It is the preseason and a football player comes into the weight room after a 30-minute sprint-agility workout conducted by an assistant football coach. This workout was unexpected and he says he feels fatigue primarily in his legs. You have him scheduled to do a power workout with the high pull, power snatch, and power clean along with some upper-body medicine ball exercises. What are your options and how do you proceed?

Options

In this situation the assistant football coach has potentially compromised the football player's ability to perform maximally in the weight room workout. Many of the high-velocity, high-power motor units were used in the workout. The upper body would have limited fatigue depending on the intensity of the training session and its impact on the player's overall fatigue. You would want to run a diagnostic test (e.g., countermovement vertical jump) to determine how much fatigue is present. Typically, you want the athlete to be at more than 90% of his best performance in order to ensure optimal training of the power motor units in the muscles to be trained. If fatigue is present, you would have to switch to anther workout within the context of the training plan for that cycle. If power capabilities are not compromised (i.e., he performed above 90% of his best countermovement vertical jump), you may want to proceed with the planned workout because the sprint-agility workout did not dramatically affect power capabilities and may have provided a dynamic warm-up. You could also delay the workout for a brief period (e.g.,

How does the fatigue after a sprint-agility workout affect a scheduled power workout?

30-60 minutes) to further improve the recovery status of the football player if the schedule permits. The key to power training is to have the athlete rested or able to perform all exercises at maximal effort in order to have the quality required for achieving training-related gains.

CASE STUDY 2

Scenario

The wrestling team comes into the weight room at 6:00 a.m. for an in-season workout. Some of the wrestlers had a meet the previous night. You have them scheduled for a power workout involving the power clean and push press along with some injury-prevention lifts for the shoulders. What are your options and how do you proceed?

Options

This will be a tough workout for the wrestlers who had to make weight and wrestle the previous night. And unless the wrestlers are accustomed to training at this time, the quality of the workout at 6:00 a.m. will not be optimal for any of them. The options are to cancel the power training workout for the wrestlers who had wrestled and send them home. You can have the other wrestlers (the ones who did not have to make weight and compete) perform the power training workout as planned; in this case you would pay close attention to their ability to train at this time of day. You should determine a time when the wrestlers who competed the previous night can perform the power training session because recovery from the meet is needed. In this scenario it becomes apparent that all team members cannot train on the same schedule. The increased need for more individualized training profiles can be accomplished with the use of the flexible nonlinear program approach.

CASE STUDY 3

Scenario

During the season, a women's cross country team comes into the weight room on a Wednesday after a moderate 5K-pace run. They have a cross country meet on Friday. Today you have them scheduled for a moderate-intensity, low-volume workout. What are your options and how do you proceed?

Options

In this scenario the runners are not significantly fatigued from the 5K moderate-pace run. The resistance training workout is of moderate intensity (e.g., 8- to 10RM zone or 70 to 80% of 1RM) and low volume. This workout should be performed as planned. It will stimulate the necessary strength maintenance as well as help to prevent injury to connective tissues. The runners should be able to recover from the workout and be ready to practice on Thursday.

Would a 5K moderate run cause significant fatigue for a cross country team athlete?

CASE STUDY 4

Scenario

The men's basketball team comes into the weight room after a preseason practice at 6:00 p.m., which is a new time for their conditioning workout. This is the time the coach has given you for your conditioning sessions with the team. All of the players have been involved in a year-round training program. You have them scheduled for a very heavy workout using 90 to 95% of their 1RM in a 1- to 3RM training zone in four multijoint exercises: hang pull, squat, bench press, and push press. What are your options and how do you proceed?

Options

Coaches set schedules and many times the schedule may not be optimal for the conditioning component of the program. The key to this scenario is whether the players are actually capable of performing the workout. You are stuck with the schedule so must proceed to see if you can achieve your workout goals with the players. An understanding of what the practice consisted of is also important and might also give you a clue about the fatigue level of the players. A hard scrimmage or high number of high-intensity drills would result in a great deal of psychological and physiological fatigue. One option is to proceed with the workout. If the players cannot perform the reps with the resistances in the load ranges prescribed (i.e., cannot perform the number of reps with the prescribed resistances), they can switch to a lighter-resistance, power-oriented workout. Since this is a new time slot for conditioning sessions for these athletes, you need to work with the coach and monitor practice stress so that you can get in your needed workouts in order to achieve the goals for the training cycle. You might also need to examine the priority of the preseason weight training cycle, considering its part in the total season's overall training goals.

CASE STUDY 5

Scenario

A volleyball player comes into the weight room at 3:00 p.m. for an off-season lower-body power training workout consisting of plyometric jumping drills. He tells you that he had only 4 hours of sleep the previous night after cramming for an exam. He had the exam at 10:00 a.m. What are your options and how do you proceed?

Options

Chronic sleep loss can compromise physiological performance, but limited sleep deprivation from typical sleep patterns has been shown to create a higher physiological state (unpublished data). This higher physiological state is created by increased nervous system sensitivity and higher levels of catecholamines, which are chemical compounds that circulate in the bloodstream. These chemical compounds are released by the adrenal glands in situations of stress, such as psychological stress or low blood sugar. Thus, the volleyball player may be ready to train for power if his psychological readiness and concentration are there after the exam. Some preliminary testing should be used to determine his training readiness. If he has a 90% or greater maximal vertical jump capability, you could go forward with the workout. If not, you would switch to an alternative workout to achieve one of the workout goals of the training cycle. You should also educate him on the importance of maintaining consistent sleep habits.

CASE STUDY 6

Scenario

The swim team comes into the weight room for an in-season workout at 2:00 p.m. after doing an unexpected high-volume 10,000-meter workout at 6:00 a.m. You have them scheduled for a session using a 12- to 15RM training zone for each exercise in a two-circuit protocol with a 1-minute rest period between sets. They are scheduled to do another workout at 4:00 p.m. in the pool. What are your options and how do you proceed?

Options

This is a tough situation because you are just adding to the physiological and potential psychological stress of these athletes with the resistance training workout. One option is to reduce the weight training volume, but with a swim workout coming again at 4:00 p.m. your athletes will have only about 1.5 hours of rest before practice and may not be fully recovered. It appears that you might cancel

What special considerations should be given to a swimmer's training volume?
© Stockbyte

the resistance training workout and work with the coach to find a time frame for in-season resistance training that will allow recovery between swim practice and weight training sessions. It would appear that the swim coach is using a very high-volume training program that might be modified to allow more effective dry-land training in the weight room. Nevertheless, your flexible nonlinear approach would favor rest for this particular day.

CASE STUDY 7

Scenario

A football team comes into the weight room for an off-season work-out, and you have them scheduled for a heavy workout (3- to 5RM) for all of the major muscle groups and some moderate-intensity injury-prevention exercises after the major part of the workout is com-pleted. What are your options and how do you proceed?

Options

No particular external circumstances exist, so you can have them proceed with the workout. It is important not to use an alternative workout unless there is sufficient evidence to support a change. Such evidence is the inability to perform exercises with at least the resistance loads used the previous time this training protocol was performed.

CASE STUDY 8

Scenario

During an off-season program, the shot and discus throwers come into the weight room and tell you that their throwing practice session had been cancelled because of bad weather, and the indoor facility is overbooked. You have them scheduled for a moderate-intensity work-out that day. What are your options and how do you proceed?

Options

When using the flexible nonlinear approach, the first option is to see this as an opportunity to check off a power day or very heavy day because you have rested athletes who are ready to perform maxi-mally. You should use this opportunity to train at a higher intensity or perform a power training session if other circumstances do not indi-cate anything to the contrary. The key here is that in a flexible nonlinear program you do not always switch to a lower-intensity, lower-volume session or shorter rest periods, but you can go to a more challenging workout if the right conditions present themselves.

How would a discus thrower benefit from the flexible nonlinear approach?

CASE STUDY 9

Scenario

The women's gymnastics team had a change in their off-season practice schedule and you were told they will be coming into the weight room at 6:00 a.m. rather than their normal 4:00 p.m. off-season workout time. You have them scheduled for a power training day using 65% of their 1RM in the power clean and 30 to 45% of their 1RM in the bench throw. What are your options and how do you proceed?

Options

This time change in the workout schedule creates a dramatic altera-tion in the athletes' normal circadian pattern at which they are accustomed to training. Thus they are functioning in a very different physiological state, most likely in a sleep state. It has been found that the body's sleep state is highly regulated by the hormone mela-tonin. It has also been shown that power output can be lower in the early morning when athletes are not used to training at these hours.

Therefore, you could proceed with the workout, but you should use preliminary testing to see if the power output has been seriously compromised. If it has, alternate to a different workout, which could include any of the other training session options of the training cycle. Heavy or moderate workouts are very good alternatives because of their contribution to the force component of the power equation. It is essential not to have a loss in strength over a training cycle because this will affect power development.

CASE STUDY 10

Scenario

The rodeo team comes into the weight room at 8:00 p.m. for an off-season workout. You have them scheduled to use a 3- to 5RM training zone and 3-minute rest periods between sets and exercises for the exercises that night. You observe that each athlete must reduce the resistance to fall within the 3- to 5RM training zone. What are your options and how do you proceed?

Options

When you reduce the resistance to hit an RM training zone, it indicates some type of fatigue. This could be due to the time of day at which the athletes are training. Individuals who are not accustomed to training at night or the early morning may see their workout compromised. If this is a standard training time, then some type of residual fatigue exists and you might consider lightening the resistance even further and targeting another RM zone (e.g., 12- to 15RM) and reduce the volume by decreasing the number of exercises or sets performed for that night's workout. If the same pattern exists when you attempt training the 3- to 5RM zone the next time, then you must carefully examine the factors that may be causing it (e.g., sickness, overtraining, conflicting schedules, or practice demands). For now, when using a flexible nonlinear approach, you would want to lighten the training resistance and reduce the volume by deceasing the number of exercises or sets to allow recovery.

CASE STUDY 11

Scenario

The football team comes into the weight room on a Wednesday for an in-season workout at 4:00 p.m. Today you have them scheduled for a high-volume, moderate-intensity workout. On Friday you have them scheduled for a low-volume, very high-intensity workout. What are your options and how do you proceed?

Options

You have an overall plan. Unless other circumstances affect an individual player or the team, you can proceed with the planned workouts.

It is not often necessary to deviate from the planned daily rotation.

Photo by AJ Macht, courtesy of the Indianapolis Colts.

CASE STUDY 12

Scenario

The baseball team comes into the weight room to perform a scheduled light-intensity off-season workout. Two of the players come up to you and say that they are not feeling well after the first two exercises. What are your options and how do you proceed?

Options

One of the golden rules is not to train when you are sick. Sometimes short rest protocols using 8- to 12RM resistances can make a person feel nauseated because he may not be able to tolerate the changes in blood and muscle acidity that occur. However, the athletes are feeling sick during the workout and it is better to be safe than sorry and call it a day and have them check with the athletic trainer or team physician. The best option is to stop the workout and rest. The other members of the team could continue with the workout.

CASE STUDY 13

Scenario

The hockey team comes into the weight room for an in-season workout on Wednesday. They tell you that they did not have practice today because of a problem with the ice rink. You had them scheduled to use light resistance and short rests between exercises, but not a power-oriented session. They had performed a power workout on Monday. What are your options and how do you proceed?

Options

This scenario brings up the concept of the opportunity to switch to a higher-intensity workout with the changes in the circumstances, in this case a cancelled practice session. You may want to default to a very heavy, low-volume workout because of the need for such

If your hockey team was not able to get on the ice for practice before their scheduled workout, how should you adapt their workout?

© Terje Rakke/The Image Bank/Getty Images

workouts to stimulate the body's high threshold motor units neurologically and maintain maximal strength throughout a training cycle. In other words, this will help maintain the force component of the power equation during the season.

CASE STUDY 14

Scenario

The wrestling team comes into the weight room on Thursday for a preseason workout. You have them scheduled for a low-rest circuit to build up their ability to tolerate the changes in blood and muscle pH (increased acidity) created by the metabolic demands of a wrestling match (i.e., blood lactic acid concentrations can go to 19 mm/L with a single match). On this day you find that the wrestlers are not able to use the same resistance for the 8- to 10RM training zone that they used on Tuesday. What are your options and how do you proceed?

Options

This gives you an indication that some type of residual fatigue exists, so you might lengthen the rest period and just do a moderate-intensity workout to see whether with more rest they can lift a similar resistance to what they have used in the past. Alternatively they may be just beginning to adapt to the short-rest program and you might want to proceed with the workout using whatever weight they can lift for the 8- to 10RM zone. The goal of the workout is to produce a change in the acid–base status of the body to help stimulate the buffering mechanisms in the muscle and blood, so the resistance used is a secondary consideration. In addition, you should pay attention to this to see if some other source of residual fatigue is affecting their workouts in the weight room (e.g., too much distance running to cut weight). Again, you do not want to see symptoms of sickness with this type of short-rest workout (e.g., nausea and dizziness), or you are moving the rest progression down too quickly over the training cycle.

CASE STUDY 15

Scenario

The basketball team comes into the weight room at their normal 3:00 p.m. training time. You find that preseason practice that day has been changed for the team from 6:00 a.m. to 4:30 p.m. You have a high-intensity workout scheduled for that day. What are your options and how do you proceed?

Options

Schedule changes are what make the flexible nonlinear method so effective. The time to do a workout is limited at best and will affect the quality of their basketball practice. So you check off a rest day and let them prepare for practice at 4:30. You also need to communicate and coordinate with the basketball coach about the practice times so that the coach understands that the athletes' practice times affect what you do in the weight room.

CASE STUDY 16

Scenario

Your jumpers on the track team come into the weight room for a power workout. Each jumper hits at least 95% of his or her best vertical jump. They are rested and ready to go. They are scheduled to perform 6 sets of 5 repetitions in weighted vertical power jump plyometric exercises. You find that with the first 2 sets your athletes are

What is the goal of this power jump exercise?

making only 1 of the 5 reps above 90% of their best jumps. What are your options and how do you proceed?

Options

The sets for power development may include too many repetitions. Research has shown that sets of 3 with 3 to 5 minutes of rest between efforts may optimize the maximal power produced in this type of exercise. The goal for any maximal-power or plyometric-type training is to produce the greatest amount of power possible in each repetition. This requires a rested athlete who is not fatigued during the workout session by too many repetitions in a set or rest periods that are too short. Use sets of 3 repetitions for 6 to 8 sets.

CASE STUDY 17

Scenario

The swim team comes into the weight room for a session before the start of the season, and all of the swimmers give you ratings of 8 to 9 on the 10-point fatigue scale. You had them scheduled for a circuit protocol with moderate-intensity workouts using 2-minute rest periods between sets and exercises. What are your options and how do you proceed?

Options

The fatigue rating gives you an indication that something is wrong. This could be due to residual fatigue from swim training or other stresses in their lives (e.g., exam schedule, sleep habits) that cause this psychological stress response. You may want to proceed with the planned session and see if they can use similar resistances as they have in the past. If they demonstrate a reduced capability with the loadings being used in the workout, you can then switch to a lighter-resistance with reduced numbers of sets but not a power training session due to the high levels of fatigue that will compromise physical capabilities. This should create a reduction in the workout stress and provide some recovery. You should also seek more information on why the swimmers are feeling so fatigued today.

CASE STUDY 18

Scenario

The women's field hockey team comes into the weight room for a scheduled heavy-resistance, low-repetition-per-set day in the off-season. You observe that each athlete is rested and hitting her intended resistance for the training zone for the first several sets. What are your options and how do you proceed?

Options

The workout is going as planned. Let it proceed. In this scenario an alteration is not necessary because the overall plan can be achieved and you should make changes only when needed on a team or individual basis.

Too often the temptation is to alter a planned workout when using the flexible nonlinear approach.

CASE STUDY 19

Scenario

The football team comes into the weight room for an in-season workout on Monday after a team meeting following an unexpected loss on Saturday. You have a heavy resistance day scheduled. What are your options and how do you proceed?

Options

This brings up the concept of psychological fatigue. In some cases this can affect the workout and reduce the quality of the session. Conversely, in other cases this can drive athletes to take out their frustrations during the workout and actually help to improve the quality of the workout. You would want to proceed with the workout and see how they respond. In addition, let them know it is all right to take it out on the weights by giving a maximal effort and putting their anger into the effort of the training session. Take care under such circumstances to make sure proper technique is used in all exercises and that no exhibitions of intense anger carry over into irresponsible movements and actions (e.g., throwing weights down). If done correctly, it may function as a good stress relief for the team under such negative circumstances. It is also very important that you do not let the football coaches use the weight room workouts for any punishment related to their loss.

CASE STUDY 20

Scenario

The women's crew team comes into the weight room for an off-season workout. You have them scheduled for a heavy day using a 3- to 5RM training zone. Using the prior heavy day's resistances, the athletes find that they can do more than 5 reps with the load. What are your options and how do you proceed?

Options

This is a case in which you are using an RM training zone, so you must adjust the load to allow for the number of repetitions in that 3-repetition zone. Ideally, do not go to failure because this causes greater workout stress (higher heart rates and blood pressures due to breath holding) and joint compression. Limiting the number of sets to failure due to compression effects on the joints is important, but you need to have them increase their resistance until they can do only 3 to 5 reps. The athletes have adapted to the training, and this change can be very dramatic if the training level of the individual is rapidly changing. This normally happens early in a training program or with beginners. In this case, increase the resistance to get them back into the RM zone you have planned.

CASE STUDY 21

Scenario

The baseball team is on the road for a spring swing set of games. They have 3 days off before the next game. You have them scheduled for a heavy-resistance, low-repetition-per-set workout at the visiting team's weight room, but because of a schedule change you are allowed to use the weight room only from 7:00 to 8:00 p.m. after a 5:00 p.m. dinner. What are your options and how do you proceed?

Options

This is a common problem with travel of all types, but especially for athletic teams on the road, where you may not be in control of your facility schedules. You could switch to a rest day while you try to reschedule the facility for the next day. Another option is to go ahead and do injury-prevention exercises such as rotator cuff exercises and other small-muscle-group exercises that will not tax the entire body after a meal. With some rest between the meal and the workout, resistance training can be performed but this will depend on the amount of food taken in and the metabolic intensity of the workout (i.e., short-rest workouts with moderate intensity are contraindicated). Typically, athletes need 2 to 3 hours after a full meal before they can take on a demanding resistance training workout.

CASE STUDY 22

Scenario

A fitness enthusiast comes into the weight room on Thursday after a big exam to do a heavy workout of 3- to 5RM. She thinks that she did badly on the exam. In the first set of the warm-up set in the squat exercise she does 5 reps, ending with failure on the fifth rep with 180 pounds (~81.6 kg). Interestingly on Monday she performed 10 reps with this same weight and did not even have to squeeze out the last rep. What are your options and how do you proceed?

Options

The warm-up set can tell you lot. In this case there is a dramatic change in performance capability. The load should be heavier for the 3- to 5RM zone than the 8- to 10RM zone, so definitely some type of fatigue exists, whether psychological stress from the test or from some other source. It could be a question of the lifter's mental focus caused by the distraction of the exam, which is compounded with the feelings of a poor performance on the exam. One option is to reduce the resistance and volume of the workout and perform a low-intensity, low-volume workout, which may not take as much mental focus. In addition, attend to the concerns of the individual's academic performance, which can be a problem in many school scenarios, to allow greater focus on a workout.

CASE STUDY 23

Scenario

A recreational lifter and fitness enthusiast comes into the weight room after having the flu for the past week. What are your options and how do you proceed?

Options

A person coming back from an illness has a depressed immune system. In addition, exercise stress of high intensity and high volume can also cause immune depression, making the individual more susceptible to illness (e.g., touching someone who has a cold or the flu, touching the mouth, nose, or eyes after surface contact that is contaminated with bacteria or viruses) for up to 6 hours after a workout. You need to start with low-intensity and low-volume workouts or a high-intensity and very low-volume workout to start to develop toleration to the workout stresses. You also need to monitor other physical activity, such as cardiorespiratory training, so that for the first week or so physical activity is not too stressful to make the individual susceptible to another illness due to reduced resistance to infections.

What are some basic precautions to take when an individual is returning to workouts after an illness?

© Bananastock

CASE STUDY 24

Scenario

A basketball player comes into the weight room for a Monday in-season workout. She had turned her ankle during a game on Saturday night. She rested all day Sunday and had some therapy for the injury. She is scheduled for a power training session today. She says she feels OK. What are your options and how do you proceed?

Options

This is an example in which injury is present in some unknown level of severity. In any case you do not want to proceed with the workout until she has been completely cleared by the team physician and athletic trainer. You cannot take the word of a trainee about how she feels regarding a known injury because the person's perception may not match the actual medical condition. She needs to be cleared for the workout by the team physician and then you need to consult with the athletic trainer regarding her exercise status and any needed exercises for rehabilitation and injury prevention.

Travelling for basketball games presents many challenges for the athlete and trainer.

CASE STUDY 25

Scenario

A personal training client who is a passionate city recreation basketball player has missed the last two scheduled training sessions of heavy-day workouts in an off-season training cycle. He is now scheduled for a power workout. What are your options and how do you proceed?

Options

In the power equation (force × distance ÷ time), the force component must be maintained and developed in order to optimize the changes in power. Missing the previous two training sessions you had intended for development of strength will result in a possible deficit for strength in the mesocycle, so it may be prudent to alternate to the heavy day again to ensure development of the needed strength (force component) that will set the base for power training sessions and power development.

How does the power equation help you assess a personal training client?

CASE STUDY 26

Scenario

A cross country runner comes into the weight room on Wednesday and is scheduled for a light resistance workout. He had a meet cancelled on Monday and the team performed a moderate-paced training session for 10K but had no weight training on Monday. They have a meet on Sunday. What are your options and how do you proceed?

Options

You might see this as an opportunity to get in a heavy or very heavy resistance workout with low volume in order to help the runners keep their strength levels up as well as maintain their connective tissue strength. This strength is so vital in the toleration of the physical pounding they take with their high-intensity endurance training.

CASE STUDY 27

Scenario

A 400-meter sprinter comes into the weight room and is scheduled for a preseason short-rest circuit training session to improve his toleration of the dramatic increases in muscle and blood acidity that occur with 400-meter racing. In your interaction with him, you find out he ran 5 miles (~8 km) just before the workout to cut some weight. What are your options and how do you proceed?

Options

Prior exercise can compromise the quality of a subsequent workout. The goal of this workout is to challenge the acid–base system to stimulate improvements in buffering capability so that toleration to changes in pH with middle-distance sprinting and training will be enhanced. One option is to proceed with the workout because many of the motor units of the lower body used in this workout will be different from those used in running the 5 miles as well as upper-body motor units. In addition, you would want him to make sure he rests and fully hydrates before and during the resistance training workout because chronic dehydration is a major problem with athletes. It has been shown that many athletes do not drink enough water, and most are chronically dehydrated. Adequate hydration before and during any workout is vital for optimal body functioning and performance.

CASE STUDY 28

Scenario

In an off-season training cycle you have scheduled a very heavy resistance training day for the shot and discus athletes on the track and field team. On the first set of the squat exercise, after the warm-up set, several of the athletes cannot lift their previous resistances used for the 1- to 3RM training zone. What are your options and how do you proceed?

Options

This indicates that the athletes' maximal strength is down, which might be a sign of acute overtraining. Your best option is to send them home and reschedule this same workout for the next session to see if they have recovered. You can also switch to a light day with a low volume of exercise. If it is an acute overtraining phenomenon, 1 or 2 days of complete rest can help to restore the acute losses of strength. Nevertheless, a dramatic reduction in intensity and volume and a complete rest day are warranted in this scenario.

What are the signs of acute overtraining?

CASE STUDY 29

Scenario

The football team comes into the weight room for a power training workout for an off-season workout. You find out from the players that an assistant football coach had called a special practice just before the scheduled weight room workout. What are your options and how do you proceed?

Options

This is an acute circumstance that might negatively affect a planned workout because of residual fatigue. You need to check with the players or, better yet, the assistant football coach to find out what kinds of exercises made up this practice session. Because it is the off-season, if the football coach just had a light exercise session to do a walk-through or "chalk talk" to teach the players football plays, it is possible to continue on with your planned power workout. However, if a significant amount of exercise was part of the practice session, you can switch to another workout. Power workouts are most sensitive to even minor amounts of residual fatigue and therefore would not be optimal if the assistant football coach had the players perform a significant amount of conditioning activities. Very heavy and heavy workouts may still be possible with some reduction in volume if the exercise stress was not severe in the practice conducted by the assistant football coach. It would also be possible to test the players to see if they can achieve an acceptable score on a power test before the weight room session to see if they are ready for a power training session. So many options exist in this situation.

CASE STUDY 30

Scenario

An 800-meter track athlete comes into the weight room and is scheduled for a short-rest circuit to help develop her buffering mechanisms for toleration of the acidic changes that occur with an 800-meter race. After three exercises she feels nauseated and dizzy. What are your options and how do you proceed?

Options

Stop the workout and allow the athlete to recover and hydrate before you release her to go home and rest. Note the rest time and resistances used in the session, and make changes in the progression with longer rest periods the next time this workout protocol is implemented.

Nausea and dizziness indicate an intolerance to the training session.

CASE STUDY 31

Scenario

The women's crew team comes into the weight room for a 6:00 a.m. session on a Friday in a preseason workout. This is the third work-out of the week. On the previous day, the group had a hard practice with low yardage and high intensity and short rest periods between intervals. They are scheduled for another sprint practice at 4:00 p.m. Fatigue ratings are high and you have a moderate-intensity workout scheduled with an emphasis on shoulder exercises. What are your options and how do you proceed?

Options

Your best option is to go to a rest day. In any program you do not want to add to the overall training stress and create a situation in which recovery of the neuromuscular system is difficult and poten-tially compounded by other workout stresses.

CASE STUDY 32

Scenario

The basketball team comes into the weight room for a power workout. You give them a preworkout test in the vertical jump and only 2 out of the 15 players can reach 90% or greater of their best vertical jump. What are your options and how do you proceed?

Options

One of the first options is to individualize the workout by allowing the two players who are capable of performing the power workout to continue and perform the power workout. The other group can switch to another workout based on the most needed type of workout for check-off in that training cycle or week. Remember that the purpose of the flexible nonlinear program is to be responsive to the circumstances surrounding each individual to optimize workouts over a training cycle and create more effective adaptations to exercise.

Using flexible nonlinear workouts can create a situation in which not all of the players will be on the same workout progression because of differences in training recovery and physical potential on a given day.

© University of Connecticut Office of Athletic Communications.

CASE STUDY 33

Scenario

On a Monday following the second football game of the season, you had a heavy resistance workout scheduled after practice as players typically do a walk-through and go over the opponent's offensive and defensive sets. Because the team lost on Saturday night, you see that the players were drilled hard and had a full scrimmage game for about 60 minutes during the Monday practice session. What are your options and how do you proceed?

Options

You had expected to get a group of well-rested players after a walk-through practice, but the coach used practice as a punishment session for a poor performance. You need to help players rest, and if you cannot send them home to eat and rest, your best option is to implement an injury-prevention set of exercises (e.g., rotator cuff, ankle, hamstring exercises) using light to moderate resistances and low volume and then send them home to rest and recover. Sometimes coaches make a wrong decision out of an emotional response to the competitive environment and should be counseled if possible. You can work with the athletic training staff to create a workout that will be beneficial because the head coach might not let the players rest completely. Recovery is the key factor, both physically and psychologically. Many times the strength and conditioning coach needs to help restore the athletes' morale when dealing with the rigors of competition.

CASE STUDY 34

Scenario

A personal training client has a target of an 8- to 10RM zone for 4 sets using his previous weight of 200 pounds (~90.7 kg) in the bench press. On the first set he completes all 10 reps, and on the second set he completes only 6 reps. What are your options and how do you proceed?

Options

The expected training goal is achieved only on the first set. This could mean there is some form of residual fatigue or the length of rest periods between sets is too short. The first option is to increase the length of the rest period after the set and see if that results in an 8- to 10RM zone performance. If the trainee does hit the 8- to

10RM zone on the last two sets, take precaution by providing more rest between sets during the next training session using this load. If not, then you need to consider a light day for the current session and check to see what else might be causing the fatigue (e.g., too much cardio training or work stress).

CASE STUDY 35

Scenario

The women's volleyball team comes in for a workout after a volleyball practice. You find out that the coach held a contest during practice in which groups of three were timed when doing 300 block jumps reaching over the net. You had scheduled them for a power workout.

Options

You see that the coach has pretty much wrecked the power training session you had planned for that day. Your best option is to switch

What are your options and do you proceed with a power training session when players' lower-body musculature is fatigued?

to another workout with some sensitivity to the fact that the players' lower-body musculature will be quite fatigued. It may be that an active rest day or upper-body workout is the best option. Alternatively, if the workout sequence over the training cycle has been met, you might allow a complete rest day.

CASE STUDY 36

Scenario

The women's field hockey team is scheduled for a rest day on Wednesday after a hard practice on Monday and a heavy resistance training day on Tuesday. They come into the weight room and you find that the practice was shortened because of rain on Monday, and on Tuesday your assistant coach put them through a light resistance workout. What are your options and how do you proceed?

Options

One of your first options is to implement the heavy resistance day that was missed on Tuesday. In the flexible approach to periodization, you can quickly adjust for a missed workout in a sequence of planned sessions for a given training cycle.

CASE STUDY 37

Scenario

Some track and field athletes come into the weight room. They have been having really hard practices all week in preparation for the conference championships. The coach has not used any tapering in her team's preparation for the meet. Several athletes also complain of being very tired and thirsty all the time. You had them scheduled for a light resistance training session to help with the anticipated tapering for the meet. What are your options and how do you proceed?

Options

Since this is an in-season maintenance workout, the athletes' physical potential for the end-of-season meet is the first concern. They are tired and thirsty, which is a sure sign that they are dehydrated. Rest, food, and fluid intake may be the best option to help these athletes maintain physiological readiness to compete. It appears that the coach worked them too hard and more exercise will just compromise their readiness to compete and peak for the conference meet.

It is well known that by the time the thirst mechanism is activated, that person is already partially dehydrated.

© University of Connecticut Office of Athletic Communications.

CASE STUDY 38

Scenario

A personal trainer's 62-year-old client has a target of an 8- to 10RM zone for 4 sets using his previous weight of 120 pounds (~54.4 kg) in the bench press. On the first set he completes all 10 reps, on the second set he completes 12 reps, and on the third set he completes 13 reps. What are your options and how do you proceed?

Options

Instruct the trainee to increase the weight whenever he goes beyond the RM training zone. If you are using the RM training zone approach with an exercise, keep the rep number to those zone reps. Again, going to failure on each set can cause joint compression and stiffness in many individuals and also greater cardiovascular stress and is not necessary for progress. With older individuals this can be a big concern. However, assessing that a trainee is in the training zone is vital for optimizing the loads lifted for each set of an exercise and for progress over time.

CASE STUDY 39

Scenario

A football player comes into the weight room for an in-season work-out and is scheduled for a heavy day and hits all of his 3- to 5RM target reps with an increased weight in the squat. On the bench press he feels some shoulder pain in his warm-up set and lets you know this. What are your options and how do you proceed?

Flexible nonlinear periodization should address this dynamic and differential set of circumstances among body parts.

Photo by AJ Macht, courtesy of the Indianapolis Colts.

Options

In many sports, the loading of exercises helps in revealing sport injuries that do not show up on the practice field. The injury is a targeted shoulder injury that requires immediate attention by the training staff and follow-up with the team physician. Your best option is to cut the workout and take him to the athletic training room for evaluation and follow-up. Upon the athlete's return to the weight room, you would need to have a full prescription from the team physician regarding what the player is capable of doing and what rehabilitation program the player is on. Progression in the squat and other exercises may be possible if the shoulder injury is isolated, and a rehabilitation program can be implemented for this one joint without compromising other exercise movements or vice versa. You may have to train the other parts of the body differently with regard to the progressions and loads used.

CASE STUDY 40

Scenario

You have properly targeted a maximal power protocol of 6 sets of 3 reps for the high pull exercise using 65% of 1RM resistance. During an observation, the pulls do not appear to be at maximal speed and there is a lot of variance between pulls; the bar sometimes gets to chest height and other times there is an apparent reluctance to pull the bar as hard as possible as it moves past knee level. The lifter is having obvious trouble with bar control and return to the platform. What are your options and how do you proceed?

Options

The lifter might not be accustomed to pulling such a light weight at maximal speed and therefore is hesitating on the lift because it is very different from pulls done with heavier loads. One option is to have the lifter practice and start to ramp up to the lifting speed of the bar. Make sure that the lifter learns to be comfortable with the increased bar speed and pull distance and then can safely return the weight to the platform. With this exercise, a lifter can go considerably higher on the body than is typical of most clean-type exercises, and the lifter needs to practice to control the bar as it moves up the body and back to the platform. The inability to control a very dynamic bar may be inhibiting the lifter's power training. Technique in every exercise is important for optimizing adaptations.

CASE STUDY 41

Scenario

You are in a 2-week, 5-day-a week overreaching cycle. You are using a planned high-volume, moderate-intensity 8- to 10RM overreaching protocol. At the start of a workout, each athlete is unable to complete the 3 sets using the resistance he or she had used previously. What are your options and how do you proceed?

Options

Since the intention of an overreaching workout is to cause an acute decrease in force production potential, this should be expected. However, you would only allow this to happen during the 2-week overreaching cycle. Studies have shown that the expected strength rebound after the overreaching cycle can occur when heavy resistances with low volume are used and when a trainee reverts to a normal frequency of training 3 or 4 days a week.

CASE STUDY 42

Scenario

The women's gymnastics team had to reschedule their workout for 6:00 a.m. The planned workout was a power workout to help them in their physical development for the floor exercise. In testing in the vertical jump for power training viability, it was noted that each of the women had power outputs less than 80% of their tested maximum countermovement vertical jump heights from an afternoon testing done the previous week. What are your options and how do you proceed?

Options

You would cancel the workout because the power output data do not show enough high-quality power capability in order to perform a power workout that will be effective in improving their maximal power output. Another issue raised in this scenario is the fact that if individuals are not accustomed to exercising in the morning or late at night, their normal circadian patterns will affect the quality of the workout. The hormone melatonin is telling their bodies that they are not awake, and unless a tremendous amount of adrenaline is present to override this hormonal message, they will not see very impressive performances.

Keep circadian patterns in mind for competitions because athletes need to adapt to the competitive time frame for optimal performance.

CASE STUDY 43

Scenario

In early September after preseason summer practices and an initial game, the men's soccer team finished a 2-hour in-season practice on Wednesday. The coach has just sent them to you in the weight room for an unexpected workout. Not all of the soccer players have been lifting as freshmen and no other weight workouts have been done since summer off-season training. What are your options and how do you proceed?

Options

The athletes are fatigued and adding to their fatigue would not help them cope with the already high amount of stress created by soccer practice and games. It appears that working with some low-intensity medicine ball exercises and flexibility will best serve the coaches' in-season practice program, which is creating a significant amount of exercise stress. In addition, freshmen players may be at a greater risk of injury because of a lack of preseason and in-season resistance training. Communication with the soccer coach is vital for developing a more appropriate conditioning program for the all-year macrocycle.

CASE STUDY 44

Scenario

The baseball team just got off of a 7-day road trip where they used handheld weights and rubber-band resistances to work out. They are back home a few days early and ready for their weight room work-outs. What are your options and how do you proceed?

Options

You should refer to the priorities of the overall training cycle, but it does present an opportunity to do some full-body multijoint exer-cises with heavy loadings. This would help to offset any detraining and maintain strength and power through the season. Since the players were in an organized cycle before the spring trip, you can implement some of these workouts to enhance their fitness base for

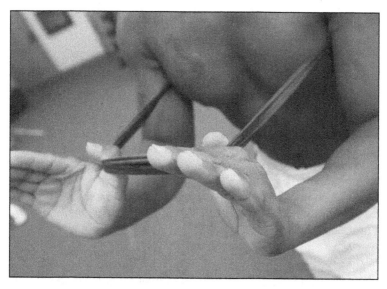

How does flexible nonlinear periodization function when travel schedule changes occur?

the in-season program. Essentially you will be starting an in-season workout routine after the road trip, which is at the beginning of the season.

CASE STUDY 45

Scenario

A rugby player comes into the weight room. He has missed the previous 6 weeks of training and practice because of a family emergency. The player had been working on a 12-week training cycle prioritized for power. What are your options and how do you proceed?

Options

You must start the player out with an initial progression that will help him recover basic strength and toleration of exercise training sessions. You should monitor progress and ability to complete the workouts, which should be prioritized for basic strength. Using flexible nonlinear periodization and training log data from previous sessions, you can see how much detraining has occurred. Essentially this much time off has been shown to produce a detraining effect, especially with anaerobic short-rest workouts. Thus, it is important to start at the beginning of a training sequence for basic strength and not try to force the athlete to come back too soon.

CASE STUDY 46

Scenario

The women's tennis team comes into the weight room for a scheduled in-season power workout focusing on whole-body power exercises (e.g., hang clean, jump squat). The team had a match the day before. What are your options and how do you proceed?

Options

In this case you would proceed. Some preliminary power testing in the vertical jump to see how much residual fatigue exists from the match would help in your evaluation of whether or not this workout is viable. In addition, some tennis players will rate their fatigue high on a scale, but when they are tested, no deficit in physical performance is observed. There is a possible disconnection from their physical perceptions, but again psychological overtraining can occur and this underscores the need to monitor the workout very carefully. Move forward with the workout, but be ready to switch to another workout if you observe actual decrements in power.

CASE STUDY 47

Scenario

In an off-season workout, you have the football team coming in for a heavy resistance day on a Monday. They start with the power clean using 90% of 1RM, which is a 3- to 5RM training zone. Every player appears to be achieving his targeted rep number and using the same or greater loads as the last time this resistance range was used.

Options

When it all works as you have planned, continue the workout and feel the satisfaction of everything moving forward. Be careful to check individual performances so that the overall impression is true for all of the players.

What are your options and how do you proceed when the players achieve their target rep numbers?

CASE STUDY 48

Scenario

The head football coach has the football team during the off-season running about 3 to 5 miles (~4.8-8 km) a day for the past 8 weeks after overhearing someone talk about the benefits of aerobics. You have prioritized a 12-week off-season training cycle for power, but after testing the team, you find that many of the players have actually gotten worse in their vertical jump power performance. What are your options and how do you proceed?

Options

It is apparent that a little information can be dangerous when a coach is not educated in exercise science. Cardiorespiratory (aerobic) fitness is important, but when aerobic training is prescribed at too high a volume, the effect is a reduction in power of the muscle groups performing the aerobic training. In fact, when marathon runners detrain, their vertical jump power actually increases. (For review on exercise compatibility see Fleck & Kraemer, 2004.) You need to educate the coach and replace the distance running with sprint intervals to help them condition their cardiorespiratory system but not affect their power performance. You then need to begin the program with a strength priority before attempting to address a power prioritization.

CASE STUDY 49

Scenario

The women's soccer team comes in from a 90-minute practice where the conditions were hot and humid. They are scheduled for a moderate resistance workout about an hour after soccer practice. What are your options and how do you proceed?

Options

First make sure that they are hydrated and that each was educated about hydration during the practice and after practice before coming into the weight room for a workout. It is possible that with even a 3% weight loss physical deficit can be observed, especially in the smaller muscle groups. Each player should be weighed so that you can determine if a significant amount of weight has been lost. Carefully move forward with the workout, which is moderate in intensity. Decrease the volume if needed in order to allow recovery from the total training stress.

Hot and humid conditions indicate special workout cautions.

CASE STUDY 50

Scenario

The softball team comes into the weight room for a scheduled very heavy resistance day in a 1- to 3RM training zone. After the first set of squats, several players are able to perform 5 reps with the previous week's starting training load. What are your options and how do you proceed?

Options

The resistances need to be increased in order to maintain the very heavy training zone of 1- to 3RM. This is an easy adjustment that can be made during the workout, and each individual should be instructed to do so when the loading is too light.

Appendix: Training Log

Keeping a training log is critical when using nonlinear and flexible nonlinear programs, because the acute program variables will change regularly. With nonlinear plans, some acute program variables, such as the exercises performed and resistance used, can change on a session-by-session basis. In this appendix we've provided a blank training log for your personal use. (See table 7.1 for an example of a completed log and a more detailed description of its use.)

Your loading information should be entered in the *Training Zone* section (i.e., light, heavy, power). The *Rest* column should be indicated in minutes.

A well-kept training log is vital in monitoring training progress and in making modifications to the training sessions in a nonlinear resistance training program.

WEEK 1

Monday: EXERCISES Training Zone:	Rest	Resistance/Reps for each set	RM Zone	Wednesday: EXERCISES Training Zone:	Rest	Resistance/Reps for each set	RM Zone	Friday: EXERCISES Training Zone:	Rest	Resistance/Reps for each set	RM Zone
		/ / /				/ / /				/ / /	

WEEK 2

WEEK 3

WEEK 4　WEEK 5

From W. Kraemer and S. Fleck, 2007, *Optimizing strength training* (Champaign, IL: Human Kinetics).

WEEK 6

WEEK 7

WEEK 8

WEEK 9

From W. Kraemer and S. Fleck, 2007, *Optimizing strength training* (Champaign, IL: Human Kinetics).

213

Glossary

active recovery phase—A period of the training cycle in which resistance training is decreased and other light forms of exercise activities used in order to allow the body and the mind to rest and partially recover.

acute program variables—Factors that define a resistance training workout: choice of exercises, order of exercises, number of sets, intensity or resistance used, and amount of rest between sets and exercises.

acute training effects—The changes occurring during exercise.

adaptation—The adjustment of an organism to its environment or the changes in the function or body structures to meet the demands of greater stress.

adenosine triphosphate (ATP)—A biochemical substance used by all cells as an immediate source of energy.

adolescence—The transitional stage of development between childhood and full adulthood, representing the period of time during which a person is biologically adult but emotionally not at full maturity. The ages considered to be part of adolescence vary by culture. In the United States, adolescence is generally considered to begin around age 13 and end around 24.

adrenaline—A hormone released by the adrenal glands often associated with the fight or flight response, also termed epinephrine.

aerobic—Using oxygen. Also a term to describe cardiorespiratory exercise.

afferent—Toward the central nervous system.

agonistic muscles—Muscles that initiate and carry out motion.

alpha-motor neuron—Also called a motoneuron, which is a nerve cell innervating muscle cells.

alternating sequence—Refers to performing exercises for alternating muscle groups in succession, such as the typical arm-to-leg exercise order.

alternative workout—A workout done in place of a regularly scheduled workout.

amino acids—Organic compounds (the building blocks) that constitute proteins.

anabolic—Promoting anabolism.

anabolism—Synthesis of complex substances from simple ones; the opposite of catabolism.

anaerobic—Without oxygen.

antagonist muscle—A muscle producing tension in opposition to the tension of another muscle (agonist).

atrophy—A decrease in muscle size.

axon—A nerve fiber.

ballistic stretching—A rapid stretching movement; a form of a dynamic warm-up.

base program—A beginning program using relatively light resistances (12- to 15RM) and lower training volumes.

bilateral—Indicates both sides of the body or the use of both arms or both legs in an exercise.

calorie (cal)—A quantity of energy, especially heat. Amount of heat needed to raise one gram of water one degree Celsius.

cardiorespiratory endurance—The ability to perform whole-body exercise for an extended time. Also refers to endurance capabilities and long-duration exercise capability.

catabolism—The disintegration of complex substances into simpler ones; the opposite of anabolism.

catecholamines—Chemical compounds that circulate in the bloodstream. These chemical compounds are released by the adrenal glands in situations of stress, such as psychological stress or low blood sugar.

central factors (in force production)—The coordination of muscle activity by the central nervous system, including intramuscular and intermuscular coordination.

circuit training—Programs that consist of several exercises performed in succession with little or no rest between exercises.

clean and jerk—One of two lifts constituting the sport of weightlifting (Olympic style), in which the barbell is first lifted from the floor to the shoulders (clean phase) and then overhead (jerk phase).

closed chain—An exercise in which the end segment of the exercised limb is fixed. The leg press and push-up are examples of this type of exercise.

competition phase—In-season training.

compliance—The ratio of change in length per unit to change in applied force per unit.

compound resistance—Resistance provided by a combination of two or several sources, such as lifting a heavy barbell that is connected to the floor by a rubber band.

concentric (or miometric) muscle action—Muscle shortening under tension; the external resistance forces act in the direction opposite from the motion. Also known as the lifting or pushing phase of a repetition.

connective tissues—Supporting tissues of the body, such as tendons, ligaments, bone, and cartilage.

contralateral—Pertaining to the opposite side of a body.

core—Referring to the abdominal, hip, and lower back muscles.

core stability—Stabilization of the trunk and pelvis necessary for performing movements of the extremities.

coronal plane—The imaginary plane that divides the body into front and back sections. Also known as the frontal plane.

creatine phosphate—See *phosphocreatine.*

cross-sectional area (of a muscle)—The area of muscle fibers on a plane perpendicular to their longitudinal axes.

cross-training—An individualized combination of all aerobic training methods, characterized by a variety of intensities and modes.

dehydration—Excessive loss of body water, which is maintained for longer than 24 hours.

delayed-onset muscle soreness—The pain and soreness that may occur 12 to 48 hours after training workouts; see *DOMS.*

delayed (training) effects—The changes manifested over a certain time interval after a performed training routine.

detraining—A cessation (stopping) or reduction of training or a decrease in physical performance caused by a cessation or reduction in training.

DOMS (delayed-onset muscle soreness)—Muscle soreness or discomfort that appears 12 to 48 hours after exercise. It is most likely due to microscopic tears in the muscle tissue, and it usually requires a couple of days for the repair and rebuilding process to be completed. The muscle tissue grows back stronger, leading to increased muscle mass and strength.

dynamic muscle action—Muscle lengthening or shortening under tension; see *concentric muscle action* and *eccentric muscle action.*

eccentric muscle action—Muscle lengthening under tension; the external forces act in the same direction as the motion. Also known as the lowering or releasing phase of a repetition.

efferent—Conducting impulses from the central nervous system toward the periphery.

electrolytes—Salts (ions) found in bodily fluids. During exercise, the body loses electrolytes (sodium and potassium) in perspiration. These electrolytes need to be replaced in order to keep concentrations constant in the body, which is why many sport drinks include electrolytes.

electromyography (EMG)—Record of electric activity within or on the surface of a muscle.

endurance—The ability to bear fatigue.

energy—Capacity to perform work.

explosive strength—The ability to exert maximal forces in minimal time.

extensor—A muscle that extends a limb or increases the joint angle.

external force—A force acting between an athlete's body and the environment.

fascia—A fibrous membrane.

fast-twitch (Type II) fibers—Muscle fibers that display high force, high rate of force development, and low endurance.

feedback—The return of information concerning output of a system to regulate future output, used to control the output of a system.

female athlete triad—A health condition composed of the following three factors: disordered eating (severe restriction of food intake or bingeing and purging), amenorrhea (cessation of menstrual cycles), and osteoporosis (a weakening of the bones that can lead to stress fractures).

fitness (physical fitness)—Slow-changing motor components of an athlete's preparedness.

flexibility—The measure of the range of motion, or the amount of movement possible, at a particular joint.

flexible nonlinear periodization—A nonlinear periodization model that allows adjustment in training intensity and volume in relation to other physical and psychological stresses.

flexor—A muscle that flexes a limb or decreases the joint angle.

force—An instantaneous measure of the interaction between two bodies. Force is characterized by magnitude, direction, and point of application.

frequency—The number of workouts per week (or unit time) or number of times a muscle group is trained per week (or unit time).

glycolysis—An ATP-generating metabolic process in which glucose is converted in a series of steps to pyruvic acid and then to lactic acid if oxygen is unavailable.

Golgi tendon organ—A tension-sensing nerve ending located in series (in the tendon) with a muscle.

growth hormone—Hormone made by the pituitary gland that controls the growth of the body.

hormone—A chemical substance that is secreted into blood and transported to another organ, where it produces a specific effect.

human strength curve—See *strength curve.*

hyperplasia—An increase in the number of cells.

hypertrophy—An increase in size of cells or organs, especially muscle.

immediate (training) effects—Effects that occur as the result of a single training session.

individualization—Efforts to train according to the interests, abilities, and other characteristics of an individual.

inertia—Resistance due to the property of a body to remain at rest or to continue its movement in a straight line unless acted on by an external force. A force is required to overcome inertia and to accelerate the body.

intensity—Also called training intensity. The external opposing force or resistance used in an exercise movement.

intra-abdominal pressure (IAP)—Pressure within the abdomen.

isokinetic—With constant speed. May refer to the rate of change of muscle length, velocity of the load being lifted, or angular velocity of the joint.

isokinetic muscle action—Muscle shortening at a constant speed. Usually applied either to the constant angular velocity of a joint or to the constant linear velocity of a lifted load.

isometric (static)—Without change in muscle (or muscle plus tendon) length.

lactic acid—A by-product of anaerobic glycolysis and anaerobic metabolism of glucose (carbohydrate).

lactic acid threshold—The pace that can be maintained with minimal increase in tissue lactic acid or increasing acidity.

learning effects—Changes in a function based on practice and better neural functioning.

load—Weight lifted or resistance used.

local muscular endurance—The ability of a certain muscle or muscle group to perform repeated contractions against a submaximal resistance. Examples are performing the maximal number of repetitions in the chin-up, parallel bar dip, or push-up exercises, or a resistance training exercise using a fixed load.

long-term planning (of training)—Planning of a year or several years of training.

macrocycle—One competition season. Includes preparation, competition, and transition periods (phases) or three to four months of training.

maturation—the attainment of full functional capacity by a cell, a tissue, or an organ.

mean power—Average power output in an activity.

menstrual cycle—During a woman's reproductive years, the monthly cycle of discharge of blood and tissues from the uterus.

mesocycle—A length of training several microcycles (weeks) in length.

meta-analysis—A statistical procedure in which the results of all studies examining a particular topic, such as periodized weight training, are compared in order to reach a quantitative conclusion.

metabolic rate—The speed at which the body uses energy. Resting metabolic rate is the rate of energy use at rest.

microcycle— Typically referring to training performed in one week.

motion—A movement determined only by its geometry. If all body parts move along the same trajectory or very similar trajectories, the motion is considered the same, regardless of differences in force, time, and velocity.

motor unit—A motoneuron and the muscle fibers it innervates.

motor unit activation—The stimulation of the motor unit and its fibers.

multiple sets—Performing more than one set for an exercise.

muscle action—Development of muscle tension (force).

muscle fibers—A skeletal muscle cell. The basic contractile units in muscle tissue are classified as two basic types: Type I (slow-twitch fibers), which are the fiber best at endurance activities, and Type II (fast-twitch) muscle fibers, which are the fibers best at developing force quickly.

muscle spindle (stretch receptor)—A length-sensitive receptor located in muscle.

muscular endurance—The type of endurance manifested in exercises with heavy resistance that does not require considerable activation of the cardiovascular and respiratory systems.

neuron—A nerve cell.

nonlinear periodization—One method of periodization in which the intensity, volume, or a given set of training variables is very distinct from workout to workout.

normative movements—Movements that stimulate the primary angle of an exercise (e.g., flat bench press versus decline bench press).

open chain—An exercise in which the end segment of the exercised limb is not fixed. Most single joint exercises are open-chain movements.

peak oxygen consumption—The maximal amount of oxygen that can be taken in at the lungs and used by the body during whole-body intense exercise.

periodization—The most popular term for planned training variation. Typically involves changing the intensity (resistance used) and the volume of exercise over time. Planned days of rest are also important to the periodization concept because recovery is allowed which can prevent overtraining. A division of the training season into smaller and more manageable intervals (periods of training, mesocycles, and microcycles) with the ultimate goal of maintaining continued gains in fitness so that the trainees achieve their best possible physical condition or performance.

phosphocreatine—An organic compound, $C_4H_{10}N_3O_5P$, found in muscle tissue and capable of storing and providing energy for muscular contraction. Also called *creatine phosphate*.

planned daily rotation—The planned rotation of nonlinear workouts.

plyometric—A type of training normally involving jumping or throw movements in which a stretch-shortening cycle is involved, the goal of which is to increase power capabilities.

pneumatic—Operated by compressed air.

power—Measured in watts; calculated as force times distance divided by time, or work per unit of time.

powerlifting—A sport consisting of lifting maximal weights in the bench press, squat, and deadlift exercises.

preparation phase—Off-season training.

preparedness—An athlete's readiness to train or disposition for a competition, characterized by that person's potential sport performance.

progressive overload—The gradual increase of training stress placed on the body during any physical training program, including resistance training.

rate of force development—Force produced at various times from the initiation of the muscle action.

recovery—The ability of the body to return to a normal level of function at or above previous physiological status or performance capabilities. Reaching the original state or new state of homeostasis.

repetition—The number of times a movement is repeated within a single exercise set.

repetition maximum—Also called RM. The amount of resistance (external force) that allows a person to perform only a given number of repetitions in an exercise movement (e.g., 1RM is the amount of resistance that allows an individual to perform only one repetition).

repetition maximum (RM) zone—The amount of resistance that allows a person to perform a number of repetitions that will fall in a training zone of a specific number of repetitions (e.g., a 3- to 5RM is the maximal resistance that allows an individual to perform only 3 to 5 repetitions in an exercise movement).

resistance—An external opposing force used in exercise. Common forms are weight stacks, elastic bands, weights, barbells, dumbbells, pneumatics, hydraulics, and isokinetics.

rest interval—The time period between sets and exercises in a workout or between workouts.

sagittal plane—An imaginary plane that divides the body into left and right sections.

sarcopenia—The loss of muscle fiber size and whole muscle mass, which results in diminished strength with age.

scheduled nonlinear sequence program—The planned sequence of workouts used in a nonlinear periodization protocol.

size principle (of motor neuron recruitment)—To control the force generated by a muscle, the CNS activates the motor neurons according to their size, from small motoneurons at low forces to large motoneurons at high forces. Because small motor neurons innervate slow-twitch (Type I) fibers while large motor neurons innervate fast-twitch (Type II) fibers, the size principle implies that at low forces the slow muscle fibers are only active.

skill training—Practicing of the motor skills or movements involved in a sport or activity.

slow-twitch (Type I) muscle fiber—Muscle fiber best at endurance activities (use of oxygen to generate energy).

snatch—One of two lifts constituting the sport of weightlifting (Olympic style), in which the barbell is lifted in one continuous motion from the floor to an overhead position.

specific exercises—Training drills relevant to demands of the event for which an athlete is being trained.

specificity—The similarity between adaptation gains induced by a training drill and the adaptation required for successful performance of a sport or activity.

specificity of training—Physiological adaptations are specific to the muscles trained, type of muscle action (eccentric, concentric, isometric), speed of movement, range of motion, and energy source (aerobic, anaerobic).

stabilizer—A muscle that contracts with no significant movement of a joint but stabilizes a joint so that the agonists can perform the desired movement.

stacked sequence—Refers to performing exercises for the same muscle group in succession, such as the typical arm-to-arm or leg-to-leg order.

strength—The maximal force a muscle or muscle group can generate at a specified velocity.

strength and power periodization—Often termed *linear* or *classic periodization,* in which there is a general pattern of training intensity increasing and volume decreasing over the entire macrocycle. A major goal of this type of periodization is to peak maximal strength and power at a specific time.

strength curve—The plot of force exerted by an athlete (or the moment of force) versus an appropriate body position measure (i.e., joint angle). Also known as *human strength curve*.

stretch-shortening cycle—Muscle action in which a concentric action is immediately preceded by an eccentric action causing a slight stretch of the muscle. This type of muscle action is the basis of plyometric training.

synergist—A muscle that assists another muscle in accomplishing a movement.

task specificity—Refers to the movement pattern and strength or power output necessary to successfully complete a specific physical task.

training frequency—The number of training sessions per week in which a particular muscle group is trained or emphasized in a training session.

training plateau—A period of time when limited or no measurable progress in a fitness test (e.g., strength, power) or physiological measure is made despite the performance of training.

training variation—Changing some aspect of the exercise protocol (e.g., acute program variables) over time, including the number of days used for rest.

transition phase—In the European periodization terminology the period of training during which training is changing from one training cycle to the next, such as changing from the preparatory to competition phases.

transverse plane—The imaginary plane that divides the body into top and bottom sections. Also known as horizontal plane.

Type I muscle fibers—Slow-twitch muscle fibers. Contraction is mediated primarily by aerobic metabolism (utilizes oxygen); they are the best fibers for performing endurance activities due to their slow fatiguing properties.

Type II muscle fibers—Fast-twitch muscle fibers. Contraction is mediated primarily by anaerobic metabolism so they fatigue quickly; they are best suited for short duration high-powered activities.

unilateral—Indicates one side of the body or one arm or one leg used in an exercise.

Valsalva maneuver—A maneuver in which a person tries to exhale forcibly with a closed glottis (windpipe) so that no air exits through the mouth or nose.

variable resistance—Strength training exercises that change the amount of resistance throughout the full range of motion.

volume—The amount of work that is performed, ideally measured in joules, but estimated using sets × repetitions or more commonly sets × repetitions × resistance used.

weight—The resistance caused by mass and gravity. Typically refers to the resistance used during strength training.

weightlifting—The official Olympic sport consisting of the clean and jerk and the snatch lifts.

work—Force times distance.

workout—An exercise training session.

Bibliography

Chapter 1 References and Suggested Readings

American College of Sports Medicine. (2002). Progression models in resistance training for healthy adults. *Medicine and Science in Sports and Exercise,* 34:364-380.

Baker, D., Wilson, G., and Carlyon, R. (1994). Periodization: the effect on strength of manipulating volume and intensity. *Journal of Strength and Conditioning Research,* 8:235-242.

Fleck, S.J. (1999). Periodized strength training: A critical review. *Journal of Strength and Conditioning Research,* 13:82-89.

Fleck, S.J. (2002). Periodization of training. In W.J. Kraemer and K. Häkkinen (Eds.), *Strength Training for Sport,* 55-68. Blackwell Science.

Fleck, S.J., & Kraemer, W.J. (2004). *Designing resistance training programs* (3rd ed.). Champaign, IL: Human Kinetics.

Hoeger, W.W.K., Barette, S.L., Hale, D.F., and Hopkins, D.R. (1987). Relationship between repetitions and selected percentages of one repetition maximum. *Journal of Applied Sport Science Research,* 1:11-13.

Hoeger, W.W.K., Hopkins, D.R., Barette, S.L. and Hale, D.F. (1990). Relationship between repetitions and selected percentages of one repetition maximum: A comparison between untrained and trained males and females. *Journal of Applied Sport Science Research,* 4:47-54.

Kraemer, W.J. (1983). Exercise prescription in weight training: Manipulating program variables. *National Strength and Conditioning Association Journal,* 5:58-59.

Kraemer, W.J. (1997). A series of studies: The physiological basis for strength training in American football: Fact over philosophy. *Journal of Strength and Conditioning Research* 11:131-142.

Kraemer, W.J., Häkkinen, K., Triplett-McBride, N.T., Fry, A.C., Koziris, L.P., Ratamess, N.A., Bauer, J.E., Volek, J.S., McConnell, T., Newton, R.U., Gordon, S.E., Cummings, D., Hauth, J., Pullo, F., Lynch, J.M., Fleck, S.J., Mazzetti, S.A., and Knuttgen, H.G. (2003). Physiological changes with periodized resistance training in women tennis players. *Medicine and Science in Sports and Exercise.* 35:157-168.

Kraemer, W.J., Noble, B.J., Culver, B.W., & Clark, M.J. (1987). Physiologic responses to heavy-resistance exercise with very short rest periods. *International Journal of Sports Medicine.* 8:247-252.

Kraemer, W.J., Patton, J.F., Gordon, S.E., Harman, E.A., Deschenes, M.R., Reynolds, K., Newton, R.U., Triplett, N.T., & Dziados, J.E. (1995). Compatibility of high-intensity strength and endurance training on hormonal and skeletal muscle adaptations. *Journal of Applied Physiology,* 78:976-89.

Kraemer, W.J., Ratamess, N., Fry, A.C., Triplett-McBride, T., Koziris, L.P., Bauer, J.A., Lynch, J.M., & Fleck, S.J. (2000). Influence of resistance training volume and periodization on physiological and performance adaptations in collegiate women tennis players. *American Journal of Sports Medicine,* 28:626-633.

Marx, J.O., Ratamess, N.A., Nindl, B.C., Gotshalk, L.A., Volek, J.S., Dohi, K., Bush, J.A., Gomez, A.L., Mazzetti, S.A., Fleck, S.J., Häkkinen, K., Newton, R.U., & Kraemer, W.J. (2001). Low-volume circuit versus high-volume periodized resistance training in women. *Medicine and Science in Sports and Exercise,* 33:635-643.

Poliquin, C. (1988). Five steps to increasing the effectiveness of your strength training program. *National Strength and Conditioning Association Journal,* 10:34-39.

Rhea, M.R., & Alderman, B.L. (2004). A meta-analysis of periodized versus nonperiodized strength and power training programs. *Research Quarterly for Exercise and Sport,* 75:413-422.

Rhea, M.R., Ball, S.D., Phillips, W.T., & Burkett, L.N. (2002). A comparison of linear and daily undulating periodized programs with equated volume and intensity for strength. *Journal of Strength and Conditioning Research,* 16:250-255.

Shimano, T., Kraemer, W.J., Spiering, B.A., Volek, J.S., Hatfield, D.L., Silvestre, R., Vingren, J.L., Fragala, M.S., Maresh, C.M., Fleck, S.J., Newton, R.U., Spreuwenberg, L.P.B., & Hakkinen, K. (2006). Relationship between the number of repetitions and selected percentages of one repetition maximum in free weight exercises in trained and untrained men. *Journal of Strength and Conditioning Research,* 20:819-823.

Silvestre, R., Kraemer, W.J., West, C., Judelson, D.A., Spiering, B.A., Vingren, J.L., Hatfield, D.L., Anderson, J.M., & Maresh, C.M. (2006). Body composition and physical performance during a national collegiate athletic association division I men's soccer season. *Journal of Strength and Conditioning Research,* 1:20(4):962-970.

Willoughby, D.S. (1993). The effects of meso-cycle-length weight training programs involving periodization and partially equated volumes on upper and lower body strength. *Journal of Strength and Conditioning Research,* 7:2-8.

Chapter 2 References and Suggested Readings

American College of Sports Medicine. (2002). Aggression models in resistance training for healthy adults. *Medicine and Science in Sports and Exercise,* 34:364-380.

Bastiaans, J.J., van Diemen, A.B., Veneberg, T., & Jeukendrup, A.E. (2001). The effects of replacing a portion of endurance training by explosive strength training on performance in trained cyclists. *European Journal of Applied Physiology,* 86:79-84.

Calder, A.W., Chilibeck, P.D., Webber, C.E., & Sale, D.G. (1994). Comparison of whole and split weight training routines in young women. *Canadian Journal of Applied Physiology,* 19:185-199.

DeLorme, T.L., & A.L. Watkins. (1948). Techniques of progressive resistance exercise. *Archives of Physical Medicine,* 29:263-273.

Fleck, S.J., & Kraemer, W.J. (2004). *Designing resistance training programs* (3rd ed.). Champaign, IL: Human Kinetics.

Fleck, S.J., & Kraemer, W.J. (1997). *Designing resistance training programs* (2nd ed.). Champaign, IL: Human Kinetics.

Gettman, L.R., & Pollock, M.L. (1981). Circuit weight training: A critical review of its physiological benefits. *The Physician and Sportsmedicine,* 9: 44-60.

Hickson, R.C. (1980). Interference of strength development by simultaneously training for strength and endurance. *European Journal of Applied Physiology,* 45:255-269.

Hickson, R.C., Dvorak, B.A., Gorostiaga, E.M., Kurowski, T.T., & Foster, C. (1988). Potential for strength and endurance training to amplify endurance performance. *Journal of Applied Physiology* 65:2285-2290.

Kraemer, W.J., Fleck, S.J., Dziados, J.E., Harman, E.A., Marchitelli, L.J., Gordon, S.E., Mello, R., Frykman, P.N., Koziris, L.P., & Triplett, N.T. (1993). Changes in hormonal concentrations after different heavy-resistance exercise protocols in women. *Journal of Applied Physiology,* 75:594-604.

Kraemer, W.J., Gordon, S.E., Fleck, S.J., Marchitelli, L.J., Mello, R., Dziados, J.E., Friedl, K., & Harmon, E. (1991). Endogenous anabolic hormonal and growth factor responses to heavy resistance exercise in males and females. *International Journal of Sports Medicine,* 12:228-235.

Kraemer, W.J., Marchitelli, L., Gordon, S.E., Harman, E., Dziados, J.E., Mello, R., Frykman, P., McCurry, D., & Fleck, S.J. (1990). Hormonal and growth factor responses to heavy resistance exercise protocols. *Journal of Applied Physiology,* 69:1442-1450.

Kraemer, W.J., Noble, B.J., Culver, B.W., & Clark, M.J. (1987). Physiologic responses to heavy-resistance exercise with very short rest periods. *International Journal of Sports Medicine,* 8:247-252.

Kraemer, W.J., Patton, J.F., Gordon, S.E., Harman, E.A., Deschenes, M.R., Reynolds, K., Newton, R.U., Triplett, N.T., & Dziados, J.E. (1995). Compatibility of high-intensity strength and endurance training on hormonal and skeletal muscle adaptations. *Journal of Applied Physiology,* 78:976-89.

Kraemer, W.J., & Ratamess, N.A. (2003). Endocrine sponsors and adaptations to strength and power training. In P.V. Komi (Ed.), *Strength and power in sport* (2nd ed.), 361-368. Oxford: Blackwell Science.

Kraemer, W.J., & Ratamess, N.A. (2004). Fundamentals of resistance training: Aggression and exercise prescription. *Medicine and Science in Sports and Exercise,* 36:674-688.

Madsen, N., & McLaughlin, T. (1984). Kinematic factors influencing performance and injury risk in the bench press exercise. *Medicine and Science in Sports and Exercise,* 16:429-437.

Marcinik, E.J., Potts, J., Schlabach, G., Will, S., Dawson, P., & Hurley, B.F. (1991). Effects of strength training on lactate threshold and endurance performance. *Medicine and Science in Sports and Exercise,* 23:739-743.

McLaughlin, T.M., Dillman, C.J., & Lardner, T.J. (1977). A kinematic model of performance of the parallel squat. *Medicine and Science in Sports,* 9:128-133.

Paavolainen L., Häkkinen, K., Hamalainen, I., Nummela, A., & Rusko, H. (1999). Explosive-strength training improves 5-km running time by improving running economy and muscle power. *Journal of Applied Physiology,* 86:1527-1533.

Peterson, M.D., Rhea, M.R., & Alvar, B.A. (2004). Maximizing strength development in athletes: A meta-analysis to determine the dose response relationship. *Journal Strength and Conditioning Research,* 18:377-382.

Ploutz, L.L., Tesch, P.A., Biro, R.L., & Dudley, G.A. (1994). Effect of resistance training on muscle use during exercise. *Journal of Applied Physiology,* 76:1675-1681.

Rhea, M.R., Alvar, B.A., Burkett, L.N., & Ball, S.D. (2003). A meta-analysis to determine the dose response for strength development. *Medicine and Science in Sports and Exercise,* 35:456-464.

Robergs, R.A., Ghlasvamd, F., & Parker, D. (2004). Biochemistry of exercise-induced metabolic acidosis. *American Journal of Physiology,* 287:R502-R516.

Robinson, J.M., Stone, M.H., Johnson, R.L., Penland, C.M., Warren, B.J., & Lewis, R.D. (1995). Effects of different weight training exercise/rest intervals on strength, power, and high intensity exercise endurance. *Journal of Strength and Conditioning Research,* 9:216-221.

Wilmore, J.H., & Costill, D.L. (2004). *Physiology of sport and exercise* (3rd ed.). Champaign, IL: Human Kinetics.

Zatsiorsky, V. (1995). *Science and practice of strength training.* Champaign, IL: Human Kinetics.

Chapter 3 References and Suggested Readings

American College of Sports Medicine. (2002). American College of Sports Medicine Position Stand. Progression models in resistance training for healthy adults. *Medicine and Science in Sports and Exercise,* 34(2):364-380.

Ballor, D.L., Becque, M.D., & Katch, V.L. (1987). Metabolic responses during hydraulic resistance exercise. *Medicine and Science in Sports and Exercise,* 19:363-367.

Barnett, C., Kippers, V., & Turner, P. (1995). Effects of variations of the bench press exercise on the EMG activity of five shoulder muscles. *Journal of Strength and Conditioning Research,* 9:222-227.

Chilibeck, P.D., Calder, A.W., Sale, D.G., & Webber, C.E. (1998). A comparison of strength and muscle mass increases during resistance training in young women. *European Journal of Applied Physiology,* 77:170-175.

Escamilla, R.F., Fleisig, G.S., Zheng, N., Landers, J.E., Barrentine, S.W., Andrews J.R., Bergmann, B.W., & Moorman, C.T. III. (2001). Effects of technique variations on knee biomechanics during the squat and leg press. *Medicine and Science in Sports and Exercise,* 33:1552-1566.

Fleck, S.J. (1999). Periodized strength training: A critical review. *Journal of Strength and Conditioning Research,* 13:82-89.

Fleck, S.J., & Kraemer, W.J. (2004). *Designing resistance training programs* (3rd ed.). Champaign, IL: Human Kinetics.

Garhammer, J. (1991). A comparison of maximal power outputs between elite male and female weightlifters in competition. *International Journal of Sports Biomechanics,* 7:3-11.

Kraemer, W.J. (1983). Exercise prescription in weight training: Manipulating program variables. *National Strength and Conditioning Association Journal,* 5:58-59.

Kraemer, W.J. (1997). A series of studies: The physiological basis for strength training in American football: Fact over philosophy. *Journal of Strength and Conditioning Research* 11:131-142.

Kraemer, W.J., Fleck, S.J., Dziados, J.E., Harman, E.A., Marchitelli, L.J., Gordon, S.E., Mello, R., Frykman, P.N., Koziris, L.P., & Triplett, N.T. (1993). Changes in hormonal concentrations after different heavy-resistance exercise protocols in women. *Journal of Applied Physiology,* 75:594-604.

Kraemer, W.J., Fleck, S.J., Maresh, C.M., Ratamess, N.A., Gordon, S.E., Goetz, K.L., Harman, E.A., Frykman, P.N., Volek, J., Mazzetti, S.A., Fry, A.C., Marchittelli, L.J., & Paton, J.F. (1999). Acute hormonal responses to a single heavy resistance exercise in trained power lifters and untrained men. *Canadian Journal of Applied Physiology,* 24:524-537.

Kraemer, W.J., Gordon, S.E., Fleck, S.J., Marchitelli, L.J., Mello, R., Dziados, J.E., Friedl, K., & Harmon, E. (1991). Endogenous anabolic hormonal and growth factor responses to heavy resistance exercise in males and females. *International Journal of Sports Medicine,* 12:228-235.

Kraemer, W.J., Marchitelli, L., Gordon, S.E., Harman, E., Dziados, J.E., Mello, R., Frykman, P., McCurry, D, & Fleck, S.J.. (1990). Hormonal and growth factor responses to heavy resistance exercise protocols. *Journal of Applied Physiology,* 69:1442-1450.

Kraemer, W.J., & Ratamess, N.A. (2003). Endocrine sponsors and adaptations to strength and power training. In P.V. Komi (Ed.), *Strength and power in sport* (2nd ed.), 361-368. Oxford: Blackwell Science.

Kraemer, W.J., & Ratamess, N.A. (2004). Fundamentals of resistance training: Aggression and exercise prescription. *Medicine and Science in Sports and Exercise,* 36:674-688.

Maffiuletti, N.S.A., & Lepers, R. (2003). Quadriceps femoris torque and EMG activity in seated versus supine position. *Medicine and Science in Sports and Exercise,* 35:1511-1516.

McCall, G.E., Byrnes, W.C., Dickinson, A., Pattany, P.M., & Fleck, S.J. (1996). Muscle fiber hypertrophy, hyperplasia, and capillary density in college men after resistance training. *Journal of Applied Physiology,* 81:2004-2012.

Peterson, M.D., Rhea, M.R., & Alvar, B.A. (2004). Maximizing strength development in athletes: A meta-analysis to determine the dose response relationship. *Journal of Strength and Conditioning Research,* 18:377-382.

Pincivero, D.M., Lephart, S.M., & Karunakara, R.G. (1997). Effects of rest interval on isokinetic strength and functional performance after short term high intensity training. *British Journal of Sports Medicine,* 31:229-234.

Rhea, M.R., & Alderman, B.L. (2004). A meta-analysis of periodized versus nonperiodized strength and power training programs. *Research Quarterly for Exercise and Sport,* 75:413-422.

Rhea, M.R., Alvar, B.A., & Burkett, L.N. (2002). Single versus multiple sets for strength: A meta-analysis to address the controversy. *Research Quarterly for Exercise and Sport,* 73:485-488.

Rhea, M.R., Alvar, B.A., Burkett, L.N., & Ball, S.D. (2003). A meta-analysis to determine the dose response for strength development. *Medicine and Science in Sports and Exercise,* 35:456-464.

Rhea, M.R., Ball, S.D., Phillips, W.T., & Burkett, L.N. (2002). A comparison of linear and daily undulating periodized programs with equated volume and intensity for strength. *Journal of Strength and Conditioning Research,* 16:250-255.

Robinson, J.M., Stone, M.H., Johnson, R.L., Penland, C.M., Warren, B.J., & Lewis, R.D. (1995). Effects of different weight training exercise/rest intervals on strength, power, and high intensity exercise endurance. *Journal of Strength and Conditioning Research,* 9:216-221.

Sforzo, G.A., & Touey, P.R. (1996). Manipulating exercise order affects muscular performance during the resistance exercise training session. *Journal of Strength and Conditioning Research,* 10:20-24.

Shimano, T., Kraemer, W.J., Spiering, B.A., Volek, J.S., Hatfield, D.L., Silvestre, R., Vingren, J.L., Fragala, M.S., Maresh, C.M., Fleck, S.J., Newton, R.U., Spreuwenberg, L.P.B., & Hakkinen, K. (2006). Relationship between the number of repetitions and selected percentages of one repetition maximum in free weight exercises in trained and untrained men. *Journal of Strength and Conditioning Research,* 20:819-823.

Signorile, J.E., Zink, A.J., & Szwed, S. (2002). A comparative electromyographical investigation of muscle utilization patterns using various hand positions during the lat pull-down. *Journal of Strength and Conditioning Research,* 16:539-546.

Simao, R., de Tarso Veras Farinatti, P., Doederiein Polito, M., Sputo Maior, A., & Fleck, S.J. (2005). Influence of exercise order on the number of repetitions performed and perceived exertion during resistance exercises. *Journal of Strength and Conditioning Research,* 19:152-156.

Spreuwenberg, L.P.B., Kraemer, W.J., Spiering, B.A., Volek, J.S., Hatfield, D.L., Silvestre, R. Vingren, J.L., Fragala, M.S., Häkkinen, K., Newton, R.U., Maresh, C.M., & Fleck, S.J. (2006). Influence of exercise order in a resistance training exercise session. *Journal of Strength and Conditioning Research,* 20:141-144.

Tharion, W.J., Rausch, T.M., Harman, E.A., & Kraemer, W.J. (1991). Effects of different resistance exercise protocols on mood states. *Journal of Applied Sport Science Research,* 5:60-65.

Willett, G.M., Hyde, J.E., Uhlaub, M.B., Wendl, C.L., & Karst, G.M. (2001). Relative activity in abdominal muscles during commonly prescribed strengthening exercises. *Journal of Strength and Conditioning Research,* 15:480-485.

Wolfe, B.L., LeMura, L.M., & Cole, P.J. (2004). Quantitative analysis of single- versus multiple-set programs in resistance training. *Journal of Strength and Conditioning Research,* 18:35-47.

Chapter 4 References and Suggested Readings

Clamann, H.P., & Henneman, E. (1976). Electrical measurement of axon diameter and its use in relating motoneuron size to critical firing level. *Journal of Neurophysiology,* 39:844-51.

Fleck, S.J., & Kraemer, W.J. (2004). *Designing resistance training programs* (3rd ed.). Champaign, IL: Human Kinetics.

Henneman, E., Clamann, H.P., Gillies, J.D., Skinner, R.D. (1974). Rank order of motoneurons within a pool: Law of combination. *Journal of Neurophysiology,* 37:1338-49.

Kraemer, W.J., Koziris, L.P., Ratamess, N.A., Häkkinen, K., Triplett-Mcbride, N.T., Fry, A.C., Gordon, S.E., Volek, J.S., French, D.N., Rubin, M.R., Gómez, A.L., Sharman, M.J., Lynch, M.J., Izquierdo, M., Newton, R.U., & Fleck, S.J. (2002). Detraining produces minimal changes in physical performance and hormonal variables in recreationally strength-trained men. *Journal of Strength Conditioning Research.* 16:373-82.

Kraemer, W.J., Noble, B.J., Culver, B.W., & Clark, M.J. (1987). Physiologic responses to heavy-resistance exercise with very short rest periods. *International Journal of Sports Medicine,* 8:247-252.

Kraemer, W.J., Piorkowski, P.A., Bush, J.A., Gómez, A.L., Loebel, C.C., Volek, J.S., Newton, R.U., Mazzetti, S.A., Etzweiler, S.W., Putukian M., & Sebastianelli, W.J. (2000). The effects of NCAA division I intercollegiate competitive tennis match play on recovery of physical performance in women. *Journal of Strength and Conditioning Research,* 14:265-327.

Luscher, H.R., Ruenzel, P., & Henneman, E. (1979). How the size of motoneurons determines their susceptibility to discharge. *Nature,* 20-27; 282(5741):859-61.

Newton, R.U., Kraemer, W.J., Häkkinen, K., Humphries, B.J., & Murphy, A.J. (1996). Kinematics, kinetics, and muscle activation during explosive upper body movements: Implications for power development. *Journal of Applied Biomechanics,* 12:31-43.

Plisk, S.S., & Stone, M.H. (2003). Periodization strategies. *Strength and Conditioning Journal,* 25(6): 19-37.

Chapter 5 References and Suggested Readings

American College of Sports Medicine. (2002). American College of Sports Medicine position stand. Progression models in resistance training for healthy adults. *Medicine and Science in Sports and Exercise,* 34(2):364-80.

Clamann, H.P., & Henneman, E. (1976). Electrical measurement of axon diameter and its use in relating motoneuron size to critical firing level. *Journal of Neurophysiology,* 39(4):844-51.

Fleck, S.J., & Kraemer, W.J. (2004). *Designing resistance training programs* (3rd ed.). Champaign, IL: Human Kinetics.

Kraemer, W.J., Noble, B.J., Culver, B.W., & Clark, M.J. (1987). Physiologic responses to heavy-resistance exercise with very short rest periods. *International Journal of Sports Medicine,* 8:247-252.

Staron, R.S., Leonardi, M.J., Karapondo, D.L., Malicky, E.S., Falkel, J.E., Hagerman, F.C., & Hikida, R.S. (1991). Strength and skeletal muscle adaptations in heavy-resistance-trained women after detraining and retraining. *Journal of Applied Physiology,* 70:631-40.

Chapter 6 References and Suggested Readings

Baechle, T.R., & Earle, R.W. (2000). *Essentials of strength training and conditioning* (2nd ed.). Champaign, IL: Human Kinetics.

Brzycki, M. (1993). Strength testing: predicting a one-rep max from reps-to-fatigue. *Journal of Health, Physical Education, Recreation and Dance,* 64:88-90.

Chapman, P.P., Whitehead, J.R., & Binkert, R.H. (1998). The 225-lb reps-to-fatigue test as a submaximal estimate of 1-RM bench press performance in college football players. *Journal of Strength and Conditioning Research,* 12:258-261.

Clark, R.R., Kuta, J.M., & Sullivan, J.C. (1994). Cross-validation of methods to predict body fat in African-American and Caucasian Collegiate football players. *Research Quarterly for Exercise and Sport,* 65:21-30.

Epley, B. (1985). Poundage chart. Lincoln, NE: Boyd Epley Workout.

Fleck, S.J., & Kraemer, W.J. (2004). *Designing resistance training programs* (3rd ed.). Champaign, IL: Human Kinetics.

Jackson, A.S., & Pollock, M.L. (1978). Generalized equations for predicting body density of men. *British Journal of Nutrition,* 40:497-504.

Jackson, A.S., Pollock, M.L., & Ward, A. (1980). Generalized equations for predicting body density of women. *Medicine and Science in Sports and Medicine,* 12:175-182.

Johnson, D.L., & Bahamonde, R. (1996). Power output estimate in university athletes. *Journal Strength and Conditioning Research,* 10:161-166.

Kraemer, W.J., & Fleck, S.J. (2005). *Strength training for young athletes* (2nd ed.). Champaign, IL: Human Kinetics.

Lander, J. (1985). Maximums based on reps. *National Strength & Conditioning Journal,* 6:60-61.

Lohman, T.G. (1981). Skinfolds and body density and their relation to body fatness: A review. *Human Biology,* 53:181-225.

Mayhew, J.L., Ball, T.E., & Bowen, J.C. (1992). Prediction of bench press ability from submaximal repetitions before and after training. *Sports Medicine Training and Rehabilitation,* 3:195-201.

Mayhew, J.L., Ware, J.S., Bemben, M.G., Wilt, B., Ward, T.E., Farris, B., Juraszek, J., & Slovak, J.P. (1999). The NFL-225 test as a measure of bench press strength in college football players. *Journal of Strength and Conditioning Research,* 13:130-134.

Morales, J., & Sobonya, S. (1996). Use of submaximal repetition tests for predicting 1-RM strength in class athletes. *Journal of Strength and Conditioning Research,* 10:186-189.

Siri, W.E. (1961). Body composition from fluid spaces and density: Analysis methods in techniques for measuring body composition. Washington, DC: National Academy of Science, National Research Council.

Thorland, W.G., Johnson, G.O., & Housh, T.J. (1993). Estimation of body composition in black adolescent male athletes. *Pediatric Exercise Science,* 5:116-124.

Ware, J.S., Clemens, C.T., Mayhew, J.L., & Johnston, T.J. (1995). Muscular endurance repetitions to predict bench press and squat strength in college football players. *Journal of Strength and Conditioning Research,* 9:99-103.

Chapter 7 References and Suggested Readings

Fleck, S.J., & Kraemer, W.J. (2004). *Designing resistance training programs* (3rd ed.). Champaign, IL: Human Kinetics.

Kraemer, W.J., Bush. J.A., Wickham, R.B., Denegar, C.R., Gomez, A.L, Gotshalk, L.A., Duncan, N.D., Volek, J.S., Putukian, M., & Sebastianelli, W.J. (2001). Influence of compression therapy on symptoms following soft tissue injury from maximal eccentric exercise. *Journal of Orthopedic Sports Physical Therapy,* 31:282-90.

Kraemer, W.J., & Fleck, S.J. (2005). *Strength training for young athletes* (2nd ed.). Champaign, IL: Human Kinetics.

Chapter 8

Fleck, S.J., & Kraemer, W.J. (2004). *Designing resistance training programs* (3rd ed.). Champaign, IL: Human Kinetics.

Index

Note: The italicized *f* and *t* following page numbers refer to figures and tables, respectively.

A

abdominal exercises 160t-161t
abduction and adduction exercises 160t-161t
absolute resistance 58
acidosis 32
active and total rest days 98
active recovery 5-6, 215
acute program variables
  definition of 41, 215
  in optimal program sequencing 77-78
adaptation
  definition of 215
  physiological 11, 27-28
adductor longus 162f
adenosine triphosphate (ATP) 215
adolescence, definition of 215
adrenaline 202, 215
aerobic, definition of 215
afferent, definition of 215
aging considerations 164-165
agonistic muscles, definition of 215
alpha-motor neuron, definition of 215
alternating sequence 48, 215
alternative workouts 105-106
amino acids, definition of 215
anabolic, definition of 215
anaerobic, definition of 215
anaerobic energy source 30-31
anaerobic metabolism of carbohydrate 30-31
antagonist muscle, definition of 216
arm curling 58-59, 59t, 160t-161t
athletes
  from Eastern Bloc countries 2-3, 5, 6t
  goal of 3
  resistance-trained 3
  training on the road 186-187
ATP hydrolysis 61-62
atrophy, definition of 216
axon, definition of 216

B

back squat 58-59, 59t
Ball, T.E. 116
ballistic stretching, definition of 216
baseball players 180-181
base program, sample protocol 89
base program phase 87-89, 88f, 216
basic fatigue scale 84f
bench press
  alternative workouts 104
  choices for a resistance exercise program 160t
  comparison of training models for 10
  correct starting and finishing positions 107
  decline in performance 46-47
  local muscular endurance 120
  muscle groups stimulated by an exercise 161t
  predictions of 1RM 111
  1RM study 58-59, 59t
bench throw 92
biceps brachii 162f
biceps femoris 162f
bilateral, definition of 216
blood lactic acid 32, 48, 61-62
body and limb circumferences
  calf 135
  general procedures for measuring 133
  hip 136

About the Authors

William J. Kraemer, PhD, is a kinesiology professor in the Human Performance Laboratory in the department of kinesiology and the department of physiology and neurobiology at the University of Connecticut at Storrs. He is also a professor of medicine at the University of Connecticut Health Center's School of Medicine in Farmington, Connecticut. Dr. Kraemer is a fellow and past president of the National Strength and Conditioning Association (NSCA) and is a fellow of the American College of Sports Medicine (ACSM). He was awarded the NSCA's Lifetime Achievement Award in 1994 and the Educator of the Year Award in 2002. He is editor in chief of the *Journal of Strength and Conditioning Research* and coauthor of *Designing Resistance Training Programs, Third Edition,* and *Strength Training for Young Athletes, Second Edition.*

Steven Fleck, PhD, is chair of the sport science department at Colorado College in Colorado Springs. He was head of the physical conditioning program for the U.S. Olympic Committee, served as strength coach for the German Volleyball Association, and coached high school track, basketball, and football. Dr. Fleck is a fellow and past president of basic and applied research for the National Strength and Conditioning Association (NSCA) and is a fellow of the American College of Sports Medicine (ACSM). He was

honored in 1991 as the NSCA Sport Scientist of the Year and in 2005 was given the NSCA's Lifetime Achievement Award. He coauthored, with Dr. Kraemer, *Designing Resistance Training Programs, Third Edition,* and *Strength Training for Young Athletes, Second Edition.*

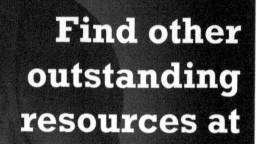